Health and Social Issues of Native American Women

Health and Social Issues of Native American Women

⟶ ∾

JENNIE R. JOE AND FRANCINE C. GACHUPIN, EDITORS

Foreword by Judith Salmon Kaur, MD

 PRAEGER

AN IMPRINT OF ABC-CLIO, LLC
Santa Barbara, California • Denver, Colorado • Oxford, England

Library of Congress Cataloging-in-Publication Data

Health and social issues of native American women / Jennie R. Joe and Francine C. Gachupin, editors ; foreword by Judith Salmon Kaur, MD.
   p. cm.
   Includes bibliographical references and index.
   ISBN 978–0–313–39713–4 (hard copy : alk. paper) — ISBN 978–0–313–39714–1 (ebook) 1. Indian women—Health and hygiene—North America. 2. Indian women—Diseases—North America. 3. Indian women—North America—Social conditions. I. Joe, Jennie Rose. II. Gachupin, Francine C.
E98.W8H43   2012
305.48′897—dc23   2012021551

ISBN: 978–0–313–39713–4
EISBN: 978–0–313–39714–1

16 15 14 13 12   1 2 3 4 5

This book is also available on the World Wide Web as an eBook.
Visit www.abc-clio.com for details.

Praeger
An Imprint of ABC-CLIO, LLC

ABC-CLIO, LLC
130 Cremona Drive, P.O. Box 1911
Santa Barbara, California 93116-1911

This book is printed on acid-free paper ∞

Manufactured in the United States of America

Contents

Foreword

Judith Salmon Kaur, MD

According to many scholars, including Devon Mihesuah, she and other Native scholars have been concerned that much of what is known or written about American Indians has been by non-Indian scholars, especially historians and anthropologists. To counterbalance this bias, Mihesuah invited the voices of several Native scholars to discuss this concern in her edited book, *Natives and Academics Researching and Writing about American Indians* (1998). Not only did the contributors provide examples of their efforts to untangle some the intellectual issues used by non-Native scholars, but they also offered critique on some of the motivation and ethics of researchers that have helped frame the image of American Indians.

In their essays, the Native scholars addressed several longstanding tools of research used to describe or analyze American Indians, including those that have produced stereotypes or have been detrimental to the communities that have been studied. The contributors drew attention to research methodology, pedagogy, ethics, and theory utilized in the non-Native analysis of American Indians. Among the outcomes from this engagement was a challenge issued by the authors to researchers (Native and non-Native), asking them to question their motives, methods, and interpretations of their work so as not to add to or construct new stereotypic images of American Indians or conduct research that had little or no application to the problems or issues faced by American Indian communities.

In this edited book, the editors also bring together a cadre of Native women scholars, all of whom are engaged in several ongoing health-related researches with Native communities. These scholars also make note of the need to recognize tribal and cultural diversities as well as the need to acknowledge some of the commonalities among tribes. One commonality expressed by the authors is the shared value held by most tribal communities, a value that perceives Native women as central and important in preserving the heart of their respective tribal cultures.

Each of the authors in this collection also calls attention to the diversity of tribes as a complex issue at multiple levels, including identification of who is an American Indian or Alaska Native (AIAN). The changing identification has numerous consequences, including how health statistics are reported or analyzed. The new demographics indicate that the AIAN population has dramatically increased in recent censuses, mainly due to changes in the way individual reported their race or ethnicity. The 2000 census places AIANs at 2.3 million, a number that is impressive but that still represents less than 2 percent of the nation's population.

The census also indicates that in comparison to other racial or ethnic groups, the AIAN population is considerably younger. For example, AIAN women comprise approximately 51 percent of the AIAN population with close to 50 percent under age 25 (IHS 2002–2003). While this is a young population, the increase in incidence and prevalence of chronic diseases as well as the mortality picture mirror the health picture of a population that is much older physiologically.

Understandably, poverty and various other determinants of poor health play a major role in the health status portrayed in the AIAN population. Thus, despite the young age, AIAN women face extraordinary challenges in all spheres of life: economic, health, social, and education. Many of these problems remain although notable transformations have taken place that reflect gains in women's rights, educational attainments, health outcomes, and employment.

The various topics covered by the authors in this edited book show that successes or gains made by women worldwide have been not been consistent for all, especially in the health arena. For example, the top five leading causes of death for Native women are either similar to or higher than rates shown for non-Native women in the United States. As noted by more than one author in this book, the five leading causes of death for Native women include cancer, heart disease, unintentional injury, diabetes, and cerebral vascular disease (stroke).

By addressing many of the health issues of Native women, the authors present a book that is a unique contribution to the literature on women's health not only because it focuses on the underserved Native American population but also because it highlights the writings of a group of all Native women researchers. This brings tremendous strength, wisdom, and insight into issues ranging from the changing roles of Native women to regional differences in cancer patterns.

Some readers might wonder why Drs. Joe and Gachupin elected to combine topics on health with social issues. Recent scientific evidence is elucidating the biologic influences of social and psychological stressors on health and health outcomes. Indeed, my area of breast cancer research has strong accumulating data for a biopsychosocial model to understand the increasing rates of breast cancer in women of color. Researchers have looked at stress and loneliness in breast cancer patients and have found increases in stress hormones such as glucocorticoids.

Animal models have shown that gene expression is changed under conditions of chronic stress, leading to more breast tumors and larger tumors. Immune reaction genes can be down-regulated, including inflammatory and lipid metabolism genes. Understanding the interactions of the social and biologic system interactions will help us understand how to intervene for positive effects on patient care. In the social and behavioral sciences literature, social support is an important independent predictor of cancer survival in several recent studies. It is intriguing to contemplate how social support is translated on the gene expression level to reduce stress, improve immune function, and ultimately improve survival. All of these tantalizing pieces of research can only be accomplished in a transdisciplinary approach to health and wellness.

Finally, it is worth repeating that Native communities are diverse and broad generalizations should be avoided. Cultural strengths, which are present in all tribes, can mitigate many of the disparities discussed in this book. Identifying interventions to improve both health and social issues are encouraging, and there are many ongoing efforts. Whether we are talking about cancer or diabetes, domestic violence or AIDS, we must understand the sociocultural contexts including the influence of federal policy on our communities. Drs. Joe and Gachupin are to be commended for bringing these social and biologic topics together to shed new light on where we are and where we should be heading.

REFERENCES

Indian Health Service (IHS). 2002–2003. *Regional Differences in Indian Health*. Rockville, MD: USDHHS, Indian Health Service, Office of Public Health Support, Division of Program Statistics.

Mihesuah, Devon. 1998. *Natives and Academics Researching and Writing about American Indians*. Lincoln: University of Nebraska Press.

Acknowledgments

We, as coeditors, would like to express our deep appreciation to our colleagues, the cadre of Native women scholars who gave of their time, energy, and scholarship to help us bring this project to fruition.

A special thank you is also due Ms. Joanne Metcalfe, who helped with reference checks and other yeoman activities. And, last but not least, we want to thank Ms. Beth Ptalis of Praeger Press for her help and guidance with this edited book.

CHAPTER 1

Introduction: Native American Women, Health, and Social Issues

Jennie R. Joe and
Francine C. Gachupin

Outside a number of periodic specific-disease-focused or government reports, there is a paucity of published works on the contemporary health status of Native American (U.S. American Indian/Alaska Native [AIAN]) women. This book is an effort to address this gap by providing a selection of social and health issues, each addressed by Native women scholars whose respective work and expertise are linked to the topics they have contributed. The effort to provide a broader perspective that incorporates relevant sociocultural context as well as an array of major health problems faced by Native American women of all ages.

In the creation of this book, Native women scholars were asked to contribute various chapters related to Native women's health or social issues, taking into consideration the abovementioned challenges. The intention of the book is to help a general audience as well as undergraduate and graduate students better understand the urgent problems, as well as some of the positive aspects of culture and resiliency, that color the lives of many Native women. The book is organized to cover major topic areas without intending to rank one issue to be of greater importance than another. Following is a brief description of topics covered by the contributors.

Following the introduction in this first chapter by coeditors Dr. Jennie R. Joe (Navajo) and Dr. Francine C. Gachupin (Jemez Pueblo), Chapter 2 by Dr. Teresa D. LaFromboise (Miami) and

Ms. Bayley Marquez (Chumash) provides a historical and contemporary background on the various events and social circumstances that have helped shaped the world of American Indian women in the lower 48 states. And because the route of colonization and history differs somewhat for Native peoples in Alaska, Dr. Rosita Worl (Tlingit) provides an overview of several significant events that have affected and continue to impact the lives of Alaska Native women in Chapter 3. In combination, these two chapters discuss how gender roles for AIAN women have changed over time and the prevailing context that shows tribal diversity as well as varying responses to pressures of colonization and western expansion. The overriding theme in both is that women in most tribal cultures shared equal status and power with men, and the valuable roles and contributions of Native women continue in the present day.

In her discourse on Native women in Alaska, Dr. Worl not only recounts 40 years of sociocultural change but also focuses on landmark changes in Alaska that stimulated and accelerated sociocultural changes for Native societies and especially for Native Alaskan women. Some of Dr. Worl's highlights include how the 1970s brought dramatic changes to Alaska and to Native Alaskans with the discovery and development of oil on the Northern Slope in Alaska and how the increased revenues from oil supported capital construction projects and also created job opportunities for many Native peoples.

Similarly, the enactment of the Alaska Native Claim Settlement Act of 1971 brought major institutional changes to the Native community with the creation of 13 regional Native corporations and 200 village corporations. The Claims Settlement act also transferred title to 44 million acres of land to Native ownership, which was followed by various economic developments of these lands and resources and incorporated the individualization of tribal groups into shareholders.

In Chapter 4, physician Dr. Terry Maresca (Mohawk) provides the background for policies and governmental actions that have developed and maintained a health care delivery system for a majority of federally recognized AIANs. This chapter also serves as an important background because, unlike other minority groups in the United States, many colonized AIANs have a unique relationship with the federal government that is anchored in numerous treaties negotiated by the federal government with tribes. In the area of health care, some of the early treaties negotiated by tribes with the federal government called for provision of health care services in exchange for the ceded tribal lands. In addition to minimum provision of health care, the treaties also include provision for other benefits such as protection of tribal lands, education, and so forth.

In her discussion of these developments, Dr. Maresca provides a brief history of the role of the federal government in providing health care to AIANs as well as how colonization not only changed the demographics of the Native populations but also impacted the contemporary sociopolitical and health landscape of most tribal communities. Her theme of social injustice is appropriate here because the health care dollars allocated annually by Congress for Native American health care programs come from discretionary funds and not from entitlement sources. Thus, dollars allocated for Indian health are not based on need but on a formula that Congress deems but the allocation has never been sufficient. The chronic underfunding is most telling when reviewed on a per capita basis: federal allocation for the health care coverage for one AIAN is half of that earmarked for one federal prisoner.

Because of the emphasis on tribal relationships with the federal government is based on a government-to-government arrangement, most tribal members who live off-reservation as well as tribal groups that do not have federal recognition do not have ready access to the federal health care system under the federal Indian Health Service (IHS). In the 1970s, however, congressional action made available limited primary health care to urbanized AIANs in selected urban communities, generally cities with sizable Native populations. These facilities are managed as not-for-profit primary care resources by Native organizations.

Understandably, no discussions about change and its impact on the contemporary health picture of Native women would be complete without giving attention to some of the leading health problems for this population, some of them due to lack of access to care or extreme poverty. Who has access to federally sponsored health care is not a simple issue. Eligibility for health care needs to be part of the larger discussion on lingering health disparities and social injustice. In addition, the history of poor health status also needs to be placed within the larger context of the collective experiences of colonization, forced cultural change, poverty, and so forth.

Starting in Chapter 5, Dr. Linda Burhansstipanov (Oklahoma Cherokee) underscores some of the leading indicators that contribute to several persistent health disparities attributable to several factors, including poverty and the chronic shortage of health resources. Dr. Burhansstipanov compares some of these leading causes of mortality and morbidity for Native American women with that of non-Hispanic white females and presents this data across different age groups. The discussion includes population, age distribution, and some sociodemographic data (e.g., life expectancy, employment, education, live births). Epidemiologic data within the chapter includes information on cancer, diabetes, heart disease, homicide, suicide, unintentional injuries, and alcohol- or drug-related health problems.

In Dr. Burhansstipanov's discussion as well as in other chapters, contributors make note of the importance of tribal heterogeneity and varying geographical locations as important markers that differentiate prevalence of various health conditions. Some of the differences are linked to the environment as well as the severity and existence of certain behavioral risk factors. Unfortunately, the overlay of tribal heterogeneity and regional difference is usually missing in many of the aggregated statistical profiles reported by various health data sources. For example, high smoking rates among Native American males and females in the Northern Plains and Alaska are a critical factor that contributes to high rates of various forms of cancer for AIANs living within these geographical regions. Regional differences, therefore, are an important variable in discussing a number of health issues in Native peoples.

Drs. Emily Haozous (Mescalero Apache) and Turner Goins (Catawba) in Chapter 6 state that in most Native American communities, chronologic age does not always imply elder status, and elders hold a special place in most communities. For example, the role of an elder is recognized as a position of great responsibility and status and is especially granted to those who voluntarily take on meaningful roles as teachers, mentors, counselors, and so forth. These elders are recognized by their communities and are perceived as repositories of wisdom and cultural knowledge, knowledge that only certain elders can deliver in a population where cultural knowledge is learned from oral history and storytelling. Indeed, within many tribes, it is the hard work and wisdom of its elders that helps maintain the foundation for the group's identity and existence.

On the topic of "Addressing Food Security and Food Sovereignty in Native American Communities," in Chapter 7, Dr. Valarie Blue Bird Jernigan (Oklahoma Choctaw) discusses how many AIAN communities lack access to high-quality and culturally appropriate foods, especially in rural, isolated reservation communities. She states that food insecurity has numerous implications for the health and welfare of AIANs and defines food insecurity as "having limited or uncertain availability of nutritionally adequate and safe foods or limited or uncertain ability to acquire acceptable foods in socially acceptable ways." She attributes food insecurity to underlying social, economic, historical, and institutional factors that affect the quantity and quality of available food and its affordability or price relative to the financial resources available to acquire it. She discusses examples of where tribal groups are taking action to address food insecurity and improve the quality of available foods by exercising self-determination and building collaborative efforts with neighboring towns to establish local farmers' markets and by encouraging the reintroduction of consumable indigenous plants through seed banks and garden projects.

In Chapter 8, another topic related to food insecurity, obesity, and physical activity, Dr. Joe provides an overview of how the epidemic of type 2 diabetes has become endemic in many tribal communities. The current epidemiological picture of diabetes shows that American Indian adults are 2.1 times as likely as white adults to be diagnosed with diabetes, and that the diabetes-related morbidity for AIANs differs regionally. For example, the diabetes-related morbidity rate among Alaska Natives is 8.1 compared to 27.6 for tribes in southern Arizona. Mortality rates for American Indian women treated for diabetes are also higher than for males. For example, the age-adjusted death rate per 100,000 in 2006 for American Indian women was 40.7 compared to 38 for males. This age-adjusted death rate for American Indian women is three times that reported for non-Hispanic white females.

In this chapter, Dr. Joe also focuses on some of the psychological impacts that are associated with some of the complications connected with type 2 diabetes, consequences that often lead to psychological as well as physical disabilities that impact not only the health of the women but also their self-image and roles as mothers or marital partners. In some instances, cultural expectations can also limit a woman's ability to maintain or develop her own social and economic independence.

In Chapter 9, "Domestic Violence in American Indian Communities: Background, Culture, and Legal Issues," Drs. Mary Rogers and Jennifer Giroux (Sicangu Oyate Lakota) discuss violence against AIAN women as a personal and public health problem that compromises women's physical and mental well-being. This chapter discusses not only the issue of domestic violence but also the complicated problem of getting help and resources to Native women who are victims of domestic violence.

Domestic violence often causes physical injuries, contributes to mental disabilities, and erodes self-esteem of women. The authors note that recent reports indicate Native women are sexually assaulted three times as often as other women, but they also caution the reader that this reported data is an underestimate because the U.S. Department of Justice notes that 70 percent of sexual assaults that occur in tribal communities go unreported.

In Chapter 10, Dr. Irene Vernon (Mescalero Apache/Yaqui) discusses HIV/AIDS risks and the sociocultural factors that either delay early diagnosis or impact prevention efforts. According to Dr. Vernon, federal reports note that although AIANs diagnosed with HIV/AIDS represented only 1 percent of all diagnosed cases in 2005, when this prevalence rate is measured against the total population of AIANs (1.5% of the U.S. population), Native Americans rank third after African Americans and Hispanics in high prevalence of HIV/AIDS.

In Chapter 11, Dr. Teshia Solomon (Choctaw) and Carol Goldtooth-Begay (Navajo) focus on cancer incidence and mortality and highlight regional variation of rates for major cancer sites. In this chapter, the authors note that Native women have lower breast cancer incidence and mortality rates than other minority women, but because of late diagnosis, AIAN women have poorer survival rates than women from other racial or ethnic groups.

In the discussion of cancer rates, the authors also make note of all the difficulties that are encountered when one wants to find reliable cancer data for the AIAN population, that is, data that is free of racial misclassification, data omissions due to small sample sizes, or data categorized as "Other Races." These data challenges hamper the ability of AIAN-focused health programs to address and advocate for resources to address key health problems like cancer.

Drs. Nina Wampler, PhD, (Eastern Band Cherokee) and Lorenda Belone (Navajo) in Chapter 12 use the storytelling approach to discuss challenges faced by three Native sisters as they try to fit in among their peers and how their efforts lead them to establish new friendships or relationships that also introduce them to high-risk behaviors such as smoking, substance abuse, and teen pregnancy. In the storytelling mode, the authors discuss how the day-to-day demands of managing an impoverished life or a stressful home environment for these young women motivate them to succumb to unhealthy peer pressure. Their stories illustrate the limited alternatives or choices available to youth and others like them in other societies.

This issue of youth and the problems faced by them is especially disconcerting as the Native population is predominately a young population. For example, the 2010 Census (Infoplease 2012) reports that the median age for AIANs on April 1, 2010, was 29.0 compared to 37.2 for the general U.S. population. With 1.3 million AIANs under age 18 years, it is important to understand that young populations not only take more health risks but are also more likely to exhibit unhealthy behaviors of peers. Given this situation, developing interventions to improve the health of our youth or provide the means for them to develop behaviors that emphasize a healthy lifestyle is a challenge that requires their input and participation, especially for strategies or programs designed for them.

In the last chapter, Chapter 13, Dr. Francine Gachupin (Jemez Pueblo) focuses on the current state of human-subject protection policies and the applicable definition of research—as a systematic investigation designed to develop or contribute to generalizable knowledge—and the policy impacts on AIANs. The changes experienced by AIANs, as a collective, over the last few hundred years have been substantive, and the long-term effects of these experiences remain unfolding and, in many instances, unknown, therefore retaining the value of research. In order to ensure better protection of subjects participating in research, ethical principles have been established so individuals are informed of the different aspects of a particular study and are voluntarily participating once given the opportunity to assess the requirements of their participation. Tribal and IHS institutional review boards (IRBs) often use the federal regulations as the floor for human-subject protection and not the ceiling. For example, federal regulations pertain specifically to the individual, but because tribes are collective entities with unique status, we should assess harms and benefits that extend beyond the individual to include assessment of family and community harms and benefits in reviews of research study protocols. This chapter reviews some important protection-of-human-subject issues to be considered by researchers when they involve Native women and children in their studies. In her "how-to" guide, Dr. Gachupin stresses the need to have researchers seek and gain community or tribal approval prior even to submission of the research grant application. Because of tribal sovereignty, the documentation of community or tribal approval is also expected by most funding agencies. The researcher-community collaboration is especially critical to avoid research abuse. In addition to an overview, this chapter also includes contact information as well as references to a list of collaborative studies that have been conducted through the Native American Research Centers for Health (NARCH).

This last chapter not only encourages investigator-community collaboration so that research outcomes are useful but also calls attention to the desire of many AIAN communities to have a greater role in studies that involve their populations.

The chapters included in this collection speak to a number of AIAN women's health concerns and, in many instance, the need for a holistic approach when it comes to healing, based on the understanding that healthy well-being requires a balance of all of the four realms of life: the mind, the body, the spiritual, and the social. Disharmonies in one or more of these realms may require attention to cultural etiologies and cultural intervention as well as diagnoses and treatment offered by allopathic medicine. Within the cultural perspective, ideally healing requires a holistic approach to reestablish the harmony or the well-being of the individual by giving attention to the mind, the body, the spiritual, and the social. The latter may entail healing that reestablishes one's sense of self or relationship with others that are a part of the ecological landscape where one lives, work, learns, and so forth.

As with any academic exercise, we hope you will take from this book a better understanding and appreciation of challenges faced by AIAN women in their collective efforts to increase the levels of well-being of self, family, community, and people. This book exemplifies a concerted effort by strong, caring, intelligent Native women to bring awareness to gaps on select social and health issues. The editors thank each of them wholeheartedly for their time and contributions.

REFERENCE

Infoplease. 2012. "American Indians: Census Facts." Pearson Education. http://www .infoplease.com/spot/aihmcensus1.html.

CHAPTER 2

Interpretation of Changing and Diverse Roles of Native American Women in Light of Twenty-First-Century Lived Experience[1]

Teresa D. LaFromboise and
Bayley J. Marquez

INTRODUCTION

When studying the gender roles of American Indian/Alaska Native (AIAN) women, the recognition of diversity and eventual change in the social structures of AIAN societies is a central concern (LaFromboise et al. 1990:455). Given that Native lifeways were drastically altered by colonization and western expansion, it is important to study the influences shaping the way outside influences shape tribes and the responses of Native women to the resultant stress experienced within their tribes over time.

Over the past two decades, an increasing number of studies have focused on AIAN women, especially in the area of ethnohistory (Mihesuah 1996; Shoemaker 1995). Yet many interpretations of the

---

1. Portions of this chapter are adapted from LaFromboise, T. D., Heyle, A. M., and Ozer, E. J. (1990). "Changing and Diverse Roles of Women in American Indian Cultures." *Sex Roles* 22(7–8):455–476. Used by permission of Springer.

roles of AIAN women remain incorrect, and limited connections are made to their present-day circumstances. Additionally, extant empirical research on contemporary AIAN women concentrates more fully on health disparities and economic indicators than on gender roles and women's rank in their culture. Although forced cultural, religious, and economic assimilation of AI/AN people has shaped their cultural practices and social structures, vibrant, diverse Native women are a dynamic cultural group whose strength, perseverance, and influence warrant more comprehensive discernment (Hudson 1980; Simoni et al. 2010). This chapter gives an overview of some of the important changes in the role and status of AIAN women as a result of colonization and other forced transformation through governmental and other policies in an attempt to more fully appreciate their spheres of influence in contemporary times.

EXAMINING AIAN WOMEN

Counter to assertions by nonindigenous, male-centered social science research, the reality of AIAN behavior and social systems, especially those of Native women, has not shown the complete picture. For example, predominantly male, "outsider" ethnographers of Native cultures have focused on males, leading to circuitous and inaccurate descriptions of Native women's beliefs and activities (Lang 1998; Leacock 1986).

Research theories and results derived from these outside observers reflect accepted ideas about AIAN women (Green 1983; Metoyer 1979) but, for the most part, also only reflect the women's roles, status, and behaviors that occurred due to the interactions with the outsiders (Brady et al. 1984). For example, because men in some tribal communities had the role of dealing with outsiders, the observers assumed that males held more power than women within their communities (Parezo 1982).

Furthermore, one could argue that Native women would be distrusting of sharing intimate parts of their lives with outsiders, considering the widespread, long-term history of violence and oppression waged against AIAN people by colonizing groups. As Brady and colleagues (1984) assert, the researchers often document the defensive maneuvers AIAN women present to observers instead of delving into their actual behaviors and personal traits.

Male-centered assumptions—both AIAN and European American—have led to interpretations of Native rituals and traditions being contested by AIAN scholars (Allen 1986; Pesantubbee 1999). Mihesuah

(2003), in her examination of works that study Native women's identities, alludes to the error made when researchers do not take into account the complex cultural context of AIAN women's lives; she contrasts that with studies and observations done by Native women themselves.

One strategy for more accurately revisioning the impact of colonization on AIAN people has been an increasing effort made by ethnographers to specifically study AIAN women through "indigenist" research methods (Barkdull 2009; Evans-Campbell et al. 2007; Napholz 2000). Indigenism as a research methodology requires the critical eye and scholarly knowledge of indigenous researchers. Prior to this advancement, ethnographic analysis was heavily influenced by stereotypes and folklore that limited Native women to princess/squaw drudge roles (Green 1975; Morris 2005; Welch 1987).

WOMEN'S ROLES IN TRADITIONAL NATIVE LIFE

A woman's identity in traditional AIAN life was firmly rooted in her spirituality, extended family, and tribe (Welch 1987), and considerable value was ascribed to the role of Native women. Benally (1988), for example, points out that Native women's self-image shows them as both collective beings as well as harmonizing influences connected to the realms of the spirit and society. In their biological roles, women are valued as mothers who raise healthy families, while in their spiritual role they are viewed as extension of the Spirit Mother. The latter role is seen essential for the continuation of the tribe's future generations.

Women's role also carried the responsibility for being the repository of cultural knowledge whose role was to educate and take care of their children and kin. In the economic role, women also contributed to the family and community's subsistence activities (Niethammer 1977). While much commonality may have existed in the roles of AIAN women, some scholars point out that generalizations about gender roles only mask the diversity of their lived experiences. For example, the vast majority of Native American women may have been faced with oppression through colonization, but their reactions to this oppression may have been constrained by their social class, the norms of their tribe, or even intertribal factionalism (Mihesuah 1996).

Many western tribes—such as the Klamath and the Lenni Lenape— divided roles between the genders in an egalitarian manner (Blackwood 1984; Caffrey 2000). Kidwell and colleagues (2008) note that "the roles of men and women in such societies complemented each other—men hunted and women gave birth and raised children. Food collection and reproduction constituted the most basic elements of a social group. Each function was essential to the whole" (p. 316). The heterogeneity of tribes must be included in this critique of past research. Current research demonstrates that, although status and power were not divided exactly between men and women in all tribes, the critical contributions of AIAN women have been greatly underestimated.

Other researchers, including Allen (1981) and Beiswinger and Jeanotte (1985), focus on the importance of relationships between tribal members and the spirit world and the effect these relationships have on gender roles. According to this perspective, all aspects of the self originate from this relationship, including power and social status (Tanner 1979 depicts this phenomenon for a Mohawk medicine woman). Researchers like Jenks (1986) and Zak (1988; 1989) report that in many tribes, women spirits were central to the maintenance of tribal religious beliefs, to their identity, and as guides for understanding life as well as rules for how tribal members were to behave. Among some of the well-known spirit women include Thought Woman of the Keres of the Northern Pueblos in New Mexico, the Clay Lady of the Santa Clara Pueblo, Changing Woman of the Navajo, and White Buffalo Calf Woman of the Sioux. LaFromboise and colleagues (1990) add that "Although tribes may have had conventional ideals of behavior for each gender group, nonconformity was identified and sanctioned through dreams or ceremonial connections with particular spirits" (p. 458).

In her discussion of the gender-differentiated position of power for men and women, Medicine (1978; 1980), a Lakota Sioux scholar, observed that the social and governing sphere for women in most tribes was shaped by her tribe's social structure and traditions. Medicine and others also indicate that although there were distinct areas of division of labor concerning male and female production, these role expectations were flexible (Blackwood 1984; Hamamsy 1957; Lang 1998; Roscoe 1998; Welch 1987). The nonconformist role is also acknowledged. For example, Allen (1981; 1986) notes that there was generally a free expression of sexuality and nonconformist gender roles in most tribes, where nontraditional males and females, gays, and lesbians were accepted to varying degrees within the group (LaFromboise et al. 1990:458).

Where institutionalized alternative roles for women were recognized and accepted, these women coexisted alongside other women who were fulfilling the "normal" female roles and who were often submissive in a marital relationship. For example, among the Canadian

Blackfeet, women who took on alternative roles favored independence and often took on manly duties and were likely to earn the title of a "manly hearted woman," or a "warrior woman." Other alternative roles might describe a woman who was sexually promiscuous as a "crazy woman" (Brave Heart 1999; Buchanan 1986; Lang 1998; Liberty 1982; Medicine 1983; LaFromboise et al. 1990).

Alternative roles also allowed women in some tribes to enter all-male occupations or live as lesbians. The term often used to describe such cross-gender roles is *berdache*[2] (Lang 1998; Lewis 1941; Roscoe 1998). A woman who took up cross-gender roles held a socially sanctioned position, a change that allowed her to shift predominately to a male-oriented social and occupational role, some-times accompanied by homosexual marriage or sexual relationships (Allen 1981; Blackwood 1984; Callender and Kochems 1983; Lang 1998; LaFromboise et al. 1990). Also, according to Callender and Kochems (1983), unlike gender identification in European society that specified female tasks based on gender, precolonial tribal groups did not specify such role expectations. Instead, in many Native communities, a woman's wish to transition to a male gender role was initiated by the woman's interest in a male-oriented role (Callender and Kochems 1983; Lang 1998).

Champagne and Brown (1997) refer to this gender-role transition as a "spiritual calling." In other situations, a family without a son may encourage one or more of their daughters to assume a male role. Kaska families, for example, have been observed to encourage a child with the most inclination to become "like a man" to assume a male role and would support the daughter to participate in the required puberty initiation ceremonies and customs for boys instead of girls. It should be noted, however, that this observation among the Kaska has recently been disputed (Goulet 1997).

Like puberty ceremonies for young women, formal initiation for a woman who desired to be initiated into a male role varied from tribe to tribe. According to Callender and Kochems (1983), it was custom-ary for cross-gender women in the Cocopah tribe to follow a male

---

2. Even though the term *berdache* is often used in the extant literature, many recent scholars have criticized its use as its definition refers only to males emphasizing sexual acts rather than gender roles. The "berdache's" assumed lesbianism is a subject of debate; thus it is also termed a "cross-gender" role (Blackwood 1984). The preferred term in the current literature for AIAN lesbian, bisexual, transgender, or cross-gender individuals is two-spirit (Jacobs et al. 1997; Thomas and Jacobs 1999; Walters et al. 2006; Wilson 1996).

custom of nose piercing in place of having their chin tattooed as did other women (LaFromboise et al. 1990:459).

LaFromboise and colleagues (1990) indicate that there is ongoing anthropological debate on cross-gender status, including how to define the characteristics or social acceptance of women in alternative roles, and point to the fact that some of the early observations made by ethnographers have biased the debate, especially when such description carried moral judgment by describing cross-gender roles as disgusting. LaFromboise and colleagues (1990) recount a number of data sources for this position by noting that Lang (1998), Roscoe (1998), and Callender and Kochems (1983) "all provided a review of the contradictory literature on cross gender roles and highlight the methodological biases and limitations of the assessment of this alternative role" (p. 460). LaFromboise and colleagues (1990) conclude that "the outsider cultural biases against transvestitism, cross-gender roles, and cross-sexual behavior, have resulted in research that condemned rather than examined the existence of these individuals" (p. 460).

Gatschet (1891) and Swanton (1911) also each note that observer bias contributed to Native reluctance toward gender role change and perhaps led to the within-tribal sanctions against cross-gender individuals. However, due to the lack of specificity in many ethnographic accounts, there is not adequate evidence to deduce whether cross-gender roles were common occurrences and widely accepted or if the roles were treated with ambivalence (Shoemaker 1995; 2010).

AGING AND STATUS OF WOMEN

The status of Native women increased as they aged (in contrast with American emphasis on youth). A postmenopausal woman, as a Winnebago tribal member puts it, was "just like a man" (Witt 1974:32). Older women's age and wisdom were revered, and their knowledge of sacred matters, tribal history, and herbal medicines cherished (Lurie 1972; Metoyer 1979). "Thus, in some tribes it was possible for women to achieve status levels equal to men, but they earned equal status by accumulating years or success in cross-gender tasks" (LaFromboise et al. 1990:460). There are ample examples of Native women who had an important role in economic, political, and spiritual spheres of life in their communities, in most instances without age or cross-gender bias (Allen 1986; Kidwell 1979; Lynch 1986). Moreover, LaFromboise and colleagues (1990) note that

In these tribes, matrilineal patterns of inheritance were observed and in those with agricultural economies, the land, crops, houses, and tools were owned by the women while the men cultivated the gardens and were responsible for much of the labor. (p. 460)

According to Seton and Seton (1953), even in nonagricultural economies, women's close relationship to food and the supply of food conferred great power upon them. In citing the works of Allen (1986), Beauchamp (1900) and Brown (1970), LaFromboise and colleagues (1990) observe that

> Women sometimes exercised formal governing authority on the basis of their spiritual power, as was the case in the pre-colonization Cherokee gynocracy, or "petticoat government," whose Women's Council had a significant influence on tribal decisions. The "Beloved Woman of the Nation," or head of the Women's Council of the Cherokee, was believed to speak the words of the Great Spirit (Allen 1986). Another cited example of women exercising visible political power (Beauchamp 1900; Brown 1970) is that of Iroquois Clan Mothers, who chose the leaders among the men of their tribe. (p. 460)

It is obvious that, although in most tribes males occupied the public sphere as political leaders or chiefs, most important familial or community decisions involved the female voices (Friedl 1967). This decision-making process, however, often made the reality of power different from what took place publically (LaFromboise et al. 1990:461). In order to understand the culture of AIAN people, it is important to recognize Native women's control over the domestic sphere because this sphere was often pivotal in the information flow and resource mobilization within a community (Kidwell et al. 2008).

COLONIZATION'S EFFECTS ON GENDER ROLES, POWER, AND STATUS

While the impact of assimilation on AIAN gender roles varied due to the conditions before colonization, overall, most Native communities have had devastating disruptions to male-female egalitarianism accompanied with a rise in attempts by Native males to assert authority over Native women (Brady et al. 1984; Welch 1987). Additionally, assimilation removed a number of central spiritual roles from Native women; many lost the ritual power associated with life events (such as puberty, menstruation, and childbearing) along with modified domestic responsibilities (Allen 1986). However, many scholars have suggested that the assimilation strategies that were imposed upon tribes often led women to become cultural mediators or agents of transculturation in order to preserve the traditions of their tribe (Kidwell 1992; Morris 2005; Pesantubbee 1999).

LaFromboise and colleagues (1990) observe that colonizers considered tribal gender role flexibility, matrilocal and extended family patterns, complemented gender power relations, and sexual freedom on the part of women as subversive to the intended European-style political, social, and religious order (p. 461). Colonization, however, took away much of this freedom. For example, Livingston (1974) reports that Montagnais-Naskpai and Iroquois men collaborated with the colonizers in subjugating Native women through the introduction of male-dominated religious and social organization.

Building on the Anderson (1985) analysis, LaFromboise and colleagues (1990) discuss Anderson's description of the relationship between the advent of commodity exchange and production systems and the subordination of women through an examination of the interaction between seventeenth-century French missionaries and the Montagnais-Naskapi and Huron tribes along the St. Lawrence River. LaFromboise and colleagues (1990) note that "the power of the missionaries to support the tribes' matriarchal and egalitarian social systems in which women were in no way subservient to men fundamentally lay in the colonizer's ability to capitalize on environmental conditions and then completely control the tribe's livelihood and society" (p. 462).

Forced culture change also decreased women's status and position of power, not only in the family but also within the larger kinship circles in many tribes. Hamamsy (1957) documents this change for the Navajos, where women and men had historically held complementary roles with a system of female inheritance. Under colonization, Navajo women lost their role as the family's financial decision maker and most of their other influences (LaFromboise et al. 1990:462). The change in the traditional Navajo family structure was impacted by wage labor, which forced women to become increasingly dependent on their husbands. Hamamsy (1957) describes the new dependency that forced many women to have to depend on erratic and irresponsible providers, especially when men declared that wages were theirs and not for other non-wage-earning members of the family. According to LaFromboise and colleagues (1990), this change resulted in disintegration of the traditional complementary role for Navajo women. Wage labor also pushed women away from the extended family kin network into more independent and separate family households. The separation took women away from the famil-iar kinship cooperation and work-sharing chores such as childcare and other assistances (p. 462).

Higher rates of hypertension have been reported among elderly Navajo women than Navajo men due to acculturation,[3] especially among the women who were most educated and isolated (Kunitz and Levy 1986). However, one recent study of off-reservation Navajo fami-lies noted that Navajo fathers spent proportionally more time doing work within the home compared to other ethnic groups (Hossain 2001).

SCHOOLING AND CULTURE CHANGE

The nineteenth-century American educational system acted as another agent of assimilation. Specifically, many American Indian chil-dren were removed from their homes and sent to boarding schools run by the Bureau of Indian Affairs (BIA). Many staff within these schools inflicted psychological trauma upon American Indian youth, as numer-ous studies can attest (Beiser 1974; Adams 1995; Kleinfeld and Bloom 1977; Lomawaima 1995; Campbell and Evans-Campbell 2011). A study that focused on American Indian women who attended boarding schools found that these women had lower self-esteem and inhibitions associ-ated with maternal capabilities due to the stress they experienced having to attend school so far from their homes (Metcalf 1976). The impact of this stress also might have transcended generations, with recent research indicating that offspring of boarding-school attendees in Canada appear to be at a greater risk of depression (Bombay et al. 2011).

In the boarding schools, American Indian women were trained for a life of domesticity and subservience. Generally they served as no more than domestic labor for the school as well as for local private citizens

---

3. Acculturation and assimilation are similar constructs in that both focus on the acquisition of the majority group's culture by members of a minority group in a unidirectional and hierarchical manner. However, there are key differences, and we define assimilation as a process that assumes members of the minority culture will be absorbed completely by the majority culture and lose their own cultural identification. Acculturation refers to the individual becoming adept in the majority culture while maintaining his or her cultural identity (LaFromboise et al. 1993:397).

and businesses. American Indian girls received an education that was strictly controlled. For example, they were beaten if they refused or resisted working as domestic laborers, and they did not receive as much classroom instruction as did American Indian boys (Szasz 1980).

It was common for these young women to run away. However, once they returned to their reservations, they were teased and ridiculed for their "white ways." It also soon became apparent to them that their "domestic" skills were not appropriate in the context of the reservation. Upon their release from Carlisle Indian Industrial Training School, they were given a propaganda book entitled *Stiya: A Carlisle Indian Girl at Home* (Bergess 1881) to inoculate them against their family's "primitive ways." Some left the reservation to journey to the cities to pursue employment that was too often underpaid (Trennert 1982).

The U.S. government made a concerted effort to train Native women to work and act like European American women with projects like the boarding schools and the BIA field matron program. The goal of these programs was to save American Indian women from their backward traditional ways (Trennert 1982). Even the policies of the Indian New Deal, which attempted to give American Indian women similar rights to European American women, completely disregarded the roles, both political and social, played by Native women (Bernstein 1984; Osburn 1995). A widespread belief was that if Native women were taught the advantages of "modern" lifestyles, then they would "civilize" their own people when they returned to their reservations.

Some evidence exists that Native women were better able to adapt to white acculturation and assimilation strategies than Native men in spite of their painful and disorienting experiences with boarding schools and other methods of assimilation (Kidwell 1995; Perdue 1995; Spindler and Spindler 1958). However, a recent study of Cheyenne River Sioux health-risk behavior contradicts earlier observations in this arena. Han and colleagues (1994) found that women who were more traditionally engaged in terms of lifestyle and language fluency were healthier than less traditional women. Yet among the men, those who were more acculturated were healthier than more traditional men. One can only speculate about these divergent reports.

When faced with forced acculturation, Native women may have been overlooked in favor of Native men as the target of change. Thus Native women were able to preserve cultural traditions where Native men were not. For example, among the Choctaw, Protestant missionaries paid little attention to women's actions within the home but focused instead on regulating the activities of Choctaw men. Choctaw women were then able to continue practicing traditional childrearing, telling Choctaw stories, and organizing Choctaw ceremonial meetings within the context of the Protestant church (Pesantubbee 1999). When faced with acculturation, Native women also may have been seen not only as less visible but as less threatening than Native men. Finally, Native women were often accustomed to a certain level of flexibility in their roles, which aided them in adapting to the work roles common in mainstream U.S. culture that Native men were reluctant to pursue.

LAND OWNERSHIP AND POLITICAL PARTICIPATION

In some tribes, women were more successful than men as landowners and political leaders who could negotiate with white Americans. This often led to an increase in their power and status (Mead 1982; Powers 1986). For instance, the women of the Northern Paiute and Oglala Sioux were more able to fill government roles than their male counterparts because they were given training in the areas of education and social welfare (Lynch 1986). Because, over time, Native women have been more likely to be gainfully employed than Native men, they have been able to have more stable households and greater influence within their family structure than men (Fiske 1995; Kuokkanen 2011).

Acculturation also led to Native women acquiring power as cultural brokers (Kidwell 1992). AIAN women often acted in ways to both preserve their culture and incorporate those parts of European cultural practices that they thought were beneficial to their tribe (Harmon 2010; Morris 2005). However, although there are reports of positive effects for some Native men (who also lost power and status due to acculturation), overall, acculturation has had major negative effects on the status, authority, and role flexibility of Native women.

THE IMPACT OF ACCULTURATIVE STRESS ON EDUCATION AND MENTAL HEALTH

Living in two different cultural worlds, the American Indian heritage culture and mainstream American culture can be "a feast of appreciation for human ingenuity, or it can be the bitterest trap" (Witt 1981:11). Despite the necessity of maintaining a way of life, a place of residence, or a profession inconsistent with traditional cultural role expectations, most Native women still preserve a sense of homeland and duty to their people. Hill and colleagues (1995) contend that efforts at assimilation in boarding schools inadvertently exposed Native women to women's roles in the dominant society and also facilitated their understanding of multiple tribal cultures. Rather than acquiesce to the demand for assimilation, Native women blended those experiences to develop a sense of pan-Indianism, which not only strengthened their own ethnic and cultural identity but helped them develop adeptness in interacting with individuals from a broad array of diverse cultural communities (Harris 2000).

It is unclear today whether bicultural involvement increases individual vulnerability to illness or psychological distress (Walters and Simoni 2002) or that individuals who operate in bicultural contexts may experience less life stress and be psychologically healthier than those who do not (Albright and LaFromboise 2010; LaFromboise et al. 2010). While Native women were able to improve their economic circumstances by moving to cities, enrolling in postsecondary education, joining the armed forces, or using other methods of adapting to the mainstream U.S. culture, these same adaptations proved to be cause of increased tension and stress (Barter and Barter 1974; LaFromboise et al. 2010). What is clear from these studies is that context is important in determining the relationship between operating biculturally and the mental health of Native women.

Despite the high incidence of acute social and economic problems on reservations, AIAN woman who remain within their own environment retain at the very least the social support of their kin and a community of like-minded people with share cultural practices. Women who leave their reservation and family may feel isolated both psychologically and geographically and find it exceedingly difficult to cognitively and socially adapt to the mainstream U.S. culture (Barrios and Egan 2002) or the cultures outside the United States (see "Fences against Freedom" in Silko 1996).

SOME CONTEMPORARY ISSUES

By and large, traditional customs and kinship ties are of secondary importance in the mainstream of American culture, which advocates individual achievement, competitiveness, and accumulation of material wealth, property, and status. Furthermore, youthful comportment and economic prosperity tend to be highly valued by mainstream U.S. culture as opposed to the valuing of elders, who are highly respected in AIAN communities (Barrios and Eagan 2002). U.S. mainstream values and societal pressures clearly conflict with primary AIAN concerns emphasizing collective self-esteem, which is the esteem generated by a person's membership in a group that is valuable and emotionally salient to that person (Tajfel 1981). Collective self-esteem of AIAN women includes, for example, recognition of the importance of individuals being responsible for extended family and friends, protection and access to sacred sites, upholding treaty rights, language revitalization, the redress of health and economic disparities, and even Native mascot abolition.

Studies that examine young adolescent Native females find that when competing against Native males they will inhibit their own performance, rather than focus on their own success, particularly when their male counterparts underachieve (Weisfeld et al. 1982; 1983). This behavior often derives from cultural norms emphasizing caregiving, cooperation, and group unity. In mainstream U.S. cultural contexts such as universities or businesses, which reward individuals who succeed in competition, the more reticent behavior of AIAN girls could hamper their own advancement or achievement.

AIAN students, many of whom come from communities plagued by high dropout rates, are inconsistently represented on college campuses. Their high school completion rate is lower than that of all other racial groups except for Hispanics (Chapman et al. 2010). However, the educational achievement of AIAN students is improving, as are their college completion rates (Ortiz and Heavy Runner 2003). In fact, the high school completion rate for 18- to 24-year-old AIAN women was 88.2 percent in 2008 (it was 74.7 percent for AIAN men). The dropout rate for AIAN women was 7 percent less than for AIAN men (Chapman et al. 2010). Among tribal colleges, over 80 percent have majority female populations that exceed the national gender ratio average (the national average is 57 percent female enrollment) (Li 2007).

Yet Native women must battle formidable social and psychological obstacles merely to be admitted to college, including poverty, racism, and teen pregnancy (Bowker 1993; Deyhle and Morgonis 1995; Deyhle 2009). These women face numerous and conflicting bicultural pressures in the college environment, and they often struggle to adapt to and succeed in higher education institutions that espouse a doctrine of individual success. AIAN women may face disapproval from family or community members who disagree with their decision to attend college and attempt to dissuade them from matriculating, especially to colleges far from their home reservation. Moreover, AIAN women who attend college may be less able to find an AIAN spouse as Native men who do not have college degrees rarely marry a woman with a higher degree of educational attainment.

Despite these obstacles, more and more women are succeeding in school and pursuing higher education. Recent research has highlighted the commonalities among AIAN women who succeed in higher education. These women often find strength in their spirituality, their identity as AIAN women, and their belief that they are helping their family and community (Barrios and Eagan 2002; White Shield 2009). Among Navajo women, matrilineal networks may provide integral support for those who choose to continue with their schooling (Deyhle and Margonis 1995). Finally, in a study of successful Ute women in social welfare leadership roles, all participants cited using culturally specific reasoning skills, social connectedness, and passion for improving the lives of tribal people to aid them in their work (Barkdull 2009).

Bearing in mind the prevalence of heightened life stress in AIAN communities, it is impressive that so many AIAN women are exerting impressive reservoirs of strength (LaFromboise et al. 2006; Willeto 2007). These coping mechanisms are dependant on factors such as age, tribe, and environment. For example, while older women from Cherokee and Appalachian tribes either did not act or merely gathered information when faced with stressful occurances (Chovan and Chovan 1985), Native female university students instead sought out support from social networks, which reflects the more traditional (and successful) coping strategies of many AIAN cultures (Attneave and Speck 1974).

American Indian women who attend college use many methods to cope with academic stress, the most common of which are seeking social support, using cognitive methods such as recalling personal and cultural beliefs associated with spirituality, other forms of self-talk, and problem solving. They also frequently use behavioral means of coping such as working harder or physically exercising to relieve tension (LaFromboise 1988). Among a sample of 88 American Indian women enrolled at the University of Oklahoma, the University of Nebraska–Lincoln, Harvard University, and Stanford University who participated in an interview and survey study of academic stress and coping, LaFromboise (1988) found that 17 percent turned to formal support systems such as mental health services, Alcoholics Anonymous, or the university financial aid office for assistance. Only 5 percent of these participants coped with stress by eating, smoking, or using drugs or alcohol.

Acculturation stress and pressures from multiple cultures often cause contrasting roles for AIAN women, particularly when the obligations of the dominating culture take precedence over community-based roles. In the discourse shared by Native women throughout interviews in the study noted above, many questioned whether psychological well-being would be possible if some integration of traditional roles and student roles were not achieved. Efforts to reassess the relative importance of each role, relinquish some roles, or reframe the experience of role enactment were frequently recounted during the interviews. At times, some participants admitted that they had needed to "stop out" for a while to fulfill valued family and community obligations.

Many AIAN women who have become successful leaders in their communities often indicate that their necessary bicultural lifestyle precipitates numerous challenges. In a study by Barkdull (2009), Ute women who occupied welfare leadership roles in their community felt that they had to achieve balance between learning the skills necessary to succeed in the mainstream U.S. culture and maintaining their own sense of cultural integrity. Living a bicultural lifestyle often meant that these women both felt misunderstood by the mainstream U.S. culture because of widespread stereotypes or prejudice about AIANs and were also misunderstood within their own tribal culture due to complications associated with frequent engagement away from the community (Benedek 1995).

Often, a Native woman who undergoes bicultural stress feels isolated from her tribe and community and no longer receives the social and cultural support she may need to help her resolve bicultural conflict. This situation has been improved by "reconstituted" tribal networks and the broadening definition of the extended family. Reconstituted, intertribal extended families are becoming increasingly common (Ramirez 2007). Extended families and intertribal networks supply many AIAN women with childcare, as well as encouragement and social support, which is needed to help combat bicultural stress. Additionally, informal networks of AIAN professional women provide contacts and support, and reimagined family roles offer traditional cultural roles, such as aunt/caretaker or mentor, to women whose professional lives and personal choices do not ordinarily allow for them.

RETRADITIONALIZED ROLES OF
CONTEMPORARY NATIVE WOMEN

One current effort Native women have made to mix traditional and contemporary roles in a constructive and culturally consistent manner is through the process of retraditionalization (Green 1983). Retraditionalization can be defined as "the extension of traditional caretaking and cultural transmission roles to include activities vital to the continuity of American Indian and Alaska Native communities within the larger American society" (LaFromboise 1998). This change is in accordance with the non-Western feminist perspective, which argues that adhering to traditional cultural norms or practices is not taking a step backward. Rather, adherence to traditional roles can be empowering in certain social contexts (Mohanty 1988) when roles are updated in order to adjust for social change and the overall structure of the culture remains integral to the process.

Over time, AIAN women have become more prominent in professional roles such as physicians, military personnel, lawyers, stockbrokers, researchers, writers, activists, social workers, teachers, and political leaders with the intent of serving their communities and tribes both on and off reservations. Often, these women's accomplishments rely upon their self-sufficiency, self-confidence, competitiveness, and emotional control. In fact, the process of retraditionalization has been recognized as a potential strategy for intervention when counseling urban AIAN women (Napholz 2000). AIAN women have been able to integrate their cultural heritage into their professional lifestyle and as a result have increased the respect and recognition of AIAN people in addition to gaining professional recognition for them.

The political influence of AIAN women in many tribes is noteworthy and still increasing, prompting calls for further research on the leadership styles of female tribal leaders (Lynch 1986; McCoy 1992). Native women's interest in politics has evolved from traditional roles that emphasize caregiving and concerns for their tribe, with an underpinning in current or vestigial gender-based systems of power within the tribe (Mankiller and Wallis 1993).

In the case of the Oglala Sioux, where women are progressively filling more political leadership positions, women's leadership has been attributed to traditional family skills and experiences that came with their roles as mothers, caregivers, or cultural brokers. A judge on the

Oglala Sioux reservation stated that as a mother, she was used to making unpopular decisions and forcing others to "stick" to them (Powers 1986). Many Oglala Sioux women of all ages have participated in political activism including leading and participating in protests for treaty rights. Yet hardly any would define themselves as political activists. Instead they perceive themselves as aiding their community and securing needed resources for their tribe (Mihesuah 2003).

Urban AIAN women have also adopted retraditionalized roles and have become leaders in their communities. In a study of the Native community in Chicago, Valentino and Straus (2004) describe how American Indian women played an integral role in the establishment and continuance of services for Native people who rely on the resources of urban centers. In 1990, women headed every major American Indian center in the Chicago area. AIAN women have held both official roles and acted as unofficial catalysts for programs throughout the United States in order to improve the lives of those in their community.

Finally, AIAN women have demonstrated their leadership in the area of environmental activism (LaDuke 1994). Due to the gendered division of labor present in many Inuit communities, women often have specific knowledge about the effects of climate change on the Arctic environment that is different from that of men (Dowsley et al. 2010). Similar to AIAN women, women in these areas are also adversely affected by contaminants of traditional food sources, which can affect reproductive health (Kafarowski 2004). Therefore, they have become key actors for the fight against climate change, and their contribution to environmental activism merits further study.

AIAN women have continued to expand their leadership capabilities into new arenas, such as law enforcement, business and finance, and law. For example, in 2004 the number of companies owned by AIAN women had increased by 69 percent since 1997 (National Women's Business Council 2006). In the arena of tribal policing, women have become key players. Within tribal police departments, 15.2 percent of the leadership positions are filled by a woman, which is a larger proportion than the total percentage of women serving in tribal law enforcement (only 5.4 percent less than the percentage of men, who hold the majority of positions). In the Navajo Nation Police Department women comprise 20 percent of all officers and hold 19 percent of the total number of leadership positions (Luna-Firebaugh 2007).

The continuation of the "warrior woman" paradigm is evident in the strong leadership of these women within the tribal police force as well as the many AIAN women who have joined the armed services, including Lori Ann Piestewa (Hopi), who was the first American woman killed in the invasion of Iraq. As of 1994, over 1,500 AIAN women have served in the U.S. military (U.S. Department of Defense n.d.). The visibility and influence of Native women in these roles may help redefine and offer alternatives to common cultural biases that are held about AIAN women by mainstream U.S. culture.

In the area of the law, AIAN women have become more visible and influential despite considerable obstacles. From 1969 to 1978, the number of AIAN women who entered law school more than tripled (Kidder 2003). While Native women face challenges such as discrimination based on race and gender, invisibility in the profession, and impediments to advancement, there are an estimated 900 AIAN women lawyers today, and they comprise approximately 40 percent of all AIAN attorneys (Multicultural Women Attorneys Network, Federal Bar Association, and Native American Bar Association 1998).

Native women generally view their leadership engagement as a personal decision rather than as a result of structural demands from within the tribe. Yet their positions of authority can also be seen as an inevitable evolution of their traditional caretaking role. Native women wish to be consistent and humble leaders who are driven by a sense of integrity rather than thirst for position (Campbell 1988). It is noteworthy that efforts at retraditionalization made by Native women are frequently in conflict with some goals of the current women's movement in mainstream U.S. culture. The majority white feminist movement tends to stress independence and personal achievement as demonstrations of gender equality, whereas Native women view their own achievements in the context of their tribe and their kin (Kidwell et al. 2008). Cultural maintenance and revitalization is just as important to AIAN women as their personal successes or failures, though professional commitments and the valued role of work are obviously very important to Native women.

AIAN women are in the process of redefining identities long obscured by the stereotypes and misconceptions of others (Fryberg et al. 2008). This process is facilitated by the increasing scholarship of Native women (as verified by this volume) and studies that have begun to break down analytic samples of AIAN by gender (Brave Heart 1999; Walls and Whitback 2011). As advances in research methodology concerning small samples sizes are made, there will be a greater opportunity for this type of work.

A common thread that runs across the experience of Native American women is that of "survivance." The concept of survivance rejects the place of AIANs as victims and asserts their own action as agents of survival, resistance, and ultimately sovereignty (Vizenor 1994; 1999). Throughout the process of colonization, acculturation, and retraditionalization and the changes brought about by a multicultural world, AIAN women have continually enacted survivance, and they will continue to do so by remaining a strong force in their own land.

REFERENCES

Adams, David W. 1995. *Education for Extinction: American Indians and the Boarding School Experience*. Lawrence: University Press of Kansas.

Albright, Karen and Teresa D. LaFromboise. 2010. "Hopelessness among White- and Indian-Identified American Indian Adolescents." *Cultural Diversity and Ethnic Minority Psychology* 16(3):437–42.

Allen, Paula G. 1981. "Lesbians in American Indian cultures." *Conditions* 7:67–87.

Allen, Paula G. 1986. *The Sacred Hoop*. Boston: Beacon Press.

Anderson, Karen. 1985. "Commodity Exchange and Subordination: Montagnats-Naskapi and Huron Women, 1600–1650." *Signs—Journal of Women in Culture and Society* 11(1):48–62.

Attneave, Carolyn L. and Ross V. Speck. 1974. "Social Network Intervention in Time and Space." Pp. 166–86 in *The Group as Agent of Change*. Alfred Jacobs and Wilford W. Spradlin (Eds). New York: Behavioral Publications.

Barkdull, Carenlee. 2009. "Exploring Intersections of Identity with Native American Women Leaders." *Journal of Women and Social Work* 25(4):120–36.

Barrios, Patricia G. and Marcia Eagan. 2002. "Living in a Bicultural World and Finding the Way Home: Native Women's Stories." *Journal of Women and Social Work* 17(2):206–28.

Barter, Eloise R. and James T. Barter. 1974. "Urban Indians and Mental Health Problems." *Psychiatric Annals* 4(11):37–43.

Beauchamp, W. M. 1900. "Iroquois Women." *Journal of American Folklore* 13(49):81–91.

Beiser, Morton. 1974. "A Hazard to Mental Health: Indian Boarding Schools." *American Journal of Psychiatry* 131(3):305–6.

Beiswinger, James N. and Holly Jeanotte. 1985. *Medicine Women*. Grand Forks: University of North Dakota Press.

Benally, S. 1988, August. "Guest Editorial." *Winds of Change*.

Benedek, Emily. 1995. *Beyond the Four Corners of the World: A Navajo Woman's Journey*. New York: Alfred A. Knopf, Inc.

Bergess, M. 1881. *Stiya, a Carlisle Indian Girl at Home*. Cambridge, MA: Riverside Press.

Bernstein, A. 1984. "A Mixed Record: The Political Enfranchisement of American Indian Women during the Indian New Deal." Pp. 13–20 in *Indian Leadership*. Walter L. Williams (Ed). Manhattan, KS: Sunflower University Press.

Blackwood, Evelyn. 1984. "Sexuality and Gender in Certain Native American Tribes: The Case of the Cross-Gender Females." *Signs–Journal of Women in Culture and Society* 10(1):27–42.

Bombay, Amy, Kimberly Matheson, and Hymie Anisman. 2011. "The Impact of Stressors on Second Generation Indian Residential School Survivors." *Transcultural Psychology* 48(4):367–91.

Bowker, Ardy. 1993. *Sisters in the Blood: The Education of Women in Native America.* Newton, MA: Women's Educational Act Publishing Center.

Brady, Victoria, Sarah Crome, and Lyn Reese. 1984. "Resist! Survival Tactics of Indian Women." *California History* 63:140–151.

Brave Heart, Maria Yellow Horse. 1999. "Gender Differences in the Historical Trauma Response among the Lakota." *Journal of Health and Social Policy* 10(4):1–21.

Brown, Judith K. 1970. "Economic Organization and the Position of Women among the Iroquois." *Ethnohistory* 17(3/4):151–67.

Buchanan, Kimberley M. 1986. *Apache Women Warriors.* El Paso: Texas Western Press.

Caffrey, Margaret. 2000. "Complementary Power." *American Indian Quarterly* 24(1):20–44.

Callender, Charles and Lee M. Kochems. 1983. "The North American Berdache." *Current Anthropology* 24(4):443–70.

Campbell, Christopher D. and Tessa Evans-Campbell. 2011. "Historical Trauma and Native Child Development." Pp. 1–26 in *American Indian Children and Mental Health: Development, Context, and Treatment.* Michelle Sarche, Paul Spicer, Patricia Farrell, and Hiram Fitzgerald (Eds). Santa Barbara, CA: Praeger.

Campbell, L. 1988. "The Spirit Need Not Die: A People in Peril." *Anchorage Daily News, Special Issue.*

Champagne, Duane and Lester B. Brown. 1997. "Preface: Sharing the Gift of Sacred Being." *Journal of Gay and Lesbian Social Services* 6(2):5–18.

Chapman, Chris, Jennifer Laird and Angelina KewalRamani. 2010. *Trends in High School Dropout and Completion Rates in the United States: 1972–2008* (NCES 2011-012). Washington DC: National Center for Education Statistics, Institute of Education Sciences, United States Department of Education. Retrieved from http://nces.ed.gov/pubsearch.

Chovan, Martha J. and William Chovan. 1985. "Stressful Events and Coping Responses among Older Adults in Two Sociocultural Groups." *Journal of Psychology* 119(3):253–60.

Deyhle, Donna. 2009. *Reflections in Place: Connected Lives of Navajo Women.* Tucson: University of Arizona Press.

Deyhle, Donna and Frank Margonis. 1995. "Navajo Mothers and Daughters: Schools, Jobs, and the Family." *Anthropology and Education Quarterly* 26(2):135–67.

Dowsley, Martha, Shari Gearheard, Noor Johnson, and Jocelyn Inksetter. 2010. "Should We Turn the Tent? Inuit Women and Climate Change." *Etudes Inuit Studies* 34(1):151–65.

Evans-Campbell, Teresa, Karen I. Fredriksen-Goldsen, Karina L. Walters, and Anthony Stately. 2007. "Caregiving Experiences among American Indian Two Spirit Men and Women: Contemporary and Historical Roles." *Journal of Gay & Lesbian Social Services,* 18(3/4):75–92.

Fiske, Jo-Anne. 1995. "Political Status of Native Indian Women: Contradictory Implications of Canadian State Policy." *American Indian Culture and Research Journal* 19(2):1–30.

Friedl, Ernestine. 1967. "The Position of Women Appearance and Reality." *Anthropological Quarterly* 40(3):97–108.

Fryberg, Stephanie A., Hazel Rose Markus, Daphna Oyserman, and Joseph M. Stone. 2008. "Of Warrior Chiefs and Indian Princesses: The Psychological Consequences of American Indian Mascots." *Basic and Applied Social Psychology* 30(3) 208–18.

Gatschet. Albert S. 1891. "The Karankawa Indians, the Coast People of Texas." *Papers of the Peabody Museum of Archaeology and Ethnology* 1(2).

Goulet, Jean-Guy A. 1997. "The Northern Athapaskan 'Berdache' Reconsidered: On Reading More Than There Is in the Ethnographic Record." Pp. 45–68 in *Two-Spirit People: Native American Gender Identity, Sexuality and Spirituality*. Sue-Ellen Jacobs, Wesley Thomas, and Sabine Lang (Eds). Urbana: University of Chicago Press.

Green, Rayna. 1975. "The Pocahontas Perplex: The Image of Indian Women in American Culture." *Massachusetts Review* 14(6):698–714.

Green, Rayna. 1983. *Native American Women: A Contextual Bibliography*. Bloomington: Indiana University Press.

Hamamsy, Laila S. 1957. "The Role of Women in a Changing Navaho Society." *American Anthropologist* 59(1):101–11.

Han, Paul K. J., James Hagel, Thomas K. Welty, Randy Ross, Gary Leonardson, and Arliss Keckler. 1994. "Cultural Factors Associated with Health-Risk Behavior among the Cheyenne River Sioux." *American Indian and Alaska Native Mental Health Research* 5(3):15–29.

Harmon, Alexandra. 2010. *Rich Indians: Native People and the Problem of Wealth in American History*. Chapel Hill: University of North Carolina Press.

Harris, LaDonna. 2000. *LaDonna Harris: A Comanche Life*. Lincoln: University of Nebraska Press.

Hill, Brenda, Courtney Vaughn, and Sharon B. Harrison. 1995. "Living and Working in Two Worlds: Case Studies of Five American Indian Women Teachers." *The Clearing House* 69(1):42–49.

Hossain, Ziarat. 2001. "Division of Household Labor and Family Functioning in Off-Reservation Navajo Indian Families." *Family Relations* 50(3):255–61.

Hudson, Grace. 1980. "Participatory Research by Indian Women in Northern Ontario Remote Communities." *Convergence: An International Journal of Adult Education* 13(1):24–33.

Jacobs, Sue-Ellen, Wesley Thomas, and Sabine Lang (Eds). 1997. *Two-Spirit People: Native American Gender Identity, Sexuality, and Spirituality*. Urbana: University of Illinois Press.

Jenks, Kathleen. 1986. " 'Changing Women,' The Navajo Therapist Goddess." *Psychological Perspectives* 17(2):202–21.

Kafarowski, Joanna. 2004. "Contaminants in the Circumpolar North: The Nexus between Indigenous Reproductive Health, Gender and Environmental Justice." *Pimatisiwin* 2, 39–52.

Kidder, William C. 2003. "Struggle for Access from Sweatt to Grutter: A History of African American, Latino, and American Indian Law School Admissions 1950–2000." *Harvard BlackLetter Law Journal* 19(1):1–42.

Kidwell, Clara S. 1979. The Power of Women in Three American Indian Societies. *Journal of Ethnic Studies* 6:113–21.

Kidwell, Clara S. 1992. "Indian Women as Cultural Mediators." *Ethnohistory* 39(2):97–107.

Kidwell, Clara S. 1995. "Choctaw Women and Cultural Persistence in Mississippi." Pp. 115–34 in *Negotiators of Change: Historical Perspectives on Native American Women*. Nancy Shoemaker (Ed). New York: Routledge.

Kidwell, Clara S., Diane J. Willis, Deborah Jones-Saumty, and Dolores S. BigFoot. 2008. "Feminist Leadership among American Indian Women." Pp. 315–29 in *Transforming Visions and Diverse Voices*. Jean Lau Chin, Bernice Lott, Joy K. Rice, and Janis Sanchez-Hucles (Eds). Oxford: Blackwell Publishing.

Kleinfeld, Judith and Joseph D. Bloom. 1977. "Boarding Schools Effect on the Mental Health of Eskimo Adolescents." *American Journal of Psychiatry* 134(4):411–17.

Kunitz, Stephen J. and Jerold E. Levy. 1986. "The Prevalence of Hypertension among Elderly Navajos: A Test of the Acculturation Hypothesis." *Culture, Medicine, and Psychiatry* 10(2):97–121.

Kuokkanen, Rauna. 2011. "Indigenous Economies, Theories of Subsistence, and Women: Exploring the Social Economy Model for Indigenous Governance." *American Indian Quarterly* 35(2):215–40.

LaDuke, Winona. 1994. "Traditional Ecological Knowledge and Environmental Futures." *Colorado Journal of International Environmental Law and Policy* 5(127):144–45.

LaFromboise, Teresa. 1988. Cultural and Cognitive Considerations in the Coping of American Indian Women in Higher Education. Unpublished manuscript, Stanford University School of Education.

LaFromboise, Teresa D., Karen Albright, and Alex Harris. 2010. "Patterns of Hopelessness among American Indian Adolescents: Relationships by Levels of Acculturation and Residence." *Cultural Diversity and Ethnic Minority Psychology* 16(1):68–76.

LaFromboise, Teresa D., Hardin Coleman, and Jennifer Gerton. 1993. "Psychological Aspects of Bicultural Competence: Evidence and Theory." *Psychological Bulletin* 114(3):395–412.

LaFromboise, Teresa D., Analiese M. Heyl, and Emily J. Ozer. 1990. "Changing and Diverse Roles of Women and American Indian Societies." *Sex Roles* 22(7/8):455–76.

LaFromboise, Teresa D., Dan R. Hoyt, Lisa Oliver, and Les B. Whitbeck. 2006. "Family, Community, and School Influences on Resilience among American Indian Adolescents in the Upper Midwest." *Journal of Community Psychology* 34(2):193–209.

Lang, Sabine. 1998. *Men as Women, Women as Men: Changing Gender in Native American Cultures*. Austin: University of Texas Press.

Leacock, Eleanore B. 1986. "Women, Power and Authority." Pp. 107–35 in *Visibility and Power: Essays on Women in Society and Development*. Leela Dube, Eleanore B. Leacock, and Shirley Ardener (Eds). Delphi: Oxford University Press.

Lewis, Oscar. 1941. "Manly-Hearted Women among the Northern Piegan." *American Anthropologist* 43:173–87.

Li, Xiaojie. 2007. *Characteristics of Minority-Serving Institutions and Minority Undergraduates Enrolled in These Institutions* (NCES 2008-156). Washington DC: National Center for Education Statistics, Institute of Education Sciences, United States Department of Education.

Liberty, Margot. 1982. "Hell Came with Horses: Plains Indian Women in the Equestrian Era." *Montana* 32(3):10–19.

Livingston, K. 1974. "Women and Contemporary Iroquois Work: A Study of Consequences of Inequality." Cornell University: Ph.D. dissertation.

Lomawaima, K. Tsianina. 1995. *They Called it Prairie Light: The Story of Chilocco Indian school*. Lincoln: University of Nebraska Press.

Luna-Firebaugh, Eileen. 2007. *Tribal Policing: Asserting Sovereignty, Seeking Justice*. Tucson: University of Arizona Press.

Lurie, Nancy O. 1972. "Indian Women: A Legacy of Freedom." Pp. 29–36 in *Look to the Mountaintop*. Robert L. Iacopi and Bernard L. Fontana (Eds). San Jose, CA: Oousha Publications.

Lynch, Robert N. 1986. "Women in Northern Paiute Politics." *Signs–Journal of Women in Culture and Society* 11(2):352–66.

Mankiller, Wilma P. and Michael Wallis. 1993. *Mankiller: A Chief and Her People*. New York: St. Martin's Press.

McCoy, Melanie. 1992. "Gender or Ethnicity: What Makes a Difference? A Study of Women Tribal Leaders." *Women & Politics* 12:57–68.

Mead, Margaret. 1982. *The Changing Culture of an Indian Tribe*. New York: Columbia University Press.

Medicine, Beatrice. 1978. *The Native American Woman: A Perspective*. Austin, TX: National Educational Laboratory Publishers, Inc.

Medicine, Beatrice. 1980. "American Indian Women Spirituality and Status." *Bread and Roses* 2(1):15–18.

Medicine, Beatrice. 1983. "Warrior Woman: Sex Role Alternatives for Plains Indian Women." Pp. 267–80 in *The Hidden Half: Studies of Plains Indian Women*. Patricia Albers and Beatrice Medicine (Eds). Lanham, MD: University Press of America.

Metcalf, Ann. 1976. "From Schoolgirl to Mother: The Effects of Education on Navajo Women." *Social Problems*, 23(5):535–44.

Metoyer, Cheryl. 1979. "The Native American Woman." Pp. 329–35 in *The Study of Women Enlarging Perspectives on Social Reality*. Eloise C. Snyder (Ed). New York: Harper and Row.

Mihesuah, Devon A. 1996. "Commonalty of Difference: American Indian Women and History." *American Indian Quarterly* 20(1):15–27.

Mihesuah, Devon A. 2003. *Indigenous American Women: Decolonization, Empowerment, Activism*. Lincoln: University of Nebraska Press.

Mohanty, Chandra Talpade. 1988. "Under Western Eyes: Feminist Scholarship and Colonial Discourses." *Feminist Review* 30:61–88.

Morris, Michael. 2005. "Emerging Gender Roles for Southeastern Indian Women: The Mary Musgrove Story Reconsidered." *Georgia Historical Quarterly* 89(1):1–24.

Multicultural Women Attorneys Network, Federal Bar Association, and Native American Bar Association. 1998, August. *The Burdens of Both, the Privileges of Neither: A Report on the Experiences of Native American Women Lawyers*. http://www.americanbar.org/content/dam/aba/migrated/minorities/ftp/nativeamerbudens.pdf-20k-2011-06-29.

Napholz, L. 2000. "Bicultural Resynthesis: Tailoring an Effectiveness Trial for a Group of Urban American Indian Women." *American Indian and Alaska Native Mental Health Research* 9(3):49–70.

National Women's Business Council. 2006, June. *Native American/Alaska Native Women and Entrepreneurship*. www.nwbc.gov/NWBC-native_american _factsheet-1.pdf.

Niethammer, Carolyn J. 1977. *Daughters of the Earth*. New York: MacMillan.

Ortiz, Anna M., and Iris HeavyRunner. 2003. "Student Access, Retention, and Success: Models of Inclusion and Support." Pp. 215–40 in *The Renaissance of American Indian Higher Education: Capturing the Dream*. Maenette Kape'ahiokalani Padeken Ah Nee-Benham and Wayne J. Stein (Eds). Mahwah, NJ: Lawrence Erlbaum Associates.

Osburn, Katherine M. B. 1995. " 'Dear Friend and Ex-Husband': Marriage, Divorce, and Women's Property Rights on the Southern Ute Reservation, 1887–1930." Pp. 157–75 in *Negotiators of Change: Historical Perspectives on Native American Women*. Nancy Shoemaker (Ed). New York: Routledge.

Parezo, Nancy J. 1982. "Navajo Sandpaintings: The Importance of Sex Roles in Craft Production." *American Indian Quarterly* 6(1/2):25–48.

Perdue, Theda. 1995. "Women, Men and American Indian Policy: The Cherokee Response to 'Civilization.' " Pp. 90–114 in *Negotiators of Change: Historical Perspectives on Native American Women*. Nancy Shoemaker (Ed). New York: Routledge.

Pesantubbee, Michelene E. 1999. "Beyond Domesticity: Choctaw Women Negotiating the Tension between Choctaw Culture and Protestantism." *Journal of the American Academy of Religion* 67(2):387–409.

Powers, Marla N. 1986. *Oglala Women Myth, Ritual, and Reality*. Chicago: University of Chicago Press.

Ramirez, Renya K. 2007. *Native Hubs: Culture, Community and Belonging in the Silicon Valley and Beyond*. Durham, NC: Duke University Press.

Roscoe, Will. 1998. *Changing Ones: Third and Fourth Genders in Native North America*. New York: St. Martin's Press.

Seton, Earnest T. and Julia M. Seton. 1953. *The Gospel of the Redman: An Indian Bible*. Santa Fe, NM: Seton Village.

Shoemaker, Nancy. 1995. *Negotiators of Change: Historical Perspectives on Native American Women*. New York: Routledge.

Shoemaker, Nancy. 2010. "The Rise or Fall of Iroquois Women." *Journal of Women's History* 2(3):39–57.

Silko, Leslie M. 1996. *Yellow Woman and a Beauty of the Spirit*. New York: Touchstone.

Simoni, Jane M., Teresa Evans-Campbell, Michele P. Andrasik, Karen Lehavot, Dellanira Valencia-Garcia, Karina Walters. 2010. HIV/AIDS Among Women of Color and Sexual Minority Women. Pp. 335–366 in *Handbook of Diversity in Feminist Psychology*. Hope Landrine and Nancy Felipe Russo (Eds). New York: Springer Publishing Co.

Spindler, Louise and George Spindler. 1958. "Male and Female Adaptations in Culture Change." *American Anthropologist* 60(2):217–33.

Swanton, John R. 1911. "Indian Tribes of the Lower Mississippi Valley and Adjacent Coast of the Gulf of Mexico." *Bureau of American Ethnology Bulletin* 43:1–387.

Szasz, Margaret C. 1980. " 'Poor Richard' Meets the Native American Schooling for Young Indian Women in Eighteenth-Century Connecticut." *Pacific Historical Review* 49(2):215–35.

Tajfel, Henri. 1981. *Human Groups and Human Categories*. Cambridge, UK: Cambridge University Press.

Tanner, Helen H. 1979. "Coocoochee Mohawk Medicine Women." *American Indian Culture and Research Journal* 3(3):23–41.

Thomas, Wesley and Sue-Ellen Jacobs. 1999. " '…And We Are Still Here': From Berdache to Two-Spirit People." *American Indian Culture and Research Journal* 23(2):91–107.

Trennert, Robert A. 1982. "Educating Young Girls at Non-reservation Boarding Schools." *Western Historical Quarterly* 13, 271–90.

United States Department of Defense. n.d. *Native American Indian Heritage Month: Native American Women Veterans*. Accessed August 14, 2011. http://www.defense.gov/specials/nativeamerican01/women.html.

Valentino, Debra, and Anne Terry Straus. 2004. "Gender and Community Organization Leadership in the Chicago Indian Community." *American Indian Quarterly*. 27(3):523–32.

Vizenor, Gerald Robert. 1994. *Manifest Manners: Postindian Warriors of Survivance*. Middletown, CT: Wesleyan University Press.

Vizenor, Gerald Robert. 1999. *Manifest Manners: Narratives on Postindian Survivance*. Winnipeg, MB: Bison Books.

Walls, Melissa L. and Les B. Whitbeck. 2011. "Distress among Indigenous North Americans: Generalized and Culturally Relevant Stressors." *Society and Mental Health* 1(2):124–36.

Walters, Karina L., Teresa Evans-Campbell, Jane M. Simoni, Theresa Ronquillo, and Rupaleem Bhuyan. 2006. " 'My Spirit in my Heart': Identity Experiences and Challenges among American Indian Two-Spirit Women." Pp. 125–49 in *Challenging Lesbian Norms: Intersex, Transgender, Intersectional, and Queer Perspectives*. Angela Pattatucci Aragon (Ed). Binghamton, NY: Harrington Park Press.

Walters, Karina L. and Jane M. Simoni. 2002. "Reconceptualizing Native Women's Helath: An "Indigenist" Stress-Coping Model." *American Journal of Public Health* 92(4):520–24.

Weisfeld, Carol C., Glenn E. Weisfeld and John W. Callaghan. 1982. "Female Inhibition in Mixed-Sex Competition among Young Adolescents." *Ethology and Socialbiology* 3(1):29–42.

Weisfeld, Carol C., Glenn E. Weisfeld, Ronald Warren, and Donald Freeman. 1983. "The Spelling Bee: A Naturalistic Study of Female Inhibition in Mixed-Sex Competition." *Adolescence* 18(71):695–708.

Welch, Deborah. 1987. "American Indian Women: Reaching beyond the Myth." Pp. 31–48 in *New Directions in American Indian History*. Collin G. Calloway (Ed). Norman: University of Oklahoma Press.

White Shield, Rosemary. 2009. "Identifying and Understanding Indigenous Cultural and Spiritual Strengths in the Higher Education Experiences of Indigenous Women." *Wicazo Sa Review* 24(1):47–63.

Willeto, Angela A. 2007. "Native American Kids: American Indian Children's Well-Being Indicators for the Nation and Two States." *Social Indicators Research* 83(1):149–76.

Wilson, Alex. 1996. "How We Find Ourselves: Identity Development and Two Spirit People." *Harvard Educational Review* 66(2):303–18.

Witt, Shirley Hill. 1974. "Native Women Today Sexism and the Indian Woman."
    Civil Rights Digest 6(3):29–35.
Witt, Shirley Hill. 1981. "Past Perspectives and Present Problems in Ohoyo Resource
    Center Staff." Pp. 11–20 in *Words of Today's American Indian Women*. Ohoyo
    Makachi (Ed). Wichita Falls, TX: Ohoyo, Inc.
Zak, Nancy C. 1988. "The Earth Mother Figure of Native North America." *Revision*
    70(3):27–36.
Zak, Nancy C. 1989. "Sacred and Legendary Women of Native North America."
    Pp. 232–45 in *The Goddess Re-Awakening: The Feminine Principle Today*. Shirley
    J. Nicholson (Ed). Wheaton, IL: Theosophical Publishing House.

CHAPTER 3

Alaska Native Women: 40 Years of Sociocultural Change

Rosita Kaahani Worl

INTRODUCTION

The 1970s brought dramatic changes to Alaska and to Alaska Natives with the discovery and development of oil on the North Slope; the infusion of increased revenues into the State of Alaska coffers supported capital construction projects throughout the state and created a vast number of job opportunities. The enactment of the Alaska Native Claim Settlement Act of 1971 (ANCSA) also brought major institutional changes to the Native community with the creation of 13 regional corporations and 200 village corporations; the transfer of title to 44 million acres of land to Native ownership followed by the economic development of those lands and resources; and the individualization of tribal groups into shareholders. During the same period, the feminist movement that sought social and economic equity for women also made inroads into the Native community. Collectively, these forces stimulated and accelerated the sociocultural changes to the fabric of Native societies and magnified the impacts on Native culture and way of life. This paper focuses on select indicators of differential rates of change evident among Alaska Native women in the last 40 years.

TRADITIONAL ROLE OF ALASKA
NATIVE WOMEN

Within the traditional societies of Alaska Natives, women maintained prominent roles in the economic sphere. They participated in hunting and fishing activities and conducted all the gathering activities, such as collecting berries and plants. Women were responsible for processing and preserving food as well as making all the clothing and some of the hunting equipment such as the skin boats used in marine mammal hunting. Among the Inupiat Eskimo of the Arctic and the northwestern regions of Alaska, women played critical roles in whaling and other marine mammal hunting activities. The Yup'ik Eskimo women of western Alaska were responsible for the processing and preserving of subsistence harvests, whether seals, salmon, or herring, and the gathering of material and weaving of the essential utilitarian baskets. Likewise, the work of Aleut women living on the Alaska Peninsula and Aleutian chain were essential as they made the specialized clothing that hunters needed in their maritime hunting. The Athabascan women living in the interior regions of Alaska fished alongside men and processed and preserved all the subsistence foods for the long, cold winter months. The Tlingit and Haida women of southeastern Alaska were also responsible for smoking and drying the food resources from the sea. Additionally, in these clan-based societies, property transferred through the maternal line. Women had the authority to approve trading transactions with neighboring tribes as well as those with the Europeans and Americans who began to frequent their coastal communities in the 1800s.

The divisions of labor in hunting, fishing, and gathering activities are gender based, and the labor, knowledge, and expertise of Native women are essential to the survival of their families and communities. Too often, the perception exists that women's work in subsistence economies is labor intensive but uncomplicated. Frink (2009:21, 24), who studied the technologies and techniques of women in Native subsistence economies, found that women's subsistence tasks are arduous and required a lifetime of training and practice but that not all women were able to achieve master status. She also emphasized the importance of the resident elder woman whose knowledge is embedded in her and the environmental and cultural experience and expertise gained over a lifetime of work. Women, in essence, served as the managers of subsistence camps and made the decisions on butchering, storing, and distribution of subsistence resources. Women were also critical in the apprenticeship system that ensured their knowledge was transferred to the younger generations.

The arrival of Americans after the purchase of Alaska from Russia in 1867, and the forcible attempts to impose their ideologies on Native societies through the school systems and churches, initiated the process that led to the erosion of the status of Native women. It was not long before Native women faced the same economic and social inequities endured by non-Native women. In her address to a statewide convention of Native women, Worl (1979), a Tlingit from southeastern Alaska, challenged the commonly held assumption that indigenous women moved from a state of inequality in their traditional societies to equality as they assimilated into Western societies. On the contrary, she noted that Native women endure double discrimination, first because they are Native and second because they are women.

Alaska Native women began to challenge the inequities they endured because of their status. They openly joined the feminist movement through their participation in the May 1977 statewide women's meeting in Anchorage. Although Native women represented a small minority of the women attending the conference, they were remarkably successful in electing 5 Native delegates of the 12 delegates who were selected to participate in the National Women's Conference in Houston in November 1977. The Native women recognized that they shared many of the same concerns as other women, but they also maintained that they had different issues that were unique to them as Alaska Native women. They contended that the value of women in their subsistence hunting and fishing societies was not generally recognized by outsiders, including the anthropologists who studied their societies. However, more importantly, they argued in the convention caucuses that their cultural survival was interrelated with subsistence and was threatened by federal and state policies and special interest groups that failed to recognize or opposed their subsistence rights and practices. The Native women successfully persuaded the national conference to include in the national plan of action a somewhat unusual feminist objective—the protection of hunting, fishing, and whaling rights (Worl 1977).

The Native women then took their concerns to the statewide Native organization, the Alaska Federation of Natives (AFN). The AFN was organized in 1966 to pursue the settlement of the aboriginal land claims of Alaska Natives. Alaska Natives divided themselves into 12 geographical regions, and the AFN governing board drew representatives from each of these regions. The Native women met during the AFN statewide convention and discussed their concerns, which included a broad range of issues from bilingual education to violence waged against Native women. They also noted their lack of representation in leadership positions at AFN and in Native corporations. The Alaska Native corporations (ANCs) were established by Congress to implement ANCSA. The Native women attending AFN adopted a comprehensive and conciliatory proclamation (in response to the concerns expressed by Native men that the Native women would join the radical feminist movement of the 1970s) that is worthy of citing in its entirety as it clearly outlines the goals and objectives Native women established for themselves to ensure the survival of their traditional cultures and to achieve equity both within the Native societies and organizations and in the new non-Native society in which they found themselves (Worl 1977):

Alaska Native women will continue to support the objectives of the Alaska Federation of Natives. However, it is our plan and purpose that henceforth our participation in the political process and affairs that affect all Alaska Natives will become increasingly visible.

As Alaska Native women, we cherish our role within our traditional cultures, and it is our intent to do everything within our power to protect our positions and our cultures. We have profound admiration for our Alaska Native men. We are honored to be accorded respect in our traditional cultures. We would ask that this same respect be extended to us in a nontraditional setting.

Our world continues to change as we come into increasing contact with our new and external influences. We feel that if Alaska Native cultures are to survive, then we as primary transmitters of our cultures must accelerate and increase our involvement to accommodate those changes. It is time for us to equalize our positions within AFN, within our villages and regional and nonprofit corporations, and within our state and national legislative bodies. We must insist that we take a greater role and responsibility in these affairs. We owe this obligation not only to ourselves as Alaska Native women, but to our communities and cultures as well.

The Alaska Native woman is in a unique position. She maintains a role in the traditional culture, but also encounters the same problems that face non-Native women, and tragically, she endures them on a greater and intensified scale. She is the object of educational, employment and political discrimination, not only as a woman, but also as a Native. She is often the object of violence, which is as devastating as being the object of jokes and ridicule.

We cannot begin to address the discriminatory actions waged against us as Alaska Native women in the larger society without first bringing to the attention of the AFN and Alaska Native men the inequities which today are so evident. We seek to resolve these inequities.

FEMALE FLIGHT: RURAL/URBAN MIGRATION

At the time of contact with Westerners in 1741, the indigenous population did not conceive of themselves as a single group or identify themselves as Alaska Natives. This singular classification of the indigenous population was conceived by Westerners. In actuality, the Alaska Natives represented four distinct cultural groups that were dispersed throughout Alaska including the Inupiat and Yup'ik Eskimo, Aleut, Athabascan, and the Tlingit and Haida of southeastern Alaska. A group of Tsimshian Indians were brought by a missionary from Canada to Annette Island in southeastern Alaska in 1891 (Philp 1981:312). While Native people did not abandon their cultural identity, the references and designation of Alaska Natives in federal law and policies and finally the legal definition of Alaska Native in ANCSA solidified the social designation and identity of indigenous peoples as Alaska Natives.

The first enumeration of the Alaska Native population was conducted in 1880, and the census revealed that the Native population had declined from its estimated contact number of 80,000 in 1741 (Langdon 1987:4) to 33,000 as a result of the epidemics of infectious diseases. It continued to decline until 1910, and it was not until 1947 that the Native population rebounded to the 1880 number (Milan and Pawson 1975:275). By the 2010 census, the Native population had grown to over 138,000 (Department of Labor 2011).

Natives traditionally inhabited all geographic regions of Alaska and migrated throughout all of Alaska. During the winter months, almost all Natives groups lived in permanent villages, but during the summer months they dispersed to summer camps. The last group to abandon a nomadic lifestyle and elect to settle in a permanent community were the Inupiat caribou hunters who established the community of Anaktuvuk Pass in the North Slope in the 1950s.

Today Alaska is broadly divided between rural and urban Alaska. Rural Alaska is generally described as communities that are not connected by road systems or are located outside of the road network. Rural Alaska includes nearly 200 villages, primarily concentrated in the Arctic, western and southwestern Alaska, and a scattering of villages throughout the interior regions and along the coast in southeastern Alaska. Village populations are less than 800, and the associated regional hubs have populations ranging from 1,000 to 5,000. The villages and regional centers are predominantly Alaska Native (Howe 2009:71) while the urban centers are predominantly non-Native.

Leask, Killorin, and Cravez (2006:4) reported that in 2000, 40 percent of Alaska Natives lived in urban areas, and they predicted that by 2020 that number would rise to 50 percent. In actuality, the urban Native population reached the 50 percent mark by the 2010 census, and Anchorage, the largest urban community, was identified as the largest Native village in the state (Dunham 2011).

Sex ratios among Natives have historically fluctuated, due primarily to differences in gender mortality from various environmental or health forces. For example, high hunting accident rates, exacerbated by the dangers of hunting on the ocean sea ice, accounted for higher deaths among men. However, in the more recent period, differential outmigration between Native men and women from rural to urban centers began to impact the sex ratio for both rural and urban Alaska (Hamilton 2008:2). Martin and colleagues (2008:5) report that from 1980 through 2006, more Native women than men migrated from rural to urban areas, leaving rural Alaska with a greater Native male population and urban Alaska with a larger Native female population in contrast to Native males. The term *female flight* was coined to describe this phenomenon characterized by the disproportionate out-migration of Native women from rural villages to the urban centers (Martin 2010:151). The term *bachelor cultures* was adopted to describe the young men who are left behind in the villages and who cannot find partners (Kleinfeld and Andrews 2006a:113).

Martin (2010:153–54) reports that the primary reason Native women give for leaving rural Alaska is to seek better education for themselves or their children. Those who were victims of sexual or other assault also want to leave the villages. Hamilton (2010:3) also points to the social problems, most often stemming from alcohol, and the pressure they create on women and girls as another reason for outmigration from villages. Hamilton and Seyfrit (1994:190) also found persistent gender differences in migration expectations with more girls than boys saying they would move away from rural communities to seek higher education. Later research would confirm that, overall, young Native girls achieve their educational aspirations. Hamilton and Seyfrit (1997:291) identify another reason Native women leave rural villages. They report that Native women are equally likely to marry Native or non-Native men while fewer Native men marry non-Natives. However, when Native women marry non-Native men, they are more likely to leave rural Alaska, which further contributes to the gender imbalance in rural communities.

The differential outmigration along with the higher mortality rate of Native men contributes to the gender imbalance in rural communities and has serious implications for the overall health of the community. One study found that young males between the age of 20 and 30 accounted for 60 percent of the population in several villages (Hamilton and Seyfrit 1994:192). The 2000 census reports that in 18 of the smallest villages, with populations less than 100, there were no women aged 20 to 29. Another 23 communities reported only 1 woman in that age group (Martin et al. 2008:5). The result is the absence of marriage partners for Native males. In one Arctic village, the shortage of marriage partners was evident with 41 percent of the men unmarried while only 10 percent of the women were unmarried (Milan and Pawson 1975:282).

The consequence of the bachelor culture, or Native males not having marriage partners, and the evident disparity between Native men and women marriage possibilities deserves further exploration. It raises the question of whether this condition is a factor in the high alcohol and substance abuse and the high suicide rate of Native males in rural communities. During the period of 1999 to 2005, Native men 15 to 24 years of age were almost nine times as likely to die of suicide as white men in this age group in the United States and five times as likely to die as white men in this age group in Alaska (Alaska Native Tribal Health Consortium 2010:1).

Female flight is a real and widespread phenomenon. Martin (2009:65) suggests that the outmigration appears to be an irreversible process. With women and children leaving the village, the stabilizing effects arising from family responsibilities are diminished. Furthermore, the departure of children from the village may lead to the closure of schools, which are generally the largest employer in the village. The school jobs disappear, prompting other people to migrate, thus leaving the survival of the village in jeopardy.

EMPLOYMENT

The discovery of oil at Prudhoe Bay in the North Slope of Alaska in the late 1960s brought massive and accelerated change to Alaska's economy. Native women entered the wage labor force in increasing numbers. During the decade from 1970 to 1980, the participation of Native women in the labor force increased by 50 percent, although they tended to be in the lower paying occupations in contrast to white women (Chilkat Institute and Institute of Social and Economic Research [ISER] 1983:9). During this period, the rate of Native women's employment approached parity with Native men; through the 1990s, their employment continued to increase, and by 2000 they had a slight edge on Native men (ISER 2004:10). However, Native men's and women's employment was far less than that of non-Natives. The ISER (2004) study reported that less than half of adult Natives have jobs compared with 73 percent of non-Native men and 64 percent of non-Native women. Additionally, the Native jobs were more likely to be part time or seasonal.

The Alaska Department of Labor reported that from 2000 to 2006, the number of Alaska Natives dropped about 3 percent in the remote rural regions but was up nearly 25 percent in Anchorage. The lack of economic opportunities in rural Alaska was the major reason, but other likely factors included better access to medical care and improved and higher education (Kruse and Kruse 2007:2). Adult Native women in the age group of 20 to 64 outnumbered adult Native men in urban areas by 17 percent (ISER 2004:3). The lower number of Native males living in the city coupled with the statewide gender imbalance reflected by a 52 percent non-Native male population (Wells 2004:8) means that Native women have a greater likelihood of meeting marriageable white men.

Alaska Native women moved from villages to urban areas for jobs. The jobs held by women were first in health care, followed by education and public administration. Jones (1976) studied the work adaptation of Alaska Native men and women to urban employment and found that Native women readily adapted to the urban environment. She attributed the more stable work adjustment of low-skilled Native women to the fact that their socialization to become a wife and mother was compatible with adapting to low-status jobs in urban Alaska. Jones noted, however, that they had received little preparation in the village for playing a major economic role in the family. The lack of training did not deter them from entering the labor market, but it tended to keep them in the low-skilled jobs.

The Alaska Native birth rate was more than twice the national average and was 53 percent higher than that of non-Natives in Alaska in 1980 (ISER 1984:4). Although the Native women's fertility rate declined in the 1980s, the large increase of Native women in their childbearing years more than offset the drop in the fertility rate. The ISER study reported that by 1980, the statewide population of Alaska Native women from age 20 to 34 comprised 14 percent of the population compared to just 10 percent ten years earlier.

The relatively high birth rate, coupled with the increasing population of Native women in their childbearing years, resulted in children constituting a larger portion of the Alaska Native population. In 1980, 23 percent of the Native population was under the age of 10. Unfortunately, the proportion of Native women living in households with their own children but no husband increased from 11 percent in 1960 to 22 percent by 2000. Native women were more than twice as likely to serve as the head of household than Native men. Similar changes had occurred in households nationwide, but the changes in Native households were more dramatic, according to an ISER study (2004:4). One in five Native children and one in seven non-Native children are growing up in households headed by women. Native children in urban Alaska are more than likely to live in households headed by women. These households are by far the most likely to be poor (ISER 2004:5).

EDUCATION

Educational opportunities improved in rural Alaska with the opening of University of Alaska campuses and the availability of both technical training programs in the regional hubs and online university course. The number of Natives with some college credit jumped from 752 in 1970 to 26,151 in 2000. Alaska Native women were especially eager to pursue educational opportunities. In 2000, nearly 35 percent of Native women had some college credit in contrast to the 26 percent of Native males (ISER 2004:15).

The gender gap in postsecondary education is a phenomenon that is evident in many nations, but the disparity between Alaska Native males and females is dramatic. The gender gap among Alaska Natives is seen from the early education years to precollege and in postsecondary education.

As noted earlier in the discussion of the outmigration of Native women from rural Alaska, young Native girls are highly motivated to seek higher education. Their motivation is reflected in efforts to prepare themselves for college. The University of Alaska Rural Alaska Honors Institute (RAHI) was established as a college preparation program for promising Alaska Native students. Kleinfeld and Andrews (2006a:118) report that 66 percent of the 1,036 students who have attended RAHI since its inception were female. The gender gap continues among the RAHI student who have gone on to seek higher education and received degrees. Of those obtaining doctorates, 100 percent were female. At the master's degree level, 71 percent have been female and 78 percent obtaining bachelor's degrees have been female. This same disparity is also evident in the Alaska Scholars Program, which offers scholarships to the top 10 percent of each school graduating class in Alaska. In 2004, among the Alaska Scholars, nearly two-thirds were females, of whom 70 percent were Alaska Native females.

The gender imbalance is also reflected in actual college enrollment and graduation. In 2003 within the University of Alaska system, 31 percent were Native males while 69 percent were female. In the University of Alaska regional centers, the disparity is even more extreme, with Native males comprising 27 percent of the student population while Alaska Native females accounted for 73 percent. In 2004, males earned less than one-third of the bachelor degrees awarded to Alaska Natives in the University of Alaska system, giving them the most extreme gender gap of any minority group in the United States. The gender gap in the associate degree programs is almost five to one (Kleinfeld and Andrews 2006b:430–31).

It is not surprising that the Tlingit and Haida of southeastern Alaska, who have had the longest exposure of all Alaska Natives to Western society, have the highest rate of Native males seeking higher education in the University of Alaska system. Their number represent 46 percent in contrast to Athabascan males at 25 percent in 2003 (Kleinfeld and Andrews 2006b:117). Although Tlingit and Haida males may have the highest number of Alaska Native males attending the University of Alaska in contrast to other Native males, the same gender imbalance is apparent in their society. According to the Sealaska Heritage Institute records, of the total number of Native students awarded scholarships in 2009, 66 percent were females while 34 percent were males. However, men and women were equal in receiving vocational technical programs scholarships.

Kleinfeld and Andrews (2006a:113) have offered two potential explanations to account for the apparent gender disparity between Alaska Native males and females attending and completing college. According to these authors, who conducted their research among the Inupiat, women are leaving remote rural communities for employment and education in regional and urban centers, leaving behind what they have termed "bachelor cultures" of young men who cannot find partners and who engage in self-destructive behavior. The second explanation is that postsecondary education represents a functional adaptation to a mixed economy in which Native males participate in a wage and a subsistence economy while Native women are more than likely to pursue work in industries such as education and social fields and administrative services for which formal education is important. On the other hand, men pursue blue-collar labor and subsistence activities for which education is unimportant. They further offer (Kleinfeld and Andrews 2006a:432) that the "employment in occupations that require academic credentials are inconsistent with the traditional, prestigious male role as independent hunter and provider."

The evident gender gap between Native males and females in education has profound implications for employment and marriage patterns, leadership positions in Native organizations that directly affect the lives of Native individuals and communities, and societal problems. Kleinfeld and Reyes (2007:180) suggest that with women assuming greater economic responsibility, men from both Native and non-Native societies no longer appear to have clear ideas of what is expected of them as adult males. The existing data appear to support these assumptions for Native populations in that Native women are pursuing education at a greater rate than that of men and Native men's participation in subsistence activities are at a greater level than that of Native women.

LEADERSHIP

One might assume that with a higher level of education, Alaska Native women would be represented in leadership positions in Native organizations in greater numbers, or at minimum would have achieved equity with Native males. The major Native organizations in addition to the statewide AFN include the 12 regional and village ANCs organized under ANCSA and the 12 regional nonprofit organizations, which administer governmental programs for Native people. The AFN's primary function remains in political advocacy. Its focus shifted from the settlement of land claims after the enactment of ANCSA to other major issues facing the Native community such as the protection of subsistence hunting and fishing rights and promotion of the social well-being of Native communities. The Native corporations focus on economic activities. They own 44 million acres of land conveyed under ANCSA and shared in the near $1 billion settlement paid to the Native corporations for the extinguishment of aboriginal title to the remaining acreages in Alaska, amounting to 320 million acres of land. The ANCs became a major economic force in the State of Alaska, representing some of the largest corporations in the State of Alaska. In the last decade, many of them had become extraordinarily financially successful, due in large part to the government contracts they were awarded under a special program that gives preference to Alaska Native corporations.

The data indicate, however, that Native women did not necessarily achieve political equity with Native men despite their higher educational levels. In 1977, Native women targeted AFN as one of the organizations in which they would seek equity with Native men. While the last two presidents of AFN have been Native women, the policy board remains predominantly male with 14 women on the board of directors in contrast to the 23 men. In addition, only one woman has served as chair of its board of directors since its formation over 45 years ago.

The gender imbalance is dramatically notable in the senior executive positions of both the 12 profit-making and the nonprofit corporations. The CEOs are appointed by the board of directors of each organization, who are all Natives. Of the 12 regional ANCs, only two Alaska Native women serve as CEO of their corporations at the present time. This number represents a decrease from the 2007 number when five Native women were CEOs of regional ANCs (Horton 2007:1). Of the 12 regional nonprofits, Native women serve as the CEO in two of the nonprofits. This is especially surprising because Native women are overly concentrated in the social service fields.

Board members of ANCs are elected by Native shareholders, who are equally divided between males and females. This pattern of selection does not appear to have an effect on gender balance because males continue to dominate the representation on the boards of directors of ANCs. For example, within one region, the historical gender imbalance is dramatic. Since the time of the initial organization of Sealaska Corporation in southeastern Alaska some 40 years ago, only seven Native women have served on its board of directors. This number is even more extreme when considering that the size of the Sealaska board of directors, which has been extraordinarily large in contrast to other corporate boards. The size decreased from 18 members to its current level of 13 directors, of which 4 are females. The same gender imbalance is replicated in most all of the governing boards of other regional ANCs.

In reviewing the political representation of women in Native organizations at the village level in 10 communities in southeastern Alaska, Native women fare a little better than at the regional level. Women on the board of directors of village corporations are represented by 27 women, with 43 male directors. At the tribal councils, Native women represent 29 members in contrast to the 38 men. In two tribal councils, women outnumbered men sitting on the councils. Of interest is the residency pattern or evidence of the impacts of outmigration from villages, which is seen in the contrast in membership between village corporations and tribal councils. Tribal councils restrict their membership to individuals who reside in the villages. On the other hand, village corporations can elect their directors from their shareholder base irrespective of their residence. The contrast in membership between a village corporation and tribal council is particularly notable in one village. Of nine members that sit on the village corporation board of directors, five directors reside outside of the community, and four of them have college degrees. In the same village, with a tribal council of five members, all of the council members reside in the community, and none have college degrees.

The village corporation holds title to the land base that generally surrounds the village as well as other economic revenues. The historic investments of this village corporation have largely been concentrated in the community. Whether this investment approach will continue by a board of directors dominated by nonresident membership is worthy of further research as economic development and job creation are vital to the survival of the community. Other research indicates that economic opportunities can stimulate a return migration to the village.

The leadership of Native women in the cultural sphere continues to be significant even with an outmigration of Native women from rural

Alaska. Their role in traditional ceremonies continues into the present-day period. For example, clan mothers in Tlingit and other Native groups play a major role in the traditional potlatch. The prominence of Native women is also reinforced in matrilineal societies, which characterize several of the Alaska Native groups, in which descent is through women. They also play an important role in teaching oral traditions and songs. The Indians of southeastern Alaska sponsor a biennial dance festival that attracts five to six thousand participants. In this area, we see that 33, or 60 percent, of Celebration 2010 dance groups had female leaders.

Alaska Native women have also become important in the school system where Native people have been relentless in promoting the integration of culturally based curriculum and Native language instruction. During the 2003–2004 school year, female teachers outnumbered men by two to one in Alaska, and five percent were Alaska Natives (McDowell Group 2005:56). We can assume that the larger numbers of Native teachers are females considering their higher graduation rate in the University of Alaska system. Native women also serve as the language teachers and teacher aides in the special Indian education programs that are funded primarily by federal grants. A state employee in the education department recently made an observation to the author that all the educators attending a workshop in Fairbanks in late July were Native women, and the previous ones she had seen attending were predominantly Native female teachers.

RETURN MIGRATION

Studies have revealed that women are less likely to move back to rural Alaska unless job opportunities are available. Huskey, Berman, and Hill (2004:80) found that Native men are more inclined to return to their home villages to participate in subsistence activities while Native women make their decisions to return based on employment opportunities that are available in the village. Natives also return to their rural home communities to be with their families. However, more men (68%) than women (58%) reported family as the main reason for returning home (Huskey and Howe 2010:155).

Cyclic migrations characterized by those who move back and forth between village and city represent another migration pattern. More often men engage in cyclic migrations. Close to 40 percent of men in Jones's (1976:39) study compared to 24 percent of women had returned to their village at least once and usually more often since their initial move to the city. Jones found that education and training affected the return migrations. Sixty percent of low-skilled men had returned to their villages at least once compared to the 23 percent of the skilled men and 20 percent of the middle-class male workers. In a study of migration to and from northern rural communities in the period of 1985 to 1990, of every 10 people who moved from northern communities, about seven returned. This pattern was about the same for males and females. However, from 1995 to 2000, the ratio of gender migration changed with more females migrating from northern rural Alaska and more men returning (Huskey and Howe 2010:151).

Fewer women return because they marry or have jobs in urban center. Martin and colleagues (2008:12) found that in 2000 about 67 percent of Native women in urban centers have been married even though they may be separated, divorced, or widowed, in comparison with 53 percent of Native males. Eighty percent of women reported they were working compared to 79 percent of men in the labor force. The marriage rate for the Inupiat women living in the city was somewhat higher. About 71 percent of Inupiat Eskimo women living in urban centers have been married in comparison to 55 percent of Inupiat men (Huskey and Howe 2010:153). The return of Natives with education and job experience to rural communities benefits the community when Native people, who have an intimate knowledge of the people and culture, can fill the job openings that are available in a village.

SUBSISTENCE HUNTING AND FISHING

Alaska Natives have expended significant political capital, largely through the AFN and with the financial and political support of ANCs, to protect Native subsistence rights. ANCSA extinguished subsistence rights, but Congress intended for the federal government to protect subsistence hunting and fishing, and they codified this intent in the Alaska National Interest Conservation Act of 1980 (ANILCA), which established a subsistence priority for rural subsistence users. ANILCA authorized the State of Alaska to manage the wildlife resources on federal lands if they complied with the rural subsistence priority. The subsistence priority, however, was challenged by sports hunters and fishers who asserted that the Alaska State Constitution provides for equal access to natural resources. The

Alaska Supreme Court concurred that a priority right for rural subsistence users was unconstitutional. As a result, the federal government assumed control of the management of wildlife and the regulation of subsistence on federal land because the state failed to comply with ANILCA. The state continues to manage fish and wildlife on state lands and waters.

Subsistence hunting and fishing is viewed by Alaska Natives as necessary for their cultural survival. It also contributes substantially to the food security of rural communities as well as being the preferred food. Additionally, the by-products of subsistence resources, including bone, skin, fur, and ivory along with other natural resources such as tree roots and bark, are used in the production of arts and craft. The sale of arts and craft and handmade, traditional Native clothing provides an important source of revenue in villages that have limited employment opportunities.

Both males and females are involved in arts and craft production, but some fields are dominated by women. Women make almost all of the traditional clothing and ceremonial regalia that are used by Native people as well as that made for sale such as parkas, mukluks, beaded moccasins, hats, and gloves. Some traditional arts, such as spruce-root basketry, that almost became extinct are now produced by Native women. In one village, 20 women learned to make spruce-root baskets. Today they earn a modest income from their basket sales to the tourist market, and to assure that the art does not become extinct, they are teaching a younger generation of basket weavers.

Rural communities are dependent on both subsistence and a cash economy. The Alaska Department of Fish and Game estimated that, in 2000, 60 percent of rural households, including both Native and non-Native households, harvest game and 80 percent fish, and the annual harvests are several hundred pounds per person. According to the 2000 census, most households in the remote rural regions also had some income from wage work. A recent survey of Inupiat households in northern Alaska found that 78 percent of the households combined jobs and subsistence hunting, fishing, and other activities (Goldsmith 2008:1–3).

The data suggest an unanticipated and more than likely an unrecognized change in subsistence. More Native men participate in subsistence activities than Native females, and Native men continue to view subsistence hunting and fishing as prestigious activities. A larger number of men have returned to village life to participate in subsistence hunting and fishing. With Native women leaving rural Alaska in greater numbers and seeking education and employment opportunities, they are participating in subsistence activities to a lesser degree.

Today subsistence hunting and fishing is celebrated through the World Eskimo Indian Olympics (WEIO). WEIO has been held in Fairbanks since 1961 and draws an estimated 1,000 participants and visitors, primarily from the Inupiat and Yup'ik Eskimo and Athabascan communities. A large population also comes from the urban centers in Anchorage and Fairbanks. A significance of WEIO is that it serves to idealize and popularize the subsistence lifestyle, and young, beautiful Native women, competing in the Miss WEIO pageant, have become a symbol of subsistence. Both men and women participate in games of strength, endurance, and agility based on skills that are needed in subsistence activities and tolerance for pain that are required to survive in the harsh arctic and subarctic climate. The female competitors in the Miss WEIO queen competition are judged on their knowledge of traditional culture, represented by subsistence activities, and the traditional clothing they wear. Although the evening gown and swimsuit competition of the first years of WEIO have been eliminated, elements of sexism persist. One moderator in the 2011 Olympics continually repeated during the time the author was present at the games that the WEIO games are traditional games that were played by men, and that if women wished to compete, they would have to seek the permission of the male athletes. While gender roles are evident in subsistence activities, their participation was primarily related to expertise. Women could be whaling captains or hunters in the same way as men, and the permission of men was not necessary.

CONCLUSION

During the last 40 years, differential rates of sociocultural change have been evident between Native males and females. Native women left rural Alaska in large numbers, leaving villages and rural centers predominantly inhabited by men. They entered the workforce in significant numbers, and they surpassed Native males in higher educational pursuits. Their success is evident by the fact that Alaska Native women with University of Alaska bachelors and masters degrees out-earned Whites and other minorities with similar degree in 2006 (Horton 2007:3). This change came at the expense of their decreased participation in subsistence in comparison to Native males although, with their increased income, they were able to provide financial support for subsistence expenses. They also married non-Natives in large numbers. While these indicators seem to point to a higher rate of assimilation of Native women to Western society, Native women took their commitment to the Native culture into the classroom, where they taught culture-based education and Native language. They also continued their role in the traditional ceremonies still held in Native communities. While their progress in education and employment was dramatic, they failed to achieve the political equity they had outlined for themselves in 1977. They continue to be underrepresented in the leadership and management positions within the major Native organizations.

Although this review focuses on Native women, who overall appear to be doing well, the policy issues are broader and warrant action. This brief assessment raises the stark reality of the demise or survival of rural communities, and of the quality of life in these villages. The issues surrounding Native men, including their educational status and their self-destructive behavior, demand the attention of the Native community. The research reveals that greater employment opportunities will both limit the outmigration and increase return migrations of Native women and reverse the pattern of gender imbalance found in Alaska's villages.

REFERENCES

Alaska National Interest Land Conservation Act of 1980 (ANILCA). Public Law 96–487.

Alaska Native Claims Settlement Act of 1971 (ANCSA). Public Law 92–203.

Alaska Native Tribal Health Consortium. 2010. *Suicide Initiative Plan: Coming together to Reduce Suicide*. Accessed July 28, 2011. https://www.anthc.org/chs/wp/injprev/upload/Suicide-Initiative-Plan-12-10.pdf.

Chilkat Institute and Institute of Social and Economic Research. 1983. *The Economic Status of Alaska Native Women*. Anchorage, AL: Alaska Women's Commission.

Department of Labor and Workforce Development, Research and Analysis Section. 2011. "2010 Census Counts for American Indians/Alaska Natives." Accessed July 28, 2011. http://live.laborstats.alaska.gov/cen/dp.cfm#ra.

Dunham, Mike. 2011. "Anchorage Is Alaska's Biggest Native Village, Census Shows." *Anchorage Daily News*, July 11. Accessed July 28, 2011. http://www.adn.com/2011/07/10/v-printer/1961423/anchorage-is-biggest-native.html.

Frink, Lisa. 2009. "The Identity Division of Labor in Native Alaska." *American Anthropologist* 3(1):21–29.

Goldsmith, Scott. 2008. "Understanding Alaska's Remote Rural Economy." ISER University of Alaska Research Summary Number 10. Anchorage, AL: Institute of Social and Economic Research.

Hamilton, Lawrence. 2008. "Footprints: Demographic Effects of Outmigration." Accessed July 28, 2011. http://pubpages.unh.edu/~lch/Hamilton_Outmigration _chapter.pdf.

Hamilton, Lawrence. 2010. "Footprints: Demographic Effects of Outmigration." Pp 1–14 in *Migration in the Circumpolar North: Issues and Contexts*. L. Husky and C. Southcott (Eds.). Edmonton, Alberta: Canadian Circumpolar Institute.

Hamilton, L. C., and C. L. Seyfrit. 1994. "Female Flight? Gender Balance and Out-migration by Native Alaskan Villagers." *Arctic Medical Research* 53(2):189–93.

Hamilton, L. C., and C. L. Seyfrit. 1997. "Environment and Sex Ratios among Alaska Natives: An Historical Perspective." *Population and Environment* 18(3):283–99.

Horton, Terry. 2007. "The Women Leaders of Alaska Native Corporations: A Brief Introduction to the Female CEOs and Board Chairs of Multi-Million and Billion Dollar Organizations." Presentation to the Women of the Mountain Conference, Orem, UT, March 7–10.

Howe, Lance E. 2009. "Patterns of Migration in Arctic Alaska." *Polar Geography* 32(1–2):69–89.

Howe, E. Lance and Lee Huskey. 2010. Migration Decisions in the Arctic: Empirical Evidence of the Stepping Stone Hypothesis: Anchorage, AK: Center for Economic Studies, U.S. Census Working Series, pp. 10–41.

Huskey, Lee, Matthew Berman, and Alexander Hill. 2004. "Leaving Home, Returning Home: Migration as a Labor Market Choice for Alaska Natives." *Annals of Regional Science* 38:75–92.

Institute for Social and Economic Research (ISER). 1984. A Summary of Changes in the Status of Alaska Natives. Prepared for Educational Services Corporation Management Concepts, Inc. for the University of Alaska, *Anchorage Institute of Social and Economic Research*. Pp. 1–80.

Institute of Social and Economic Research (ISER). 2004. *Executive Summary: Status of Alaska Natives, 2004*. Anchorage, AL: University of Alaska.

Jones, Dorothy M. 1976. "Urban Native Men and Women: Differences in Their Work Adaptations." ISEGR Occasional Papers No. 12. Fairbanks, AL: Institute of Social Economic and Government Research.

Kleinfeld, Judith and Justin J. Andrews. 2006a. "Postsecondary Education Gender Disparities among Inuit in Alaska: A Symptom of Male Malaise?" *Études/Inuit/ Studies* 30(1):111–21.

Kleinfeld, Judith and Justin J. Andrews. 2006b. "The Gender Gap in Higher Educa-tion in Alaska." *Arctic* 59(4):428–34.

Kleinfeld, Judith and Maria Reyes. 2007. "Boys Left Behind: Gender Role Disinte-gration in the Arctic." *THYMOS, Journal of Boyhood Studies* 1(2):179–90.

Kruse, Jack and Marg Kruse. 2007. *Survey of Living Conditions in the Arctic: Results*. Anchorage, AL: Arctic Human Health Initiative.

Langdon, Steve J. 1987. *The Native People of Alaska*. Anchorage, Alaska: Greatland Graphics.

Leask, Linda, Mary Killorin, and Pamela Cravez. 2006. *Understanding Alaska: People, Economy and Resources*. Anchorage, AL: University of Alaska Institute of Social and Economic Research.

Martin, Stephanie, Mary Killorin, and Steve Colt. 2008. "Fuel Costs, Migration and Community Viability." Anchorage: University of Alaska–Anchorage, Institute of Social and Economic and Research. Prepared for the Denali Commission.

Martin, Stephanie. 2009. "The Effects of Out-Migration on Alaska Villages." *Polar Geography* 32(1):61–67.

Martin, Stephanie. 2010. "Who Moves and Why: Stylized Facts about Inupiat Migration in Alaska." Pp 147–162 in *Migration in Circumpolar North*. Lee Huskey and Chris Southcott (Eds.). Canadian Circumpolar Institute in corporation with Arctic University.

McDowell Group. 2010. "Alaska Native—12 Education Indicators." Anchorage, Alaska: Prepared for First Alaskans Institute Alaska Native Policy Center. Accessed July 28, 2011. http://www.firstalaskans.org/index.cfm?fa=documents _overview&doctype=49.

Milan, Frederick A. and Stella Pawson. 1975. "The Demography of the Native Population of an Alaska City." *Arctic* 28(4):275–83.

Philp, Kenneth R. 1981. "The New Deal and Alaska Natives, 1936–1945." *Pacific Historical Review* 50(3):309–27.

Wells, Rebecca. 2004. *Statewide Health Profiles for Alaska Natives*. Anchorage: Alaska Native Epidemiology Center, Alaska Native Health Board.

Worl, Rosita. 1977. "The Alaska Native Women's Proclamation." Presented to the 1977 Alaska Federation of Natives Annual Convention, Anchorage, Alaska.

Worl, Rosita. 1979. "Changing Times and Changing Roles: We Have a Choice." Presented to the Alaska Native Women's Statewide Convention, Anchorage, Alaska, May 10.

CHAPTER 4

The Impact of Federal Government Policies on American Indian and Alaska Native Health Care

Terry M. Maresca

INTRODUCTION

On the question of gender discrimination, a renown Navajo tribal leader, Annie Wauneka, once stated:

> The basic reason for discrimination against Indian women stems from the Federal government's intervention in Indian affairs. (Witt 1981:66)

In this chapter, the impact of selected federal policies on American Indian/Alaska Native (AIAN) health over the last 500 years will be reviewed. Certain policies were directed toward or had a disproportionate effect on AIAN women. Some historic background to the issues of an era has been included in order to better understand the human impact of the policies discussed. Some government interventions are characterized by overt deprivation of basic human rights. Other policies reflect paternalism, racism, or lack of due diligence. Still others document attempts to segregate and then assimilate AIAN populations. At times, government policy has been to reverse the consequences of its previous mandates.

Government involvement in AIAN health has had a mixed record of success for women. It altered day-to-day choices that are often taken for granted, such as what we eat, how we care for and educate our young, where we live, and our private health matters. It has negatively impacted Native women's inherent rights to maintain their fundamental roles in the economic, sociopolitical, and spiritual life of their communities. Fortunately, there is evidence of individual and collective indigenous resilience in the face of these challenges. There is also room for optimism with recent developments in tribal and federal government collaborations.

This overview is in no way a comprehensive treatise on this subject. Regrettably, the impact of policies on Native Hawaiian women's health post–1898 annexation by the United States is beyond the scope of this chapter. Given the broad time frame to cover, I have adapted titles of eras commonly used by AIAN policy scholars. The reader will note overlap between certain eras and the policies described therein.

OVERVIEW OF PRE-COLUMBIAN CONTACT HEALTH

AIAN population estimates precontact vary, but AIANs are now thought to have numbered between 5 and 2.5 million scattered between the United States and Canada (Edmunds 1995:727). The first written reports of European visitors from the East Coast to Alaska remarked on the good, if not exceptional, health of the local tribes, comparing it favorably to the chronic maladies seen in their homelands (Fortuine 1971). Observers frequently commented on the apparent efficacy of the local health practices that led to "surprising cures" (Feest 1975:153). These included herbal medicines, a variety of surgical techniques, preventive practices, family planning and childbirth assistance methods, physical medicine, and even autopsies (Lucier, VanStone, and Keats 1971). Acute infections and chronic diseases such as arthritis, however, were also known (Martin and Goodman 2000).

Health was generally seen in the context of respect and balance for one's relationship with family, tribe, the natural world, and spiritual realms. The symbol of the medicine wheel encompasses the domains of physical, spiritual, emotional, and mental wellness needed to maintain a good life and good health. Although not used by all AIANs, these concepts are common to most tribes.

The tribal health workforce included women at all levels. Their roles included family educator of children, caretaker of elders, producer and owner of crops and foodstuffs gathered, and community leader collaborating with men as equals to make community decisions. Women in extended families typically possessed common medical knowledge on prevention and treatment of everyday maladies within the family life cycle. Routine health care likely occurred in a home-based setting.

Indigenous health experts also included specialized women whose knowledge and skills were sought after as midwives, pharmacists, diagnosticians, and healers for more serious conditions. In some communities, they were the preferred surgeons due to their practiced hands "accustomed to fine needlework" (Fortuine 1985:37). Medicine women functioned as respected healers with significant spiritual, mental health, and community health roles. They trained in a process sanctioned and regulated by their communities. Each tribe had its own protocol for individuals seeking such care, which included methods of showing respect and providing compensation for the healer's work. Although the roles of men and women were different, there was general respect and equal recognition for contributions made.

There is little documentation of referral centers for health care, such as clinics or hospitals, beyond that of ceremonial sites in certain communities. No written policies associated with how health care was delivered exist. Oral tradition and artifacts found in some communities suggest an exchange of ideas between tribal trading partners and sharing of medicines.

POSTCONTACT HEALTH POLICY TO THE EARLY TREATY ERA: 1492–1830

The impact of early colonization on AIAN communities cannot be overstated, particularly the ravaging effects of infectious disease and violence perpetrated by foreign invaders against women, children, and elders. Thousands of Indians had experienced the presence of non-Indians and their diseases before actually meeting them in many regions of the country, particularly in the Southeast and Southwest. There, the diaries of Spanish invaders noted the recent abandonment of villages and evidence of epidemic deaths. Smallpox, influenza, and measles were particularly devastating because the tribes had no prior exposure to these foreign microbes. Mass fatalities caused major declines in AIAN populations. They also paved the way for European colonial powers in many areas to abuse or to enslave remaining tribal members as an unwritten policy to secure a ready-made workforce in the New World. This added to the high morbidity and mortality of the AIAN population in the first century post-Columbian contact.

Prior to the Revolutionary War, there was regular contact among various tribal nations with representatives of the American colonies, but there was no cohesive Indian policy. Nor were the diverse Eastern tribes able to negotiate collectively with the European immigrants. The U.S. Constitution of 1787 contains the first definitions of federal relationships with Indians under both Articles I and II. It allowed Congress to regulate commerce between tribes and declared the federal government to be the "ultimate arbiter" of the tribes' legal status through its treaty-making authority. Section 8 of Article I specifically prohibits states from assuming jurisdiction in tribal-federal matters. This special government-to-government relationship between the federal government and tribes effectively bypasses state jurisdiction over Indians. It was clarified by the 1831 Supreme Court decision in *Cherokee Nation v. Georgia* (1831), where the Cherokee Nation was defined as a "domestic dependent nation ... [like] a ward to his guardian."

Understanding the concept of historical treaty obligations of the U.S. government toward tribes is fundamental to understanding the unique relationship AIAN people have with the federal government. This is unique compared to any other ethnic or minority group in our country. The combination of treaties, Supreme Court decisions, executive orders, and laws forms the basis of the government-to-government federal trust relationship with tribes. There are 374 documented treaties made with various tribal nations and the U.S. government from 1778 to 1871. (Technically, Alaska Natives did not sign any formal treaties with the United States. The 1867 Treaty of Cessation gave them the same rights as Indians in the continental United States).

Treaties typically involved ceding tribal lands for cessation of hostilities and provision of certain services. Preservation of certain rights was often included—for example, access to traditional hunting or fishing territories. About two dozen treaties specifically mention the provision of health services. Stipulations included items like physician services, hospital construction, and medical supplies. The first to do so was with the Winnebago tribe in 1832.

Government motivations to assist Natives were weighted on the side of strategic planning rather than pure humanitarian instincts. For example, presidential objectives for the 1803 Lewis and Clark expedition reflected intense government curiosity about American

Indian tribes in the West, including their size, illnesses, habits, and especially their resources. Other actions document a desire to protect encroaching white settlers and outpost army personnel from the impact of epidemic disease in Indian country. In 1832, the first Congressional appropriation for Indian health was made. A sum of $12,000 went to purchase smallpox vaccine for tribes deemed cooperative with "the Great White Father" in Washington (Kaiser Family Foundation 2004:5). This would amount to over $300,000 today.

Ironically, jurisdiction for all Indian issues including health services fell under the auspices of the Office of the Secretary of War from 1789 to 1849. In 1849, responsibility for Indian affairs was transferred to the new Bureau of Indian Affairs (BIA). From the start, funds for Indian health were discretionary, based on Congressional whim and lobbying efforts, and not appropriated based upon actual need. As will be discussed later in this chapter, this process remains unchanged today.

INDIAN HEALTH POLICIES OF THE REMOVAL, RESERVATION, AND INDIAN WARS ERAS: 1830–1880

Federal policy shifted during the presidency of Andrew Jackson to one of Manifest Destiny embodied in the American Indian Removal Act of 1830. This asserted the prevailing ethnocentric worldview that removal of Indians east of the Mississippi to a reservation in the Indian Territory (present-day Oklahoma) was in the United States' economic and political interest. Forced removal to reservations launched the "Trail of Tears" associated most commonly with the relocation of Cherokee, Choctaw, Creek, and Chickasaw tribes. Others such as the Sauk and Fox, Winnebago, Ute, and Navajo were also affected in subsequent years. An estimated 25 percent of Cherokee who began the march died during or shortly after arrival (Palmer and Allen 1976). Survivors suffered weakened immunity and were more susceptible to both acute and chronic diseases, including a profound sense of defeat.

The reservation policy brought with it a cadre of new bureaucracies to govern it in the form of politically appointed Indian agents and provision merchants, many unscrupulous. Reservation conditions introduced new adverse impacts on the health of Indian people. Food insecurity, spoiled and unfamiliar food rations, and frank starvation were common. Subsistence hunting, fishing, or gathering was absent or limited in many areas. Basic needs went unmet, with scant home-building supplies, unsanitary conditions, and distribution of poor-quality clothing that could not last a winter. People suffered from lack of exercise. Perhaps most importantly, traditional male and female roles were seriously disrupted. The rampant spread of infectious disease epidemics, introduction of alcohol and commercial tobacco, and continued military conflicts near reservation areas also took a major toll on spiritual, emotional, physical, and mental health.

The year 1819 marked the beginning of federal policy involving Indian child education by new funding for missionary-run schools using the Civilization Fund. This policy would be a cornerstone after the Civil War. Expanded funding to secular boarding schools would become a major tool of acculturation. Multiple Christian missionary denominations joined Indian agents and traders on reservations to put their "civilize and Christianize" motto to practice. Over 60 mission-run boarding schools were established by 1834. Medical missionaries were sometimes assigned to these schools ("Medical Missionary Work" 1984). A typical motto was "to save them from their cruel superstitions, to heal them of their various loathsome diseases, the effects of ignorance as much as of vice, to rescue from the lives of suffering their poor women and children and yet unborn babes, as well as to save their immortal souls for Christ" ("Field Matrons" 1894:5).

Under the War Department, army doctors were sometimes assigned to tend to reservation health needs when they impacted military functions or civilians. In 1849, when federal responsibility for Indian health transferred to the new BIA, medical hires were often unlicensed. In contrast, commissioned military doctors actually met a higher standard of practice than typical contract or commercially trained doctors of the day. A medical license to work for the BIA was not required until 1878 (Olch 1982). Remarkably, a few tribes demonstrated the ability to protect their own people from unqualified medical practitioners. The Choctaw Nation passed a law regulating potential nontribal members from the practice of medicine within its borders in the 1880s (Allen 1970).

By the 1840s, federal government policy was expanded to educate "heathen" reservation women to reach the heart of their people. Officials thought that if women acquired household skills and white worldviews, they might positively influence their mates, thereby reducing armed conflict. Unfortunately, Indian wars in the West did not stop. It was deemed imperative that this new education process also reduce the influence of grandmothers in the community. They were considered tyrants of the Indian community and hindrances to civilization (Eastman 1896).

Gen. Samuel C. Armstrong was an influential leader of the time and founder of the Hampton Institute boarding school for black and Native children in Virginia. He expressed concern over girls' "inherited spirit of independence" that made them harder to train. His views and army background gave rise to militaristic educational methods and disciplinary rules as the standard within boarding schools. These were an anathema to AIAN families. Severing children's ties to their culture and families was a critical means of stopping intergenerational promulgation of "heathen rites and superstitions" by Indian women (Trennert 1982).

Thus began a major national policy of assimilation by forced removal of very young children to boarding schools, often hundreds of miles from their families. Parents were stripped of the right to raise their children. Students were forced to speak English and forgo traditional dress, foods, and customs. Children learned trade skills and Christianity and how to conform to white society's worldview. A few schools taught health-related skills such as nursing. Some curricula included the common practice of outsourcing student labor as indentured servants to local white households under the rubric of domestic science training. This exposed some AIAN girls to physical and sexual abuse in addition to that already documented within boarding schools. Neglect and death in the schools was common, and their adjacent cemeteries bear silent witness to this form of genocide.

The success of boarding schools like Hampton and Carlisle in the eyes of majority society led to the expansion of these models in the West. Native families, however, deeply mourned their children being "bleached" by the system. Despite BIA reports on the success of these programs, there is evidence to suggest that those returning home encountered problems, especially girls (Trennert 1982:286). Boarding-school policy had a devastating, rapid, and intergenerational impact on both mental and physical health of communities. Residual effects remain to this day, including loss of language, cultural disconnection, and deficits in parenting and opposite-sex relationship skills. Only recently has the relationship of historical trauma to increased rates of chronic illness such as cardiovascular disease begun to be explored by researchers.

In 1890, federal policy created a reservation-based job called the field matron. This woman would teach Indian women a variety of housekeeping skills deemed vital in American society. These included home decoration, making butter and cheese, laundry, and care of domestic animals and sick persons as well as adherence to Sunday religious rituals ("Field Matrons" 1894:9–10). Not all reservations had such personnel, but some larger nations such as the Navajo, Yakama, Sioux, and Cheyenne/Arapaho did. Approximately 20 percent of these women were Native, usually boarding-school graduates themselves, enticed by the few jobs available to them back home. The matrons' job description included undermining indigenous knowledge transmission systems because elders' teachings and medicine men were deemed evil influences. It is hard to imagine the emotional impact on the young women who did return to their homes and were caught between cultures, having lost their skills as indigenous women (Bannan 1984).

HEALTH POLICY DURING THE ASSIMILATION AND ALLOTMENT ERA: 1880–1930

The late 1880s saw another major Indian federal policy shift with passage of the Dawes Act, also known as the Land in Severalty Act of 1887. This law allowed for systematic dismantling of the reservation system in the West. It held in trust and then distributed small plots of land to American Indian men, expecting them to settle down and become ranchers and farmers. Men first had to prove they were competent to understand the responsibilities of landownership. "Excess" land of incompetent men was sold to white settlers. Severe reservation poverty and overt fraud undermined many land sales. The policy clearly discriminated against women with head-of-household status and did not acknowledge tribes with matriarchal inheritance patterns.

The Dawes Act was profoundly demoralizing to Native communities, whose cultures had always considered land protection a core element of health. The act rapidly destroyed traditional land bases and functioning tribal systems of government, and accelerated loss of historic grazing and gathering territories. Between 1887 and 1934, approximately 90 million acres were lost.

The Dawes Act also marked the first use of blood quantum to determine who was Indian for allotment registration purposes. This was not historically used by tribes for self-definition. Many began to adopt this colonial process under pressure (Edmunds 1995:724). The issue of tribal enrollment and federal recognition became linked to eligibility for government services, including education and health care. Children of mixed marriages who did not meet blood quantum criteria, non–federally recognized tribes, and those who lived in urban areas or off reservation became ineligible for such services. It was not until 89 years later when the Indian Health Care Improvement Act (IHCIA) of 1976 (P.L. 94-437) was passed that a more inclusive definition of AIAN health care eligibility was proposed.

The federal policy of prohibiting Indian ceremonial practices such as the Sun Dance was formalized by the 1883 Code of Indian Offenses, with fines of jail time or withholding rations. It also included punishment for medicine men assisting the people. The code expanded in 1892 to ban traditional medicines and ceremonies, dances, healing practices, and funeral rites as being objectionable and affecting health (Sniffen and Carrington 1914). To enforce this, the job description of BIA doctors included counteracting medicine people's community impact. A sum of $25,000 ($319,000 today) was appropriated by Congress in 1923 to stop trafficking in alcohol and deleterious drugs, including peyote, among Indians, stating that their peyote religion was simply a pretense ("Peyote" 1918).

By the end of the nineteenth century, the AIAN population on and off reservation hit a nadir of 237,196 in the 1900 census. This is a far cry from the 5 million conservative estimate of the precontact population. The threads of epidemic disease and federal removal and assimilation policies were thought by the public to be coming together to their logical end. Infectious diseases such as tuberculosis, trachoma, and epidemics of influenza, cholera, diphtheria, and malaria overwhelmed the 81 Indian service doctors serving the people in 1888 (Allen 1975). Lack of medical and basic food supplies and facilities to address community needs were a steady complaint to Indian agents. In the far north, medical relief work among Alaska Natives began after 1910. Despite physician reports "showing a deplorable situation calling for urgent action," Congress denied the bureau funding to control rampant tuberculosis and trachoma (Sniffen and Carrington 1914:23).

Remarkably, this difficult era also saw the birth of several bicultural women who made an impact not just on the health of their communities but also on the dominant society's view of "the Indian problem" through political advocacy using white power structures of the time. One such person was Susan LaFlesche Picotte, MD (Omaha). The daughter of an Omaha chief and the first American Indian woman physician, she was influenced by missionaries during her boarding-school education at Hampton Institute. She returned to her reservation in Nebraska in 1889. There, her major causes included a successful state-wide ban of the common drinking cup as a vector of disease, home preventive measures to minimize childhood illness, and temperance. She was called upon to lobby Congress by her tribe to improve health conditions using the power of her pen and in-person efforts in Washington, D.C. Due to her bicultural education, she was able to attract funding sources associated with Christian women's organizations sponsoring reservation missionary work. Poor child health conditions motivated her to build a local hospital primarily to serve the community (Mathes 1993).

During this era, there was a growing movement of nonprofit and occasionally nonsectarian Indian rights organizations made up of non-Indian men and women. They concurred with overall societal goals of ultimate civilization and citizenship for Indians. They also put political pressure on federal commissioners of Indian affairs by speaking publicly on documented abuses of Indian agents and failure of the governments' obligations in the health care arena. Bicultural Indian war veteran and advocate Sarah Winnemucca (Paiute) gave popular lectures in large cities like San Francisco to add legitimacy to these efforts.

After World War I, a pivotal law in AIAN health care was passed. The Snyder Act of 1921 (P.L. 67-85) allowed the government to "direct, supervise, and expend such moneys as Congress may from time to time appropriate, for the benefit, care, and assistance of the Indians . . . for relief of distress and conservation of health." This codified the federal government's obligation to provide health service funding to all federally recognized tribes, not just those with treaty health stipulations. This act marked a major policy shift with the additional recognition that such support would need to be ongoing. Expenditures for construction and repair of health facilities, health professional workforce development, and funds to support urban Indians were implied as allowable.

THE MERIAM COMMISSION AND THE INDIAN NEW DEAL: 1930–1948

Under growing public pressure to investigate reservation conditions, a report to the Interior Department (parent organization of the BIA) was made in 1928. The Meriam Commission report documented inadequate funding for Indian health systems and inferior health conditions attributed to bureaucratic government policies and procedures. Under the administration of President Franklin D. Roosevelt, efforts began to correct the flaws of assimilation-era policies. Reservations had simply failed to "merge in the saving sea of white civilization" (Grammer and Welsh 1912:2).

Commissioner of Indian Affairs John Collier worked with mostly white liberal reformers to advocate for and pass the Wheeler-Howard Act of 1934, also known as the Indian Reorganization Act or "Indian New Deal." This reaffirmed the sovereign status of tribes and allowed them to reestablish their own governments in the form of tribal councils that could interact again with the federal government. The same year, the Johnson O'Malley Act allowed tribes to contract with private entities for health, education, and welfare services in their communities.

Given the long history of forgotten promises, many tribal leaders did not trust the government's new policy dictating how they would self-govern. There was significant opposition to this law, called a "raw deal." Some feared that adoption of tribal constitutions modeled after the U.S. government would not reflect tribal customs and could accelerate the loss of AIAN political systems. Several Indian activists such as Alice Jemison (Seneca), Charles Eastman, M.D. (Wahpeton Sioux), and Carlos Montezuma, M.D. (Yavapai) became widely known for promoting tribal self-determination free from BIA control. Jemison also lobbied for government action on health issues such as addressing environmental pollution on Seneca territory and stopping prosecution of tribal members who exercised subsistence treaty fishing rights. Other well-known Indian women reformers of the time include Gertrude Simmons Bonnin, Ella Deloria, Ruth Bronson, and Helen Peterson, who networked with large white women's organizations like the Young Women's Christian Association (YWCA) to advocate for Native rights.

Some communities demonstrated self-determination and respect for their traditional health systems by combining Western science with American Indian healing concepts to address common health problems of the time. Several California tribes successfully tackled the problem of tuberculosis control in the 1930s. They combined modern public health concepts learned in boarding school with input from elders and traditional healers using their Indian medicine circle in the days before streptomycin was introduced (Trafzer, Keller, and Sisquoc 2006).

In 1944, the National Congress of American Indians was formed. As politically active AIANs, they stood against assimilation policies and advocated for tribal sovereignty, with health care being one of their driving issues. Women with a strong community health agenda slowly began to be elected to their tribal councils for the first time. Annie Wauneka from the Navajo Nation, the most populous reservation in the country, was among the first in 1951. She was eventually awarded the U.S. Presidential Medal of Freedom for her efforts to improve health care among her people.

Sadly, some tribes experienced environmental trauma due to destruction of land by government-condoned dam construction or hazards brought about by resource extraction. The photograph of tribal chairman George Gillette weeping as he signed over Fort Berthold land to build the Garrison Dam in 1948 is not soon forgotten. Neither is the impact of the increased rates of obesity and diabetes decades later in this same area from destruction of traditional lifeways (Jones 2011).

THE TERMINATION ERA AND THE BIRTH OF THE INDIAN HEALTH SERVICE: 1949–1970

After World War II, another shift occurred in federal Indian policy. Citing failure of the Indian Reorganization Act's restructuring 15 years earlier, the 1949 Hoover Commission called for change. This commission proposed encouraging mainstream assimilation, dismantling the failed reservation system, and converting tribes to state regulation rather than federal oversight. AIANs saw this as a clear abrogation of treaty rights.

Congressional committees created a process to determine which tribes appeared most financially successful and therefore deemed qualified to have their rights terminated first. This process was vigorously opposed by tribal leaders. Nevertheless, over 100 tribes both on and off the target list were systematically stripped of their right to self-govern ("terminated") between the years from 1954 to 1962. Tribes such as the Klamath in Oregon and Menominee in Wisconsin lost their ability to protect their land and provide health care to their people. It was not until the 1970s that some of these tribes were able to petition successfully to the U.S. government to have their status reinstated. Regrettably, other tribes have yet to have their rights restored.

The termination policy was combined with new federal efforts to assimilate Indians and relocate them to major cities under the guise of a work program called the Employment Assistance Program of 1948. Reservation inhabitants were encouraged to relocate their families to cities such as Oakland, Chicago, Phoenix, and Denver. Minimal financial support was provided for this relocation policy, thus promoting the cycle of poverty for those impacted. At that time, there were no urban Indian health facilities. Poor health for urban Natives was another major outcome with far-reaching impacts today.

In 1954, the Transfer Act moved health services for AIANs from the BIA to the U.S. Public Health Service (PHS), a division of the Department of Health, Education, and Welfare (DHEW). One year later, the Indian Health Service (IHS) was created as a separate division within the PHS. The IHS mission is to raise the health of Indian people to its highest level using its role as public health and medical service provider. IHS also acts as primary advocate for Indian health within the federal bureaucracy. The impact of this change was a much-needed increase in funding, but levels remained markedly below actual level of need.

Administratively, the IHS is broken into 12 area offices. It currently manages 163 tribal and federally controlled smaller service units, typically an entire reservation or collection of Alaska Native villages. Within these service units are over 670 facilities providing direct care, including hospitals, health centers, school health centers, satellite clinics, health stations, and Alaska village clinics (IHS 2011b).

Due to the remote nature of some areas, an IHS facility may be the sole source of care in a region. Indian health programs use a public health model that includes medical care, preventive care, health promotion, health education, community-based services, and sanitation. The IHS integrated system of care is considered by many to be an international model of rural health care delivery.

The IHS system faced many challenges in its first two decades. Initial IHS efforts focused on control of still-rampant acute and chronic infectious diseases and construction of health facilities. Another challenge was a national scandal over its procedures regulating female sterilization in the 1970s. The IHS routinely took directives from DHEW. In 1970, DHEW began subsidizing family planning and voluntary sterilization for low-income women. Before 1973, they had no published guidelines for providing family planning services or to protect a woman's' right to informed consent for such services. Ethical violations occurred when individual health care providers implemented these programs through their own sociocultural lens rather than the worldviews of AIAN women.

This issue came to a head in the mid-1970s. Indian newspapers such as *Akwesasne Notes* (1974) included reports from American Indian physicians and others who identified multiple improprieties around the nation. These included high rates of sterilization of young women, hysterectomies rather than tubal ligations for permanent contraception, and incomplete consent procedural processes (U.S. DHEW 1978). Coercive practices such as threatening loss of child custody were also cited. Grassroots advocacy to the chairman of the Senate Select Committee on Indian Affairs led to a General Accounting Office (GAO) investigation in a third of the IHS service areas.

The 1976 GAO report confirmed higher rates of sterilization compared to historic trends. IHS was cited for not conforming to Department of Health, Education, and Welfare (DHEW, but now renamed the Department of Health and Human Services, DHHS) HEW safeguards in the informed consent process. It did not corroborate reports of coercion and never interviewed any of the women involved. The report documented the need for IHS to add multiple safeguards to the surgical informed consent process, which was done. Subsequent independent studies were done by several tribes including the Navajo Nation that corroborated the GAO findings (Temkin-Greener et al. 1981). The exact number of women impacted nationally was never determined (Dillingham 1977; Lawrence 2000).

THE INDIAN SELF-DETERMINATION ERA: 1970s TO PRESENT

The decades of the 1960s and 1970s saw rising public awareness of racial discrimination and the lack of civil rights for many in the United States, the impact of poverty, and the feminist movement. Along with the rise of black nationalism came a rekindling of American Indian traditionalist movements. These promoted political activism, land protection, language revitalization, indigenous spirituality, and culture as means of individual, community, and tribal healing.

The Alaska Native Claims Settlement Act of 1971 created 12 regional corporations and 200 village corporations as an alternative to the reservation system. More than 40 million acres of land and close to $1 billion were put under this corporate control. Based upon a business structure with funding, the corporations brought broader economic authority and political power to their regions, leading to more sustained economic growth.

Following the lead of President Richard Nixon's executive order proclaiming national support for Indian "self-determination without termination," Congress passed the landmark Indian Self-Determination and Education Assistance Act (Public Law 93-638, as amended) in 1975. The "638 option," as it is widely known, gave tribes a choice to take over an array of government functions previously held at the federal level. Its companion was the Indian Health Care Improvement Act (IHCIA), also known as Public Law 94-437. This law gave the health-specific authority to support the options of Public Law 93-638. The IHCIA marked a major change in federal AIAN policy.

The intent of IHCIA is to provide the quantity and quality of health services necessary to elevate the health status of American Indians and Alaska Natives to the highest possible level. It also encourages maximum tribal participation in the planning and management of such services. For the first time, the IHCIA allowed tribes the choice to direct and operate their own health programs or to stay under federal IHS management. The IHCIA and the Snyder Act are the two major laws that form the legislative foundation for IHS-provided health care services.

Given the chance to redesign health programs to meet tribal member needs with fewer IHS regulations, some tribes began to slowly take over discrete pieces of their health systems. Control over emergency service transportation, dialysis units, and public health nursing departments became increasingly common. The majority of tribes who took advantage of these self-governance compacts and self-determination contracts found they could actually expand services to their people (Manson and Altschul 2004). New or increased collaborations with local private hospital systems and academic centers were now possible (U.S. Commission on Civil Rights 2004:57).

In the 36 years since the IHCIA was enacted, over half of the IHS budget is now administered by tribes (IHS 2011b). The frontrunner is the Alaska area of IHS, with 99 percent of its programs under direct village corporation control. Some of its programs have attracted international attention, such as Southcentral Foundation's Nuka holistic model of care that is culturally congruent to their customer-owners. The Nuka model, with its emphasis on relationship building, prevention, and integrated care teams, has vastly improved health outcomes for its users (Southcentral Foundation 2011).

In recent years, tribes have used their powers of self-governance to impact women's health in unique ways. Some tribes with successful gaming ventures have elected to direct funds for services not historically covered by his, such as long-term care, which disproportionately affects women. One example is the Archie Hendricks Sr. skilled nursing facility on the Tohono O'odham Nation in Arizona (TOLTC 2009). Other tribes have crafted their civil or criminal codes to address major community problems, such as alcoholism and domestic violence, or used tribal council resolutions to make changes. Examples of such laws are children's protection codes. These mandate reporting, court appearance, and substance abuse treatment for women living on tribal lands and pregnant with a native child who are abusing alcohol or controlled substances (Little River Traverse Band of Ottawa Indians n.d.; Native American Rights Fund 2005).

URBAN INDIANS

A vital component of the IHCIA was its Title V provisions, which formally codified inclusion of the growing AIAN urban population. In cities with sizable native populations, 34 urban Indian health organizations (UIHOs) grew to serve the needs of those who had fallen in the growing gap of service provision. Types of services range from outreach only to comprehensive primary care centers (IHS 2011b). However, there remains a significant disparity with IHS funding to these UIHOs. They have historically consistently received 1 percent or less of the entire IHS budget, but 57.4 percent of the 2,475,956 AIANs who identified only one racial category live inside metropolitan areas, according to the 2000 census (U.S. Census Bureau 2000).

Gross inequity in funding puts urban AIANs at disproportionately higher risk for health-related problems. Data collection is a vital strategy to inform future health policy and research in this arena and keep tribes visible. The Urban Indian Health Institute is a consortium that coordinates and disseminates data pertinent to the 34 UIHOs. Some of their research publications are specific to women's' health disparities such as maternal-child and reproductive health (Urban Indian Health Institute n.d.).

PERMANENT REAUTHORIZATION OF THE INDIAN HEALTH CARE IMPROVEMENT ACT (IHCIA)

The IHCIA, along with the Snyder Act, form the basic legislative foundation for health care services provided by the IHS. After more than a decade of work by tribal leaders and national Indian health advocacy groups, landmark permanent reauthorization of the IHCIA occurred as part of Public Law 111-148, the Patient Protection and Affordable Care Act, in March 2010. This act gives permanent authority to fund Indian health programs set forth in the IHCIA of 1976. A major policy change is the inclusion of urban Indian health care as a permanent part of IHS, consistent with recent AIAN population demographics. This goes beyond the Affordable Care Act's extension of health insurance coverage to an additional 32 million people nationwide, which will likely cover many AIAN urban dwellers.

The IHCIA now contains important new provisions to expand AIAN health services. These include allowing funds to be spent on long-term, community-based, and hospice care. Additional mental health services are included along with streamlined access for tribes to directly bill major government insurance programs such as Medicare, the Children's Health Insurance Program, and Medicaid. Health professional recruitment and retention programs for those working in AIAN communities are expanded and authorized. However, the House of Representatives voted to repeal the parent Patient Protection and Affordable Care Act in January 2011. This raises concerns among tribal leaders that the Senate could also vote to repeal the hard-earned permanent IHCIA reauthorization contained therein.

A NEW WAVE OF FEDERAL GOVERNMENT COLLABORATIONS

In more recent decades, Indian health program priorities have shifted to address burgeoning rates of chronic diseases like diabetes, cancer, and cardiovascular disease. Such conditions are prominent among both sexes, with disease incidence typically occurring at younger ages than in the general population. Congressional appropriations were granted to support interventions such as the Special Diabetes Program for Indians in 1997, with impact on over 300 tribal grantees (Moore et al. 2006). Federal agencies like the National Institutes of Health (NIH) have revised grant eligibility criteria to allow tribes and Urban Indian Health Organizations (UIHOs) to compete for research and demonstration project funds in women's health and other disciplines. These and other collaborations between IHS and NIH such as the Native American Research Centers for Health (NARCH) have funded training for a small but growing cadre of indigenous health researchers and clinicians

(IHS 2011d). This approach has promoted community capacity to address important issues such as healing from historic trauma and the use of cultural strategies to reduce substance abuse and violence using community-based participatory models.

Collaborations between UIHOs and reservation, state, and county governments have demonstrated effectiveness in reducing women's health disparities. One example is the Montana American Indian Women's Health Coalition, which has improved access to breast and cervical cancer screening services among urban and reservation women (Montana American Indian Women's Health Coalition n.d.). Increased collaboration at the federal interagency level has also been documented. The Veteran's Administration and IHS have exchanged electronic health-record technology and expanded services for veterans including rural in-home care and payment for selected traditional medicine services.

Internationally, the United States is a member of several indigenous health consortia to address common concerns across borders. One outcome is the 2010 Arctic Health Declaration, with its objective to ensure increased participation in health research of Arctic indigenous people across nine countries (Institute for Circumpolar Health Research 2010).

The passing of the Indian Religious Freedom Act of 1978 finally decriminalized traditional medicine and ceremonial practices that had been carefully preserved by many communities at great cost. In 1994, the IHS Traditional Health Advocacy Policy reaffirmed the need to respect such practices within its health care system. This is vital, in that many reservation and urban communities today continue to use such services (Fuchs and Bashshur 1975; Marbella et al. 1998). They are seen as more effective than standard care for treatment of substance use and mental health challenges (Walls et al. 2006). Also in 1978, the Indian Child Welfare Act was passed in response to the disproportionately high number of Indian children being removed from their homes by both public and private agencies. This added a level of safety for AIAN families under chronic stress from unjust loss of family members.

The federal government has taken action to bolster tribal law enforcement and health services that enhance the ability to prosecute crimes against AIAN women more effectively with the passage of the Tribal Law and Order Act in 2010. It includes efforts to combat sex trafficking, sexual assault, and domestic violence. Such expanded protection is necessary: one in three AIAN women has experienced sexual assault in her lifetime, the highest rate of any ethnicity in the nation (Amnesty International 2007).

In 2000, President Bill Clinton mandated all federal agencies working with tribal governments and Alaska Native corporations to adhere to a tribal consultation process on issues that will impact their communities. Many AIAN communities note higher levels of government-to-government consultation under the administration of President Barack Obama, such as the 2011 review of the federal subsistence hunting and fishing regulations. AIAN women are increasingly involved in the leadership of and participation in health systems services at all levels. This was marked by the appointment of the first female IHS director in 2009, Yvette Roubideaux, MD, a member of the Rosebud Sioux tribe.

In December 2010, the United States finally joined its international colleagues in support of the United Nation's (UN) Declaration on the Rights of Indigenous Peoples. Although not legally binding, it can be seen as a moral compass that supports government commitment to correct historic wrongs, change current laws and policies, and support greater tribal autonomy (Indian Law Resource Center 2010). This is consistent with recognizing the inherent sovereignty of the federal trust relationship between the tribes and Alaska Native corporations.

SELF-DETERMINATION WITHOUT APPROPRIATION

For the many reasons noted in this chapter, knowledgeable contemporary politicians and writers have called the IHS the first prepaid American health care system. Its cost was dearly paid for in perpetuity by the transfer of over 400 million acres of land and incalculable loss of life due to cumulative impacts of colonization. However, the great value of what has been given up has not matched the value of actual services rendered in the eyes of many Natives.

The extent of the health care services depends on local community needs and is dependent on three things: eligibility, appropriations, and medical priorities. All AIANs who wish to access federal IHS services must first meet established eligibility criteria. Economic need is not a variable. In an effort to deal with limited financial resources, only federally recognized tribal members from a list of 565 tribes and Alaska Native villages in 35 states are eligible for service. Tribal facilities and urban programs might have different patient qualification criteria. In 2011, IHS provides health care services to 1.9 million of the 3.3 million in the United States who indicated themselves as only AIAN, typically those who live on or near a reservation (IHS 2011c). This means no coverage for state-recognized tribal members, members of terminated tribes, and urban dwellers who live in areas not covered by the 34 UIHOs, among others (U.S. Commission on Civil Rights 2004).

The second issue is appropriations. Compared to other federal health programs, the IHS is chronically underfunded at only 59 percent of level of need (U.S. Commission on Civil Rights 2003). The IHS is not an entitlement program like Medicare. Funding for Indian health services must be lobbied for every year. Funds can run out by the end of the fiscal year and often do. Health care is rationed as a means of controlling costs using a priority system based on medical acuity rated from one to five. This particularly impacts contract health services, defined as any service that cannot be provided with the resources available at a given site. This in turn impacts women's health.

For example, screening mammography may be available onsite at a clinic. If a woman has an abnormal test and requires a biopsy, she may not meet contract health priority criteria to be seen by a surgeon because this procedure is not considered immediately life-, limb-, or vision-threatening to warrant a priority one designation. All preventive services are considered priority two.

As noted above, there are over 1.4 million people not covered by IHS benefits at all. This is a major gap, compounded by the fact that the types of services available to any IHS user have never been clearly or consistently defined. Further, these services are not fully portable or predictable if a person moves away from her home service unit area to another region.

Finally, significant disparities exist in per-capita expenditures for the IHS user population compared with other groups. In 2010, IHS spent $2,741 per user versus the total U.S. population rate of $6,909 (IHS 2011b). By comparison, other federal programs spent more per capita on their beneficiaries than IHS. The Federal Bureau of Prisons inmate costs were $4,412.62 per person per year during fiscal year 2007 (U.S. Department of Justice 2008), and Medicare spent $8,754 per person in 2008 (Medicare 2010). It remains to be determined how the provisions of the Affordable Care Act will provide all AIAN nationally with a defined and portable menu of comprehensive benefits. Doing so will be a major step to fight this centuries-old injustice.

SUMMARY

From the time of contact with Columbus, a myriad of historic events and government interventions have shaped current AIAN health disparities for both men and women. Misdirected and often erratic federal government policies have had a major role in creating or maintaining these disparities. The social, economic, and emotional impacts of many policies continue to be felt today. In recent decades, there have been expanded efforts on the part of the federal government to improve funding and collaboration with the tribes. However, gross underfunding of the IHS remains a major ongoing challenge.

Despite these injustices, AIAN people have consistently shown their courage, resilience, and resourcefulness to mitigate the impact of certain federal interventions in their lives. Women are regaining their traditional leadership roles in planning for and participating in health interventions at the community and national level that include elements of indigenous culture blended with Western strategies. Expanding tribal sovereignty options have empowered many tribes to make necessary changes to improve community health. The health of our tribal lands and our future generations depend upon our use of indigenous wisdom and collaborations of our choosing, as our ancestors have done before us.

REFERENCES

Akwesasne Notes. 1974, July. "Sterilization of Young Native Women Alleged at Indian Hospital." Hogansburg, NY.

Allen, Virginia R. 1970. "Medical Practices and Health in the Choctaw Nation, 1831–1885." *Chronicles of Oklahoma* 48(1):60–73.

Allen, Virginia R. 1975. "Agency Physicians to the Southern Plains Indians 1868–1900." *Bulletin of the History of Medicine* 49(3):318–30.

Amnesty International. 2007. "Maze of Injustice: The Failure to Protect Indigenous Women from Violence: End Injustice—Free Forensic Examinations." Accessed July 28, 2011. http://www.amnesty.org/en/library/asset/AMR51/035/2007/en/cbd28fa9-d3ad-11dd-a329-2f46302a8cc6/amr510352007en.pdf.

Bannan, Helen M. 1984. " 'True Womanhood' on the Reservation: Field Matrons in the United States Indian Service." *Southwest Institute for Research on Women* 18:1–25.

Cherokee Nation v. Georgia. 1831. 30 U.S. (5 Pet.) 1.

Dillingham, Brint. 1977. "Indian Women and IHS Sterilization Practices." *American Indian Journal* 3(1):27–28.

Eastman, Elaine G. 1896. "Indian Women at Home." *Indian's Friend* 6(12):9–10. Philadelphia, PA.

Edmunds, David R. 1995. "Native Americans, New Voices: American Indian History, 1895–1995." *American Historical Review* 100(3):717–40.

Feest, Christian F. 1975. "Another French Account of Virginia Indians by John Lederer." *Virginia Magazine of History and Biography* 83(2):150–59.

"Field Matrons." 1894. *Indian's Friend* 6(11):9–10. Philadelphia, PA.

Fortuine, Robert. 1971. "The Health of the Eskimos, as Portrayed in the Earliest Written Accounts." *Bulletin of the History of Medicine* 45(2):97–114.

Fortuine, Robert. 1985. "Lancets of Stone: Traditional Methods of Surgery among the Alaska Natives." *Arctic Anthropology* 22(1):23–45.

Fuchs, Michael and Rashid Bashshur. 1975. "Use of Traditional Indian Medicine among Urban Native Americans." *Medical Care* 13(11):915–27.

Grammer, Carl E. and Herbert Welch. 1912, February. "The Present Situation of Indian Affairs." *Indian Rights Association* 86(3500): 2.

Indian Health Service. 2011a. "About Us." Accessed March 4, 2011. http://www.ihs .gov/index.cfm?module=About.

Indian Health Service. 2011b. "Fact Sheets, 2011 Profile." Accessed March 12, 2011. http://www.ihs.gov/PublicAffairs/IHSBrochure/Profile2011.asp.

Indian Health Service. 2011c. "Fact Sheets: Indian Population." Accessed March 21, 2011. http://www.ihs.gov/PublicAffairs/IHSBrochure/Population.asp.

Indian Health Service. 2011d. "Research Program: NARCH." Accessed July 31, 2011. http://www.ihs.gov/Research/index.cfm?module=narch.

Indian Law Resource Center. 2010. "UN Declaration Sets New Agenda for US-Indian Relations." Accessed March 11, 2011. http://www.indianlaw.org/ content/un-declaration-sets-new-agenda-us-indian-relations.

Institute for Circumpolar Health Research. 2010. "General News: Arctic Health Ministers Sign Declaration." Accessed March 11, 2011. http://ichr.ca/2011/02/ arctic-health-ministers-sign-declaration.

Jones, Lisa. 2011. "A Flood of Ill Health." *High Country News*, May 16.

Kaiser Family Foundation. 2004. "Legal and Historical Roots of Health Care for American Indians and Alaska Natives in the United States." Accessed March 21, 2011. http://www.kff.org/minorityhealth/loader.cfm?url=/commonspot/ security/getfile.cfm&PageID=31330.

Lawrence, Jane. 2000. "The Indian Health Service and the Sterilization of Native American Women." *American Indian Quarterly* 24(3):400–419.

Little River Traverse Band of Ottawa Indians. N.d. "Children's Protection Code Ordinance." Accessed March 11, 2011. http://www.narf.org/nill/Codes/ lrcode9.htm.

Lucier, Charles V., James W. VanStone, and Della Keats. 1971. "Medical Practices and Human Anatomical Knowledge among the Noatak Eskimos." *Ethnology* 10(3):251–64.

Manson, Spero M., and Deborah B. Altschul. 2004. "Meeting the Mental Health Needs of American Indians and Alaska Natives." Cultural Diversity Series. Alexandria, VA: National Technical Assistance Center for State Mental Health Planning.

Marbella, Anne M., Mickey C. Harris, Sabina Diehr, Gerald Ignace, and Georgianna Ignace. 1998. "Use of Native American Healers among Native American Patients in an Urban Native American Health Center." *Archives of Family Medicine* 7, 182–85.

Martin, Debra L. and Alan H. Goodman. 2000. "Health Conditions before Colum-
bus: The Paleopathology of Native North Americans." Pp 19–40 in *American
Indian Health: Innovations in Health Care, Promotion, and Policy*. Everett K.
Rhoades (Ed.). Baltimore: Johns Hopkins University Press.

Mathes, Valerie S. 1993. "Susan LaFlesche Picotte, M.D.: Nineteenth-Century
Physician and Reformer." *Great Plains Quarterly* 13(3):172.

"Medical Missionary Work." 1894. *Indian's Friend* (Philadelphia) 6(12):5.

Medicare. 2010. "Medicare Payment Advisory Commission Data Book: Healthcare
Spending and the Medicare Program, June 2010." Accessed March 12, 2011.
http://www.medpac.gov/documents/jun10databookentirereport.pdf.

Montana American Indian Women's Health Coalition. N.d. "State NBCCEDP
Models of Success Highlights." Accessed January 18, 2011. http://www
.theweavingproject.org/PDFs/MAIWHC_Final.pdf.

Moore, Kelly, Yvette Roubideaux, Carolyn Noonan, Jack Goldberg, Ray Shields, and
Kelly Acton. 2006. "Measuring the Quality of Diabetes Care in Urban and Rural
Indian Health Programs." *Ethnicity and Disease* 16, 772–77.

Native American Rights Fund. 2005. "Statutes of the Grand Traverse Band of Ottawa
and Chippewa Indians, Jurisdiction of the Children's Court." Accessed March 11,
2011. http://www.narf.org/nill/Codes/gtcode/10.pdf.

Olch, P. D. 1982. "Medicine in the Indian-fighting Army, 1866–1890." *Journal of the
West* 21(3):32–41.

Palmer, Howard R. and Virginia Allen. 1976. "Stress and Death in the Settlement of
Indian Territory." *Chronicle of Oklahoma* 54(2):352–59.

Sniffen, Matthew K. and Thomas S. Carrington. 1914. "The Indians of the Yukon
and Tanana Valleys Alaska." *Indian Rights Association* 98, 23.

Southcentral Foundation. 2011. "Nuka System of Care." Accessed July 18, 2011.
http://southcentralfoundation.org/nuka/index.ak.

Temkin-Greener, Helena, Stephen J. Kunitz, David Broudy, and Marlene Haffner.
1981. "Surgical Fertility Regulation among Women on the Navajo Indian
Reservation." *American Journal of Public Health* 71(4):403–7.

TOLTC Tohono O'odham Nursing Care Authority. 2009, December 24. "Tohono
O'odham Nursing Care–Our Story." YouTube http://www.youtube.com/
watch?v=3qqT3tDgUWY.

Trafzer, Clifford E., Jean A. Keller, and Lorene Sisquoc, eds. 2006. *Boarding School
Blues: Revisiting American Indian Educational Experiences*. Lincoln: University of
Nebraska Press.

Trennert, Robert A. 1982. "Educating Indian Girls at Nonreservation Boarding
Schools, 1878–1920." *Western Historical Quarterly* 13(3):271–90.

Urban Indian Health Institute. N.d. "Reproductive Health of Urban American
Indian and Alaska Native Women." Accessed January 18, 2011. http://www
.niwhrc.org/download/uihi_report.pdf.

U.S. Census Bureau. 2000. "Census of Population and Housing, DP-1, Profiles of
General Demographic Characteristics." Accessed January 18, 2011. http://
www.census.gov/prod/cen2000/dp1/2kh00.pdf.

U.S. Commission on Civil Rights. 2003. "A Quiet Crisis: Federal Funding and
Unmet Needs in Indian Country, June 2003." Accessed July 28, 2011. http://
www.usccr.gov/pubs/na0703/na0204.pdf.

U.S. Commission on Civil Rights. 2004. "Broken Promises: Evaluating the Native American Health Care System 2004." Accessed July 30, 2011. http://www.law .umaryland.edu/marshall/usccr/documents/cr122004024431draft.pdf.

U.S. Department of Health, Education and Welfare. 1978. "Family Planning, Contraception, Voluntary Sterilization and Abortion: An Analysis of Laws and Policies in the United States, Each State and Jurisdiction (as of October 1, 1976 with 1978 addenda)." Washington, DC.: Government Printing Office.

U.S. Department of Justice. 2008. "The Federal Bureau of Prisons' Efforts to Manage Inmate Health Care: Office of the Inspector General Audit Division, Audit Report February 2008." Accessed March 12, 2011. http://www.justice.gov/oig/reports/BOP/a0808/final.pdf.

Walls, Melissa L., Kurt D. Johnson, Les B. Whitbeck, and Dan R. Hoyt. 2006. "Mental Health and Substance Abuse Services Preferences among American Indian People of the Northern Midwest." *Community Mental Health Journal* 42(6):521–35.

Witt, Shirley H. 1981. "An Interview with Dr. Annie Dodge Wauneka." *Frontiers: A Journal of Women Studies* 6(3):64–67.

CHAPTER 5

Health Disparity: The Morbidity and Mortality Picture

Linda Burhansstipanov

INTRODUCTION

The opportunity for maintaining good health is not uniformly available to all peoples worldwide, including Native Americans or American Indians and Alaska Natives (AIANs) in the United States. This chapter highlights and compares selected health disparities between AIAN adult females and adult non-Hispanic white (NHW) females. The data shows that in many areas of health disparity, Native women are more likely to have poorer health and experience more chronic diseases and disabilities than white women, and that although there have been some health improvements, Native women continue to have extensive unmet health needs due to cost, access, cultural barriers, and other factors.

Over several generations, increasing numbers of unhealthy lifestyle behaviors have also become part of the lifestyle of many Native Americans—behaviors that have become embedded so they add to the persistence of several health disparities—including increased obesity, habitual use of manufactured tobacco, and sedentary lifestyles. To counter and decrease the incidence of preventable health problems, many urban and rural tribal communities are currently engaged in various community-based health promotion initiatives to encourage a return to some of the healthy ancestral lifestyles, including consumption and preparation of healthy foods, reserving commercial tobacco for ceremonial uses only, and so forth. The health promotion initiatives also include programs such as fitness centers to help increase daily physical activity and promote fitness. The ultimate goal of these initiatives is to change the negative health behaviors in order to help reduce preventable causes of morbidity and mortality for Native women, namely cardiovascular disease, cancer, diabetes, and other chronic and disabling health conditions.

SOME NOTES ON DEMOGRAPHICS

In 2004, the U.S. Census began to make available a subset of census data (American Community Survey [ACS]) to provide relevant and reliable sociodemographic data for use by communities. The ACS on AIANs estimates the population of Native Americans at 4 million, with slightly over half (2.2 million) of this population claiming only one racial heritage—indicating membership in only one tribe or as an Alaska Native (U.S. Census/ACS 2004:1). For many others, the self-identification of AIAN includes an identity with other racial or ethnic groups (U.S. Census 2004).

The demographics for 2004 also note that, compared to whites, a higher proportion of AIANs are younger, but they also have a population profile that reflects a lower proportion of individuals over age 65. Perhaps due to the larger percentage of Native Americans under age 25, many AIANs also have never married compared to the white population (U.S. Census/ACS 2004:3). Despite age distribution or characteristics of racial identification, poverty is extreme for many. For example, 1 in 4 AIANs, compared to 1 in 10 whites, live on an income that is below the poverty level (U.S. Census/ACS 2004:3).

Approximately 20 percent of AIAN families also report having a female as single head of household, compared to 9 percent for white families (U.S. Census/ACS 2004:10). The areas of employment for AIANs include service occupations, construction, production, and transportation. Where Native women are employed, disproportionate numbers of them work in unsafe and unhealthful conditions without health benefits, retirement, proper training, protections, or knowledge about occupational health risks (Colorado Cancer Plan n.d). For many, unhealthy living conditions extend to the home as well as to the workplace. Most housing situations (approximately 12%) lack safe and adequate water supply and waste disposal facilities. The 12 percent noted is higher in comparison to the 1 percent of the homes for the U.S. general population (Colorado Cancer Plan n.d.).

Native American women also have higher fertility rates than whites: 66 per 1,000 births, compared to 50 per 1,000 births for white women (U.S. Census/ACS 2004:9). It should also be noted that a higher percentage of elderly Native women compared to white women are also caretakers of their grandchildren (7 percent and 2 percent, respectively) (U.S. Census/ACS 2004:11).

Thirty-six percent of AIAN families have income that is under 200 percent of the federal poverty level. Poverty often means unemployment, which in turn means many are underinsured or uninsured. For example, in one survey, 35 percent of Native Americans said they did not have health insurance in 1999 (Burhansstipanov 2001). In the absence of health coverage, many Native families depend on the health care resources of the federal Indian Health Service (IHS). IHS, however, is not available or conveniently located nearby for many Native families. For example, Satter and colleagues report that only 4.5 percent of AIAN adults in California (the state with the highest number of AIANs) report they are able to utilize IHS (Satter et al. 2005b; Zuckerman et al. 2004).

Having a health facility that serves as one's permanent medical home is essential to accessing needed medical attention and is where one goes to obtain preventive health care services. In California, more than one-third of uninsured AIANs indicated they do not have access to a facility when they can receive routine health care (Satter et al. 2003). And understandably, those who are uninsured or underinsured are less likely to obtain preventive services or other needed screening for various diseases.

Health literacy remains a problem for certain segment of the Native population. Literacy remains a challenge because fluency in tribal language by the younger generation of Native Americans appears to be eroding. For example, approximately 75 percent of AIANs over age 5 report that they speak only English. In certain regions of the country, tribal language, however, is still spoken as the first or second language. For example, 18 percent of AIANs indicated that they speak another language other than English; presumably this other language is their tribal language (U.S. Census/ACS 2004:12).

Despite greater use of the English language, language barriers and inadequate health literacy can still delay or inhibit access to health services. This is especially challenging for those who are not fluent in the English language. For them, the daily language barrier prevents them from learning about available services and finding answers to their health-related questions, including information on eligibility for health care. These patients are also reluctant to pick up printed health information, especially when the artwork or cover does not appear to be culturally or linguistically relevant.

HEALTH STATUS INDICATORS

Where native women lives not only impacts her quality of life health but also her health status. Not only do significant numbers of vulnerable populations live in unhealthy environments, but quality health care is often not available in many of these isolated rural environments as well in poorer sections of the urban enclaves. Although treaty obligations help with the availability of federally sponsored health care on most rural reservations, the health services available are not always adequate. For example, most federal IHS hospitals and clinics are small and do not have specialty services such as surgery, obstetrics, oncology, and so forth.

As the only racial group in the United States to have a history as wards of the federal government, many Indian people experience existing and persistent health problems that are rooted in past colonial history as well as fluctuating health resources due to lack of funding or conflicting government policies. While there have been some improvements in the health status of many AIANs, most improvements are due to medical advancements. The discovery of antibiotics, for example, has helped decrease mortality due to several communicable and infectious diseases. It is now generally acknowledged that while medical advances have helped decrease mortality and morbidity, the improvements gained are increasingly overshadowed by an array of new, costly, chronic diseases. Some of these new health problems are also the results of preventable behavioral health problems.

One measurement of improvement has been increased life expectancy, although it is not on par with that for whites. An examination of life expectancy trends for AIANs between 1999 and 2001 shows that a Native American child born today has a life expectancy that is 2.4 years less than the U.S. all-races population (74.5 years to 76.9 years, respectively) (IHS 2006). While there is some improvement in decreasing infant mortality, data examined for the period between 2000 and 2002 shows that Native infants die at a rate of 8.5 per every 1,000 live births, compared to 6.8 per 1,000 for the U.S. all-races population (IHS 2006).

Although current life expectancy for Native women is still not ideal in comparison with whites, the trends point to improvements.

Life expectancy improvement is especially noticeable when current data is compared with similar data reported in the 1990s, when the life expectancy data for Native women showed they were likely to die 10 years earlier than white women (U.S. Census Bureau 2006). The life expectancy improvements noted, however, are not uniform across all tribes or in all geographic regions of the country. Data on life expectancy rates as well as other health indicators for Native Americans continue to vary from one region of the country to the next.

In addition to life expectancy, age-adjusted death rate (from all causes) is another important indicator of the health of a population. The federal IHS reports that the age-adjusted death rate (from all causes) for the Native American population is 1,059 per 100,000, compared to 872 per 100,000 for whites, maintaining a gap that continues to pose challenges for tribal health advocates as well as for the health care delivery system serving this population (IHS 2006).

According to the Centers for Disease Control (CDC), the four leading causes of death for Native women include the following (in descending order): cancer, heart disease, unintentional injuries, and diabetes (CDC 2006c). The CDC data also show mortality due to cancer is the number one cause of death for Native women over age 45, and heart disease is a significant cause of death for Native women after age 65 (CDC 2006c). It is anticipated that most deaths due to heart diseases are related to or have developed as one of the complications associated with type 2 diabetes, now endemic in many Native communities. And as would be expected in a young population, unintentional injuries are the leading cause of death for Native women under age 44, a time when young people tend to exhibit high levels of risk-taking behaviors (CDC 2006c; IHS 2006).

The inclusion of suicide and homicide among the leading causes of death for AIANs also signals a culture of hopelessness that engulfs the lives of many Native Americans. Although there are no data to indicate what percentage of deaths are associated with hopelessness, there is ample evidence that premature death and poor quality of life haunts both men and women.

While much of the existing mortality and morbidity data is helpful in evaluating the health status of a population, some critical health information is not readily available, which limits the formation of a clearer picture of the health conditions of Native women. For example, there is no information on stages of several diseases at the time of diagnosis, or information on conditions that may be the result of improper treatment or the quality of life following diagnosis and treatment, and so on. (Urban Indian Health Commission [UIHC] 2007). Moreover, few national health data agencies report data by gender or break out data on AIANs as is frequently done with other minority populations. Thus much of what is known about the health of AIANs is based on health data reported by the IHS and some of the urban Indian health programs.

NATIVE FAMILIES IN THE URBAN COMMUNITIES

Today, over 50 percent of the AIANs in the United States live in suburban or urban communities (UIHC 2007). The migration from rural to urban areas has been occurring more rapidly since the 1950s when the federal government initiated a large-scale relocation program, promising individuals or families that the urban resettlement would offer them better economic or educational opportunities. The reality, however, was relocation from one impoverished community to another. In many instances, the urban relocatees found that jobs were not plentiful, and many were left without access to health care. Existing urban health care facilities often denied them health care, assuming that all AIANs were the responsibility of the federal government. Pregnant Native women, in particular, often lacked prenatal care and had to travel back to their reservation to deliver.

As the concern over the lack of health care for relocated Indian families increased, advocates as well as new urban Indian organizations began to seek alternatives to help alleviate this problem. Some organization started to establish storefront free clinics, staffed by volunteers and using donated medical equipment and supplies. Over time, these not-for-profit clinics began to expand and were eventually able to provide a number of health services. Most of these urban health clinics were established in the 1960s and 1970s and are located in large metropolitan areas like Seattle, San Francisco, Phoenix, and Dallas. The urban clinics established were in cities where many AIANs were relocated and where many have remained. Today there are 34 urban-based primary health care facilities across the country. As these clinics became more stable, they formed a national consortium, the National Council of Urban Indian Health (NCUIH).

Due to the requirements for federal funding, the services offered by the urban clinics are available to Native Americans as well as other residents living within their respective neighborhoods. The types of services provided by the clinics are not all equal. Depending on their service population and their proximity to existing IHS facilities, the health programs range from those that offer primarily health education and referral services to those that offer more comprehensive primary health care services, including dental, mental health, and public health. To discourage duplications, urban-based health facilities located closest to existing IHS resources are less likely to offer direct medical or dental care. The urban clinics depend largely on third-party payments to sustain their operations. Only 2 percent of their funding comes the IHS.

The resources and capability of the urban-based health programs for AIANs have slowly increased as the urban Indian population has increased. More recently, the urban programs have established their own Epidemiology Center in Seattle, Washington. The new Urban Indian Health Institute (UIHI) has initiated several efforts and studies to help improve collection and analysis of the health data in order to build a more reliable and comprehensive understanding of the health problems faced by the urban Indian population (UIHI 2010).

Some of the results of the health status of urban Indians indicate health disparity is visible for this group as well. For example, Castor and colleagues (2006) summarize some of the leading causes of death for AIANs living in urban communities, listing cardiovascular disease, cancer, cerebrovascular disease, and chronic lower respiratory diseases as the four leading cause of death for urban Indians. For the most part, this assessment of leading causes of death for Native Americans living in the cities mirrors that for AIANs living on reservations. Unfortunately, it is not known if there were gender differences in the urban data examined by the team of researchers headed by Castor (2006).

In their quest to improve health data, the NCUIH surveyed its membership to ascertain which health data the clinics find most useful (Barnes, Adams, and Powell-Griner 2010; Castor et al. 2006). The results indicated that data from the U.S. Census as well as the Census Bureau's ACS on AIANs were the most helpful and relevant. It is understandable that these resources are helpful because each produces separate reports on AIANs. Other data sources mentioned, but that received a lower ranking, included the Medical Expenditure Panel Survey, a survey conducted by the Agency for Healthcare Research and Quality, and the Centers for Disease Control's National Health and Nutrition Examination Survey. These two are among other federal or national agencies that do not always extract data on AIANs, citing possible breaches of confidentiality because the AIANs comprise a small sample. Despite some of the shortcomings, all of these

national data sources do provide useful information on health disparity for AIANs.

ACCESS TO HEALTH CARE

Enrolled members of more than 560 federally recognized AIAN
tribes and their descendants are eligible for services provided by the
IHS. According to the IHS, "approximately 55% of AIANs living in
the U.S. depend primarily on the IHS for their health care" (Haverkamp et al. 2008:1,13). Because a majority of the AIANs live off-
reservation, the 55 percent is highly unlikely but may reflect a high
percentage of return visits by those with chronic health problems.
The patient-user population for IHS is probably closer to 20 percent
of all AIANs living in the United States. Moreover, IHS, tribal and
urban Indian clinics and facilities are not in all 50 states (they are in
36 states, and as noted, not all of those provide medical services; some
are education or referral programs only). In addition, the IHS data
system is limited to people who used their system within the previous
two years. For those who have not used the service (which includes a
high percentage of those living in urban areas), no data are available.
Despite some misunderstanding, IHS is not "health insurance." For
example, beginning in 1998, the U.S. Census Bureau ceased counting
IHS eligibility as "health insurance coverage" (IHS 2006).

The annual Congressional discretionary appropriation for IHS is
funded at a significantly lower per capita rate than other federally
funded health care systems. Per capita funding for the IHS in the
2009 budget was $2,690, compared to $6,826 for the general U.S.
population (Satter et al. 2005a). Obviously, IHS is significantly underfunded (U.S. Commission on Civil Rights 2004). Where IHS does not
have the medical resources needed by a patient, IHS facilities depend
on contract dollars to pay for these needed emergency medical services. Because the contract health care (CHS) funding is limited, it is
used as a form of rationed health care (U.S. Commission on Civil
Rights 2003; Edwards et al. 2010; Espey et al. 2007; Burhansstipanov
et al. 2002; Burhansstipanov 2006).

DISPARITIES

Tony Iton, in his presentation at a workshop hosted by the Institute of Medicine's (IOM) Committee on Health Equity, stressed the

need to distinguish between health inequities and health disparities (IOM 2011). He notes that health inequities (as defined by the World Health Organization) are viewed as health conditions that are unnecessary, avoidable, and therefore unjust. He defines health disparities as the difference in health outcomes that are divorced from the context in which they are produced (IOM 2011:9). It is the context, however, that is central to the persistent health disparities for AIANs.

Discussion of health disparities, therefore, must include the context of those determinants of health that contribute to poor or good health, determinants such as place, environment, occupation, gender, disability, socioeconomic situation, health literacy, access to health care, and access to affordable healthy food. There is general agreement among many countries that resolving the determinants of poor health or health inequities is complex, expensive, and will require considerable investment of resources over decades. Acknowledging areas of health inequities or disparities, however, is less complicated. For example, Table 5.1 compares selected health disparities between Native and white women from the National Health Statistics (Barnes et al. 2010), covering the period between 2004 and 2008.

As can be seen, Table 5.1 includes data on self-assessed health status as well as selected health conditions. If one compares the information between Native and white women, the disparity in all of the categories are most glaring for Native women except for one slight disadvantage that shows chronic bronchitis as higher for NHWs. In Table 5.2, the health disparity highlights some of the key differences for health behaviors and psychological distress.

Although there are differences for both males and females across many of these health behaviors and levels of psychological stress, it is important to draw especially attention to the difference between Native and NHW women. It is interesting to note that Native women are less likely to drink alcohol but, in all other indicators, Native women are more likely to be current smokers, be overweight or obese, and be physically inactive. Although the percentage differences are small, Native women also report more psychological distress, including feeling sad, hopeless, and worthless.

It is also worth noting that although it is not always noted, the persistence of some of the health disparities for Native women can also be attributed to factors that are beyond their control, namely race, age, gender, and sexual orientation. Other data sources also

Table 5.1
Selected Health Disparity Results from March 2010 National Health Statistics Reports (U.S. 2004–2008)

	AIAN Adults, Both Genders	NHW Adults, Both Genders	AIAN Female Adults	NHW Female Adults	AIAN Male Adults	NHW Male Adults
Self-Assessed Health Status for adults 18 years of age and older						
Excellent	22.6%	31.1%	23.7%	30.6%	21.3%	31.7%
Very Good	23.6%	33.6%	24.7%	33.6%	22.9%	33.6%
Good	33.6%	24.3%	32.8%	24.5%	34.2%	24.0%
Fair	14.1%	8.2%	13.4%	8.5%	15.0%	7.9%
Poor	6.1%	2.8%	5.3%	2.9%	6.6%	2.8%
Selected Health Conditions for Adults 18 Years of Age and Older						
Heart Disease	14.7%	12.2%	15.0%	11.3%	15.5%	13.5%
Hypertension	34.5%	25.7%	30.2%	24.7%	38.7%	26.7%
Stroke	4.7%	2.4%	*2.5%	2.4%	6.9%	2.5%
Emphysema	*3.0%	1.9%	*3.2%	1.6%	*2.7%	2.3%
Asthma	14.2%	11.6%	18.2%	13.0%	10.1%	10.1%
Chronic bronchitis	4.9%	4.4%	5.2%	5.8%	4.9%	3.0%
Diabetes	17.5%	6.6%	16.2%	6.2%	18.2%	7.2%
Ulcer	11.4%	7.6%	10.8%	7.7%	12.8%	7.6%
Absence of all natural teeth	13.9%	8.0%	13.1%	8.0%	14.8%	8.0%
Hearing Loss/Deafness	5.5%	3.2%	2.7%	2.3%	9.3%	4.2%

An asterisk (*) before the percentages means the data have a relative standard error of greater than 30% and less than or equal to 50% and should be used with caution as they do not meet the standards of reliability or precision.

Table 5.2
Selected Health Disparity Results from the March 2010 National Health Statistics Reports (U.S. 2004–2008)

	AIAN Adults, Both Genders	NHW Adults, Both Genders	AIAN Female Adults	NHW Female Adults	AIAN Male Adults	NHW Male Adults
Health Behaviors for Adults 18 Years of Age and Older						
Current smokers	32.7%	22.5%	27.6%	21.0%	38.6%	24.1%
Never smoked	44.6%	54.0%	51.2%	38.2%	36.4%	49.0%
Current moderate or heavy alcohol drinkers	17.9%	22.6%	11.6%	14.7%	23.8%	31.0%
Overweight, but not obese	30.2%	34.5%	29.6%	26.6%	30.4%	42.6%
Obese	39.4%	24.3%	39.7%	23.0%	38.7%	25.5%
Engaged in regular activity	25.5%	34.0%	24.8%	32.8%	26.1%	35.4%
Inactive (physically)	43.8%	34.8%	43.1%	35.4%	43.9%	33.6%
Psychological Distress						
Serious psychological distress	3.4%	2.9%	3.1%	3.4%	*3.6%	2.3%
Feel sad most or all of the time	4.9%	2.7%	4.9%	3.2%	*4.6%	2.2%
Feel hopeless most of the time	3.0%	1.9%	*2.5%	2.2%	*3.5%	1.5%
Feel worthless most of the time	3.2%	1.7%	*2.4%	2.0%	*3.8%	1.4%

*relative standard error greater than 30% and less than or equal to 50%.

reinforce the fact that many Native Americans (of both genders) are both greatly impacted by poverty, for example in access to education, employment, unsafe neighborhoods, insufficient access to healthy foods, and health insurance that is independent on IHS. Faced with these daily challenges, it is understandable that many Native women often assume that they are powerless to change their circumstances.

HIGHLIGHTING SELECTED CAUSES OF DEATH FOR NATIVE WOMEN

Mortality is a key indicator of the end result of many unpreventable and preventable health problems. Following is a selection of some of the health disparities that are most critical for Native Americans.

CARDIOVASCULAR DISEASES

AIANs are more likely to be diagnosed with heart disease than their white counterparts. In addition, AIAN adults are more likely to be obese than white adults, more likely to have high blood pressure, and more likely to be current cigarette smokers than white adults—all risk factors for heart disease. AIANs have the highest rate of premature deaths from heart disease of all races, with 36 percent of deaths from heart disease classified as premature. That rate is nearly 2.5 times that of whites (Brown et al. 2000; O'Connell et al. 2010).

The 2010 National Health Statistic Report indicates that AIAN adults are 1.4 times as likely as white adults to be diagnosed with heart disease and that AIAN adults are also 1.3 times as likely as white adults to have high blood pressure (O'Donnell et al. 2001). A longitudinal study (the Strong Heart Study) that has been examining health and disease among a large sample of Native Americans also reports that hypertension rates among American Indian tribes in Arizona, North Dakota, South Dakota, and Oklahoma range from 21 to 41 percent (Welty et al. 2002). Without question, diabetes is a major risk factor for cardiovascular disease in all American Indian populations, resulting in cardiovascular disease being the leading cause of death. Dr. Ghodes's classic study published in 1995 documents that all heart-related deaths from 1975 to 1984 in one tribe, the Pima Indians, occurred in those with diabetes (cited in Welty et al. 2002).

CANCER

Between 1997 and 2006, short-term trends in death rates for all cancers combined decreased for all genders and racial/ethnic groups except for American Indian women (Schraer et al. 1997). And as noted, cancer incidence is still increasing among American Indians (Edwards et al. 2010; Jemal et al. 2004). In November 2007, the federal government (specifically the National Institutes of Health [NIH], CDC, and IHS) released a long-awaited report to the nation that emphasized AIAN incidence data (See Chapter 11 in this collection for more information). The report showed that the incidence of cancer had increased for Alaska Native women compared to AIANs living outside of Alaska. Regional differences also show that in the 48 contiguous states, cancer incidence was elevated for American Indians living in the Northern and Southern Plains (Espey et al. 2007).

Native cancer patients continue to have the poorest survivorship from cancer five years after diagnosis when compared with other minority, poor, and medically underserved populations (Espey et al. 2007; Horm, Devesa, and Burhansstipanov 1996; Lanier et al. 1993; Satter et al. 2005a; Burhansstipanov and Olsen [in press]). In many geographic regions, there are no accurate survival data available and quality-of-life information specific to Native American cancer survivorship issues are not collected; thus the true extent of the survivorship data is unknown (Samet et al. 1987; Burhansstipanov and Hollow 2001).

Early detection is key to successful treatment of many cancers. Results from the CDC's Behavior Risk Factor and Surveillance Survey provide some useful data on cancer screening data for NHWs and for all AIAN females. For example, a comparison of cervical cancer screening between AIAN women and whites (over age 18) shows that 78 percent of Native women compared to 84 percent of white women report having had a Pap test within the past three years. Among AIAN women, Native women living in Northern Plains states were more likely to have had a Pap test (80.4% compared to 74.0%, respectively) than Native women living in states in the Southern Plains (Steele et al. 2008).

A comparison of AIAN and NHW women (over age 40) indicates that 69.4 percent of AIAN had had a mammogram within the past two years, less than the 76 percent reported by white women. There were slight regional differences among American Indian women who lived in the states in the Northern Plains from those living in the Southern Plains: 67.9 percent compared to 66.4 percent (Steele et al. 2008).

Although most IHS facilities have or can refer Native women for cancer screening, IHS facilities do less screening than other health facilities. For example, the IHS 2006 screening rates were Pap smears, 54.4 percent, and mammograms, 38.7 percent (Burhansstipanov and Hollow 2001). These rates are significantly lower than those for the U.S. population as a whole (Steele et al. 2008). Of note, Indian health resources have steadily increased their efforts in cancer screening. For example, the Aberdeen Area Tribal Council Health Board (AATCHB) noted in their report that mammography screening for their Native population had increased to 48 percent in 2010 (AATCHB 2007).

Other cancer screening, including for colorectal cancer, is low for the Native population in the Dakota states. For example, only 22.4 percent of Natives 50 years and older had had a fecal occult blood test within the past two years, and 40.3 percent self-reported ever having had either a sigmoidoscopy or colonoscopy. These data clearly show that underscreening among American Indians living in the Northern Plains states remains a challenge (AATCHB 2007).

Being obese increases the chances of developing cancer differently in men and women. For men, an average gain of 33 pounds increased the risk of developing the following cancers: esophageal by 52 percent; thyroid by 33 percent; colon by 24 percent; kidney by 24 percent; and all other cancers including rectal cancer and malignant melanoma (Renehan et al. 2008).

For women, a weight gain of 29 pounds increased the risk of cancer for the following: uterus and gallbladder by nearly 60 percent; esophagus by 51 percent; kidney by 34 percent; and postmenopausal breast, pancreatic, thyroid, and colon cancers. The risk of leukemia, non-Hodgkin's lymphoma, and multiple myeloma rose in both sexes among those who were obese (AATCHB 2007).

DIABETES

It is estimated that 23.6 million, or approximately7.8 percent, of the U.S. population have diabetes and of these, 5 to 7 million have undiagnosed diabetes (Dabelea et al. 1998). The prevalence of diabetes is higher among the AIAN population (16.5%) than any other major racial or ethnic group in the United States, and the prevalence of diabetes continues to increase among all U.S. races (CDC 2010).

Type 2 diabetes is caused by the body's resistance to the action of insulin or by impaired insulin secretion. A test that measures levels of blood glucose over 90 days (hemoglobin A_{1c}) can suggest an increased risk for the development of diabetes (Renehan et al. 2008). Type 2 diabetes, the most common type of diabetes, can be managed with healthy eating, physical activity, oral diabetes medications, or injected insulin. Most AIANs with diabetes have type 2, which usually develops in adults but is now found among increasing numbers of children and adolescents (Diabetes Monitor n.d.). Only a small number (2–4%) of AIANs have type 1 diabetes (Gilliland et al. 2002; Barnes et al. 2010).

Until recently, type 2 diabetes has been most common among people over 50, but incidence and prevalence of this disease is changing. For example, the largest relative increases in AIANs with diabetes has occurred among those between the ages of 20 and 34 during the period between 1994 and 2002. This rate rose from 1.8 percent to 3.1 percent (Denny, Holtzman, and Cobb 2003). About 15 percent of AIANs who receive care from IHS have diabetes, a total of 105,000 people, making them 2.6 times more likely to have diabetes in comparison to NHWs of similar age (CDC 2003). These are underestimates, and some regions report 40 to 70 percent of American Indian adults age 45 to 74 had diabetes in three geographic areas (National Diabetes Information Clearinghouse 2002; Lee et al. 1995). Rates vary across regions, with almost one in three American Indian adults in southern Arizona having diabetes (Diabetes Monitor n.d.). For example, among the Pima Indians, the most widely studied American Indian group, the prevalence of type 2 diabetes was approximately 50 percent in individuals ages 30 to 64 (Women's Health 2011b).

As noted before, American Indians with diabetes have significantly higher rates of hypertension, cerebrovascular disease, renal failure, lower-extremity amputations, and liver disease than commercially insured U.S. adults with diabetes (Gohdes 1995).

GESTATIONAL DIABETES

Gestational diabetes (blood glucose levels elevated above normal during pregnancy) occurs more frequently among American Indians (in about 2–5% of all AIAN pregnancies), African Americans, and

Hispanics/Latinos. It is also more common in obese women and women with a family history of diabetes. Gestational diabetes requires treatment to normalize maternal blood glucose levels to avoid complications in the infant. Women who have had gestational diabetes have a 35 percent to 60 percent chance of developing diabetes during the 10 to 20 years following their pregnancy (O'Connell et al. 2010; CDC 2010). Children born to mothers with gestational diabetes also are at a higher risk for developing type 2 diabetes (CDC 2011; Women's Health 2011a).

The prevalence of gestational diabetes varies from tribe to tribe, from 3.4 percent for Navajo to 14.5 percent for Zuni and 5.8 percent for Yup'ik Eskimos (Diabetes Monitor n.d.). It has been reported that more than one-quarter (27.5%) of Pima Indian women who had gestational diabetes developed diabetes within 4 to 8 years following pregnancy. Almost one-third (30%) of Zuni women with gestational diabetes also developed diabetes within 6 months to 9 years after pregnancy (Diabetes Monitor n.d.).

LIFESTYLES RELATED TO MORBIDITY AND DISPARITIES

Many health problems that are a part of the picture of health disparity include conditions that can be prevented. The next section touches on two of these lifestyle behaviors that put individuals at risk for several health problems.

OBESITY

Being overweight or obese increases one's risk of heart disease, type 2 diabetes, high blood pressure, stroke, breathing problems, arthritis, gallbladder disease, sleep apnea (breathing problems while sleeping), osteoarthritis, and about one-third of all types of cancers.

Obesity is measured with a body mass index (BMI) using height and weight. BMI is only an estimate. Errors in BMI can be influenced by muscle issues. For example, someone who is physically active probably has more muscle tissue, and muscle weighs more than fat. Women with a BMI of 25 to 29.9 are considered overweight, and women with a BMI of 30 or more are considered obese. The AIAN adult obesity rate is double that of the general population (CDC 2011). AIANs of all age groups are disproportionately overweight or obese (19.7% NHW compared to 28.6% AIAN) (Galloway 2002; Gruber et al. 1995). AIAN women are 40 percent more likely than white women to be obese (Steele et al. 2008). According to the Office of Minority Health (OMH), over half of AIAN women are overweight (OMH 2005).

AIANs are 1.6 times as likely to be obese as NHWs. AIAN adults (30.4%) were as likely as black adults (30.8%) and less likely than white adults (40.9%) and Asian adults (62.8%) to be a healthy weight (OMH 2005). AIAN women (29.4%) were less likely than black women (36.6%) and more likely than white women (20.3%) and Asian women (5.8%) to be obese (OMH 2005). Persons 18 and older who self-report being obese also report their leisure time physical activity as being insufficient (Denny et al. 2003).

HABITUAL USE OF MANUFACTURED TOBACCO

AIANs have the highest prevalence of smoking (Espey et al. 2007) and the highest rates of tobacco-related health disparities (Denny et al. 2003; Henderson et al. 2004; Haverkamp et al. 2008; CDC 2005). According to the National Center for Health Statistics, 21 percent of American Indian women 18 and over currently smoke (CDC 2006a). However, there is great geographic and tribal variability. Health status reports indicate that many more AIANs from Alaska and the Northern and Southern Plains use manufactured tobacco than in other regions of the United States. Despite regional differences, a large percentage of AIAN adults (32%) smoke, more than any other racial or ethnic group (CDC 2005).

As would be expected, cancer and cardiovascular disease death rates throughout Indian country mirror patterns of habitual or addictive use of manufactured tobacco. The rate of smoking among American Indian women of reproductive age (44.3%) and the prevalence of smokeless tobacco use among men (24.6%) are higher for the Northern Plains tribes than any other population. Nearly two-thirds (60.8%) of the survey respondents reported being current smokers. Almost three-fourths (74%) reported weekly exposure to secondhand smoke inside of their home, a vehicle, or workplace (Espey et al. 2007).

SUMMARY

Health is determined by many factors, from the biological to the environmental and political. Unfortunately, and as discussed here, much of what is currently known about Native women's health is incomplete as most of the data are drawn from national data sets that combine both sexes. Without this information, it is difficult to ascertain gender differences among multiple leading indicators associated with morbidity and mortality. The lack of data exists despite considerable evidence that there are gender differences in the prevalence of many health conditions.

Native women, as women all over the world, have unique reproductive health care needs. In addition to accessing and managing the health care for their families, women also have higher rates of chronic diseases as well as higher utilization of health care resources. Because of their central role in securing health care for their families, they also are essential in improving health or closing the health disparity gap.

Unfortunately, in many areas of scholarship, the life and resiliency of Native women have been neglected. For example, little is said about healthy Native women and their families, and the commitment many of them make to help improve the well-being of their family and their community. Many Native women who were relocated to urban environments helped organize storefront clinics, and later many of them took over management of these resources.

They do not always view themselves as activists, but Native women have been and continue to be at the forefront of advocacy for, and helping implement or maintain, health resources and services to better the lives of Native families in their communities. Despite the dismal picture of poor health and poverty that haunts them, they are not passive. Today, many of them sit on policy-making boards or organizations that are working to provide quality health care, assist others to help improve their socioeconomic circumstance, or obtain better education for their children. These Native women are the sage clan grandmothers, breadwinners, and single heads of many households, and increasing numbers of them are pursuing higher education without forgetting their familial ties or their cultural roots. As with women in many cultures, Native women often prioritize their day on the basis of the needs of others and neglect their own aches and pains until they reach a point where seeking medical attention is necessary.

REFERENCES

AATCHB. 2007. "Northern Plains Comprehensive Cancer Plan." Rapid City, SD: American Indian Cancer Plan 2008–2012.

Barnes, P. M., P. F. Adams, and Eve Powell-Griner. 2010, March 9. "Health Characteristics of the American Indian or Alaska Native Adult Population: United

States, 2004–2008." National Health Statistics Reports, Number 20. http://www.cdc.gov/nchs/data/nhsr/nhsr020.pdf.

Brown, E. R., V. D. Ojeda, R. Wyn, and R. Levan. 2000. *Racial and Ethnic Disparities in Access to Health Insurance and Health Care.* Los Angeles, CA: UCLA Center for Health Policy Research.

Burhansstipanov, L. 2001. "Cancer: A Growing Problem." Pp 223–252 (Chapter 10) in *Promises to Keep.* M. Dixon and Y. Roubideaux (Eds.). Washington, D.C.: American Public Health Association.

Burhansstipanov, L. 2006. "American Indian and Alaska Native Women and Cancer." Pp. 459–71 in *Nursing Care of Women and Cancer.* K. H. Dow (Ed.). St. Louis, MO: Mosby Elsevier.

Burhansstipanov, L., A. Gilbert, K. LaMarca, and L. U. Krebs. 2002. "An Innovative Path to Improving Cancer Care in Indian Country." *Public Health Reports* 116(5):424–33. Retrieved from http://www.publichealthreports.org/.

Burhansstipanov, L., and W. Hollow. 2001. "Native American Cultural Aspects of Nursing Oncology Care." *Seminars in Oncology Nursing* 17(3):206–19.

Burhansstipanov, L. and S. Olsen. In press. "Cancer Prevention and Early Detection in American Indian and Alaska Native Populations." In *Cancer Prevention in Diverse Populations: Cultural Implications for the Multi-disciplinary Team.* Marilyn Frank-Stromborg and Sharon J. Olsen (Eds.). St. Louis, MO: Mosby/Oncology Nursing Society.

Castor, Mei L., Michael S. Smyser, Maile M. Taualii, Alice N. Park, Lawson Shelly, and Ralph A. Forquera. 2006. "A Nationwide Population-Based Study Identifying Health Disparities between American Indians and Alaska Natives and the General Populations Living in Select Urban Counties." *American Journal of Public Health* 96(8):1478–84.

Centers for Disease Control (CDC). 2003, August 1. "Diabetes Prevalence among American Indians and Alaska Natives and the Overall Population—U.S., 1994–2002." *Morbidity and Mortality Weekly Report* 52(30):702–4.

Centers for Disease Control (CDC). 2005a. "Tobacco Use among Adults—United States, 2005." *Morbidity and Mortality Weekly Report* 55(42):1145–48.

Centers for Disease Control (CDC). 2006b. "Racial/Ethnic Differences among Youths in Cigarette Smoking and Susceptibility to Start Smoking—United States, 2002–2004." *Morbidity and Mortality Weekly Report* 55(47):1275–77.

Centers for Disease Control (CDC). 2006c. "Leading Causes of Death by Age Group, American Indian or Alaska Native Females—United States, 2006." http://www.cdc.gov/women/lcod/06_native_females.pdf.

Centers for Disease Control (CDC). 2010. "Diabetes: Successes and Opportunities for Population-Based Prevention and Control: At a Glance, 2010." Accessed June 2011. http://www.cdc.gov/chronicdisease/resources/publications/AAG/ddt.htm.

Centers for Disease Control (CDC). 2011. *National Diabetes Education Program: The Diabetes Epidemic among American Indians and Alaska Natives.* Atlanta, GA: CDC.

Colorado Cancer Plan. n.d. Accessed June 16, 2011. http://www.coloradocancerplan.org/index.php/healthdisparities/overview.

Dabelea, D., R. L. Hanson, P. H. Bennett, J. Roumain, W. C. Knowler, and D. J. Pettitt. 1998. "Increasing Prevalence of Type II Diabetes in American Indian Children." *Diabetologia* 41(8):904–10.

Denny, Clark H., Deborah Holtzman, and Nathaniel Cobb. 2003, August 1. "Surveil-
    lance for Health Behaviors of American Indians and Alaska Natives: Findings
    from the Behavioral Risk Factor Surveillance System, 1997–2000." *Morbidity
    and Mortality Weekly Report*. Atlanta, GA: CDC, MMWR:52(S S07):1–13.
Diabetes Monitor. n.d. Diabetes in American Indians and Alaska Natives. Accessed
    June 2011. http://www.diabetesmonitor.com/b43.htm.
Edwards, B. K., E. Ward, B. A. Kohler, C. E. Eheman, A. G. Zauber, R. N. Anderson,
    A. Jemal, M. J. Schymura, I. Lansdorp-Vogelaar, L. C. Seeff, M. van Ballegooi-
    jen, S. L. Goeden, and L. A. G. Ries. 2010, February 1. "Annual Report to the
    Nation on the Status of Cancer, 1975–2006. Featuring Colorectal Cancer
    Trends and Impact of Interventions to Reduce Future Rates." *Cancer*. Edwards
    BK: Cancer 116(3):544–573.
Espey, D., X. C. Wu, J. Swan, C. Wiggins, M. Jim, E. Ward, and B. K. Edwards.
    2007. "Annual Report to the Nation on the Status of Cancer, 1975–2004, Featur-
    ing Cancer in American Indians and Alaska Natives." *Cancer* 110(10):2119–52.
Galloway, J. M. 2002. "The Epidemiology of Atherosclerosis and Its Risk Factors
    among Native Americans." *Current Diabetes Report* 2, 274–81.
Gilliland, Susan S., Janette S. Carter, B. Skipper, and Kelly J. Acton. 2002. "HbA1c
    Levels among American Indian/Alaska Native Adults." *Diabetes Care*
    25(12):2178–83.
Gohdes, D. 1995. "Diabetes in North American Indians and Alaska Natives." In
    National Diabetes Data Group, Diabetes in America, 2nd ed. NIH Publication No.
    95-1468, 683–701. Bethesda, MD: National Institute of Diabetes and Digestive
    and Kidney Diseases, National Institutes of Health. Data Group: Diabetes in
    America, 683–695.
Gruber, E., M. M. Anderson, L. Ponton, and R. DiClemente. 1995. "Overweight and
    Obesity in Native American Adolescents: Comparing Nonreservation Youths
    with African-American and Caucasian Peers." *American Journal of Preventative
    Medicine* 11(5):306–10.
Haverkamp, D., D. Espey, R. Paisano, and N. Cobb. 2008. *Cancer Mortality among
    American Indians and Alaska Natives: Regional Differences, 1999–2003*. Rockville,
    MD: USPHS, IHS.
Henderson, P. N., D. Rhoades, J. A. Henderson, T. K. Welty, and D. Buchwald.
    2004. "Smoking Cessation and Its Determinants among Older American Indi-
    ans: The Strong Heart Study." *Ethnicity and Disease* 14(2):274–79.
Horm, J. W., S. S. Devesa, and L. Burhansstipanov. 1996. "Cancer Incidence,
    Mortality, and Survival among Racial and Ethnic Minority Groups in the United
    States." In *Cancer Epidemiology and Prevention*. D. Schottenfeld and J. F.
    Fraumeni Jr. (Eds.). New York: Oxford University Press, 192–235.
Indian Health Service (IHS). 2006. "IHS Brochure." http://www.IHS.gov/
    PublicAffairs/IHSBrochure/Disparities.asp.
Institute of Medicine (IOM). 2011. *State and Local Policy Initiatives to Reduce Health
    Disparities: Workshop Summary*. Washington, DC: The National Academy.
Jemal, A., L. X. Clegg, E. Ward, L. A. G. Ries, X. Wu, P. M. Jamison, P. A. Wingo,
    H. L. Howe, R. N. Anderson, and B. K. Edwards. 2004. "Annual Report to the
    Nation on the Status of Cancer, 1975–2001, with a Special Feature Regarding
    Survival." *Cancer* 101, 3–27.

Lanier, A. P., J. Kelly, B. Smith, C. Amadon, A. Harpster, H. Peters, H. Tantilla, C. R. Key, and A. M. Davidson. 1993. *Cancer in the Alaska Native Population: Eskimo, Aleut, and Indian Incidence and Trends 1969–1988.* Anchorage, AK: Alaska Area Native Health Service.

Lee, E. T., B. V. Howard, P. J. Savage, L. D. Cowan, R. R. Fabsitz, A. J. Oopik, J. Yeh, O. Go, D. C. Robbins, and T. K. Welty. 1995. "Diabetes and Impaired Glucose Tolerance in Three American Indian Populations Aged 45–74 Years." *Diabetes Care* 18(5):599–610.

National Diabetes Information Clearinghouse. 2002. "Fact Sheet: National Diabetes Statistics." NIH Publication 02-3892. Accessed April 4, 2002. http://www.niddk .nih.gov/health/diabetes/pubs/dmstats/dmstats.htm.

Office of Minority Health. 2005. "Health Status of American Indian and Alaska Native Women." Accessed June 16, 2011. http://minorityhealth.hhs.gov/ templates/content.aspx?ID=3724.

O'Connell, Joan, Rong Yi, Charlton Wilson, Spero M. Manson, and Kelly J. Acton. 2010. "Racial Disparities in Health Status: A Comparison of the Morbidity among American Indians and U.S. Adults with Diabetes." *Diabetes Care* 33(7):1463–70. Accessed June 16, 2011. http://care.diabetesjournals.org/ content/33/7/1463.long.

O'Donnell, C. J., S. S. Oh, J. B. Croft, K. J. Greenlund, C. Ayala, Z. J. Zheng, M. D. Mensah, and W. H. Giles. 2001. "Disparities in Premature Deaths from Heart Disease—50 States and the District of Columbia." *Morbidity and Mortality Weekly Report* 53, 121–25.

Renehan, Andrew G., Margaret Tyson, Matthias Egger, Richard F. Heller, and Marcel Zwahlen. 2008. "Body-Mass Index and Incidence of Cancer: A Systematic Review and Meta-Analysis of Prospective Observational Studies." *Lancet* 371(9612): 569–78.

Samet, J. M., C. R. Key, W. C. Hunt, and J. S. Goodwin. 1987. "Survival of American Indian and Hispanic Cancer Patients in New Mexico and Arizona, 1969–82." *Journal of the National Cancer Institute* 79(3):457–563.

Satter, D., N. Rios Burrows, M. Gatchell, M. Taualii, and D. Welch. 2003. *Diabetes among American Indians and Alaska Natives in California: Prevention Is the Key.* Los Angeles, CA: UCLA Center for Health Policy Research.

Satter, D. E., B. F. Seals, Y. J. Chia, M. Gatchell, L. Burhansstipanov, and L. Tsai. 2005a. "American Indian and Alaska Natives in California: Women's Cancer Screening and Results." *Journal of Cancer Education* 20(Suppl.):58–64.

Satter, D. E., A. Veiga-Ermert, L. Burhansstipanov, L. Pena, and Terrie Restivo. 2005b. "Communicating Respectfully with American Indian and Alaska Natives: Lessons from the California Health Interview Survey." *Journal of Cancer Education* 20(1):49–51.

Schraer, C. D., A. I. Adler, A. M. Mayer, K. R. Halderson, and B. A. Trimble. 1997. "Diabetes Complications and Mortality among Alaska Natives: 8 Years of Observation." *Diabetes Care* 20(3):314–16.

Steele, C. B., C. J. Cardinez, L. C. Richardson, L. Tom-Orme, and K. Shaw. 2008. "Surveillance for Health Behaviors of American Indians and Alaska Natives (AIAN)—Findings from the Behavioral Risk Factor Surveillance System, 2000–2006." *Cancer* 113(S5):1131–41.

Urban Indian Health Commission (UIHC). 2007. *Invisible Tribes: Urban Indians and Their Health in a Changing World*. Seattle, WA: Robert Wood Johnson Foundation and Urban Indian Health Commission.

Urban Indian Health Commission (UIHC). 2010. *Urban Indian Health Data System: Envisioning a National Health Information System for Urban Indian Health Organizations*. Seattle, WA. Urban Indian Health Institute. March.

U.S. Census. 2004. *Census 2000 Summary Files: American Indian and Alaska Native Population for Montana Reservations by Sex and Age*. Washington, DC: Department of Commerce, U.S. Census Bureau. Table P12C.

U.S. Census/American Community Survey. 2004. *The American Community— American Indians and Alaska Natives: 2004 American Community Survey Reports*. Washington, DC: U.S. Census Bureau.

U.S. Commission on Civil Rights. 2003. *A Quiet Crisis: Federal Funding and Unmet Needs in Indian Country*. Washington, DC: U.S. Commission on Civil Rights. www.census.gov/newsroom/releases/archives/. . ./cb06-ffse06.html.

U.S. Commission on Civil Rights. 2004. *Broken Promises: Federal Funding and Unmet Needs in Indian Country*. Washington, DC: U.S. Commission on Civil Rights.

Welty, T. K., D. A. Rhoades, F. Yeh, E. T. Lee, L. D. Cowan, R. R. Febsitz, D. C. Robbins, R. B. Devereux, J. A. Henderson, and B. V. Howard. 2002. "Changes in Cardiovascular Disease Risk Factors among American Indians: The Strong Heart Study." *Annals of Epidemiology* 12(2):97–106.

Women's Health. 2011a. "American Indian Women and Cholesterol." Accessed June 16, 2011. http://www.womenshealth.gov/minority/americanindian/cholesterol.cfm.

Women' Health. 2011b. "American Indians and Diabetes." Accessed June 2011. http://www.womenshealth.gov/minority/americanindian/diabetes.cfm.

Zuckerman, S., J. Haley, Y. Roubideaux, and M. Lillie-Blanton. 2004. "Health Service Access, Use, and Insurance Coverage among American Indians/Alaska Natives and Whites: What Role Does the Indian Health Service Play?" *American Journal of Public Health* 94(1):53–59.

CHAPTER 6

Becoming an Elder: Native Women and Aging

Emily A. Haozous and R. Turner Goins

INTRODUCTION

As is true in many cultures, American Indian (AI) elders serve critical roles to communities in preservation and continuation of culture and in caregiving. Historically, many tribal groups have been matrilineal, and women have been essential to continuing the traditional lineage and preservation of family roles within their tribe. Historically and culturally, the position of women in the tribe is determined by cultural norms that distinguish tribes as either matriarchal or patriarchal. In matriarchal societies, the primarily lineage is through the women, or one's mother and mother's kin, while in patriarchal societies the lineage is through men, or the father and his kin. In general, women in matrilineal society have a more secured and powerful position so that an elderly woman, if she chooses, can have a gentle leadership role as the family matriarch, an important position that serves as a key hallmark of tribal identity for her family or clan. In contemporary times, the role of the elder woman has broadened into tribal representation to the outside world, caregiving, and preservation of cultural identity and practices. Even within nonmatrilineal tribes, the role of women in supporting and continuing cultural and health practices is widespread. Indeed, within many tribes, the hard work and wisdom of its women provide a foundation for the community's existence.

In most Native American communities, chronologic age does not imply elder status. The role of elder is recognized as a position of great responsibility and status and is granted only to those who choose to take a meaningful role within their community. Through the process of aging, women are expected to learn and share their wisdom with their community as a continuation of the cycle of life. Fortunately, women are eager to build on the knowledge they have gained through the years, and it is much more common that younger women are recognized as tribal elders than it is that elderly women are not recognized as elders.

When examining aging in Native communities, two key concepts are imperative to building context in the discussion. The first is that although chronologic age is seen as an external measure of aging in mainstream culture, the adoption of the role and title of elder within American Indian and Alaska Native (AIAN) communities is much more closely related to the individuals' role in the community and the cumulative wisdom she represents (Lewis 2010). Second, the additive effect of both stressors within the individual's life and the burden of many generations of stressors through historical trauma and weathering creates a setting in which the chronologic age of a person may give an inaccurate idea about that person's physical health. Indeed, as a result of this weathering, many Native women experience symptoms associated with aging at much younger ages than in their non-Hispanic white counterparts (Palacios and Portillo 2009).

SOME SOCIODEMOGRAPHICS AND NOTIONS OF AGING

Native American populations are younger than other ethnicities, with 31 percent of the population aged less than age 15, based on the 2000 U.S. Census. According to this same report, only 6 percent of American Indians are older than 65 years (IHS 2009). The majority (51%) of Native Americans live in six states: California, Oklahoma, Arizona, New Mexico, Texas, and North Carolina (AOA 2009). Life expectancy varies in different communities—what is considered elderly in South Dakota might not be so in New Mexico, and given the effects of weathering and historical trauma as well as repeated first-hand traumas of boarding school abuse, sexual and physical abuse, and early childbearing among Native women, a 50-year-old Native woman may very likely already be a grandparent and experiencing health and lifespan issues comparable to a non-Native woman at age 65.

Standardized definitions for aging in the general population are based on the understanding that aging is most meaningful for women over age 65. Were we to base all generalizations of aging in tribal communities on this marker, we would drastically underrepresent the true experience of aging for American Indians. Unfortunately, statistical analyses for population-based comparisons rarely include the younger-old in their reporting, so most of the data for this chapter are drawn from articles defining elderly as beginning at age 65. Indeed, comparisons of morbidity between Canadian First Nations elders and age-matched non–First Nations Canadians show that same-age First Nations people are more ill and live with more chronic diseases than non–First Nations people (Wilson et al. 2010). The same is true among American Indians (Goins and Pilkerton 2010). Although the information presented in this chapter is an attempt to provide a snapshot of the aging experience for AI women, it is important to understand that aging is a relative term, and the experiences reflected here represent a younger population of Native Americans than they would in non-Natives.

Although aging is a natural process, the role of social determinants of health in premature aging is a growing body of science. When we examine issues of aging in Native women, there are consistent themes suggesting that body size, stress, and the cumulative stress of living in resource-poor conditions contribute substantially to morbidity in this population. In this chapter, we will first describe the role of Native women elders within their communities. Next we will briefly outline the most pertinent health concerns for Native American women elders, looking at both an individual-based and a community-based view, with a particular focus on the role social determinants of health play in aging. Finally, we will relate the impact these health concerns have on the continuation of culture and role for AI communities.

THE IMPORTANCE OF AI WOMEN ELDERS

As explained previously, aging in AI culture extends beyond chronology. Aging is seen as a gift and a responsibility, and the elderly Native American individual takes on important roles within the culture that can be neither earned nor purchased. As keepers of traditional knowledge, elders are seen to act as a bridge between the living world and the spiritual world and, as such, are expected to perform specific ceremonial roles. For example, in the Apache culture, elder women are key to many rituals related to life passage, including giving a baby his first haircut, introducing a baby to her cradleboard, and acting as guide and mentor for young women as they complete their coming-of-age ceremony.

CAREGIVING

Both historically and in contemporary culture, AI grandmothers often serve as primary caregivers for grandchildren. Whether this is a choice made due to interference of substance abuse within the family or because the parents are filling the role of wage-earner during their youth, grandmother caregivers are strikingly common across Native nations (Cross, Day, and Byers 2010). As many as 60 percent of Indian children live in homes where grandparents are the primary caregivers, and it is unclear what percentage of additional AI children are placed in temporary caregiving situations with grandparent caregivers (Good 2006).

Reasons for AI elder caregiving of grandchildren are diverse but fall into several observed grandparenting styles: distance, ceremonial, fictive, custodial, foster, and cultural conservation grandparenting (Weibel-Orlando 1997). The distanced grandparent is one who lives afar and visits infrequently, and it is relatively uncommon in Indian families. The ceremonial grandparent is a temporary caregiver, charged with providing cultural and ceremonial teaching to grandchildren over brief but concentrated visits. The fictive grandparent is an adopted grandparent caregiver and would be recognized in the larger culture as a foster parent or other assumed caregiver. The custodial grandparent assumes responsibility for children when their birth parents are unable to provide care for health or legal reasons. The custodial grandparent acts as cultural conservator and sees the role of caregiving grandparent as a responsibility to continue with cultural teaching (Weibel-Orlando 1997). These categories provide a very basic framework for understanding the diverse reasons for caregiving, and not all categories are exclusive; indeed, many caregivers will take on the role for multiple reasons.

HEALTH CONCERNS OF AI WOMEN ELDERS

The cumulative stressors of living become evident with aging (IHS 2009). Diminished overall health contributes to the development of chronic disease, and as described in this chapter, many AI elder women experience a constellation of life-long stressors that increase the inevitability of chronic disease and diminished quality of life. Overall health for Native Americans is poor in comparison with other racial and ethnic groups, with AI adults experiencing poorer general health, as well as higher rates of diabetes, troubled hearing, psychological distress, and unmet medical needs (Barnes, Adams, and Power-Griner 2010). Leading causes of death for Native Americans age 65 and older are heart disease, malignant neoplasms, diabetes, cerebrovascular disease, and chronic lower respiratory disease.

A complex constellation of factors contributes greatly to increased morbidity among Native elder women. Social determinants of health such as poverty, lack of education, stress, racism, job insecurity, underfunded health care systems, and unemployment intermingle in creating a landscape of health inequity that plays out in the chronic diseases of Native elder women. In addition, comorbidities create complex health conditions that require constant attention and sophisticated medical care. In AI women elders, 57 percent of the elders had been told by a health care provider that they had three or more chronic health conditions, including vision loss, arthritis, hearing loss, depression, hypertension, and diabetes (Goins and Pilkerton 2010). Causes for these comorbidities go beyond the physiological explanatory models and have their foundation in the social environment in which Native women elders live their lives.

Although some disease appears without warning and without explanation, more often chronic illness is the result of a complex interplay between unmodifiable risk factors such as heredity, age, and sex and modifiable risk factors such as diet, physical activity, habitual tobacco use, alcohol, and obesity. Heart disease, diabetes, and some cancers can all be linked to diet and exercise. For example, cerebrovascular accidents can be linked to hypertension, which is turn is linked to sedentary lifestyle and unhealthy weight. Although highly simplistic, these examples serve to illustrate the manner in which social determinants of health act as catalysts for those individuals who might have unmodifiable risk factors for a particular health issue.

CARDIOVASCULAR DISEASE

As is true with the general U.S. population, cardiovascular disease is the leading cause of death for Native Americans age 65 and older

(IHS 2009). Cardiovascular disease is a complex constellation of diseases of the heart and blood vessels and includes hypertension, hyperlipidemia, and atherosclerosis. In addition, comorbid conditions such as diabetes mellitus increase a person's risk for cardiovascular disease as a result of arterial damage caused by hyperglycemia. Although precursors to cardiovascular disease begin early in life and are associated with known risk factors such as a diet high in saturated fats, smoking, inactivity, and obesity, morbidity from cardiovascular disease is the result of cumulative behavior and is inherently a disease of aging.

Inactivity is particularly relevant in the aging population of AIs. The Strong Heart Family Study evaluated physical activity in 3,665 AIs using both interview and data collection through seven-day pedometer use (Rhoades et al. 2007). The researchers found that older participants were predictably less active and that neither male nor female elders walked 5,000 steps per day, meaning none of the participants met the Centers for Disease Control and American College of Sports Medicine recommendations for daily physical activity (Storti et al. 2009). Examination of longitudinal data from this same cohort found increases in heart disease risk factors over time, including increases in the proportion of participants with hypertension and diabetes mellitus.

CANCER

The second leading cause of mortality, cancer is a widespread and growing problem for AI women. While non-AI groups are enjoying improvements in cancer mortality, AI mortality from cancer has been stable or increasing, particularly among women (Jemal et al. 2010). In examination of national statistics, breast, colorectal, and uterine cancer are among the top five cancer diagnoses in Native women, and colorectal cancer, lung cancer, kidney cancer, and non-Hodgkin's lymphoma rank among the top 10, with geographic variance (Wiggins et al. 2008; Jemal et al. 2010).

An important cause for disparate cancer outcomes is that Native women tend to have a much later stage at diagnosis, decreasing both treatment options and survival from cancer for this population. The late-stage cancer diagnosis is due to a constellation of causes, including systemic causes due to limited access to cancer screening; financial barriers preventing payment for cancer treatment; educational barriers limiting understanding of the importance of cancer screening; issues with rural living and transportation; cultural barriers to care, such as cancer fatalism or the belief that treatment is futile; or the tendency of Native women to prioritize the well-being of the family and community over themselves and thus delay health-seeking behaviors until the symptoms of cancer are unbearable. The combination of barriers to receiving timely and complete treatment for cancer diagnosis translates to disproportionate mortality for cancers that would have been treatable had they been caught early and treated aggressively.

In response to the high mortality due to cancer, many tribal communities are developing creative and innovative responses to increase cancer screening. Cancer navigation through lay community workers, most often women, has improved cancer outcomes in some communities. Cancer support groups among Native women have increased, which has effectively reduced the taboo that was previously limiting communication and support through cancer treatment. Innovation in dissemination of cancer-screening education has led to several community-based interventions designed to increase cancer screening and decrease late-stage diagnoses of cancers. These interventions will also improve the overall dialogue around cancer, demystifying the process of diagnosis and treatment and hopefully will lead to better health-seeking behaviors in the future.

DIABETES

Diabetes is a well-recognized epidemic in AI populations, with mortality from diabetes and diabetes-related causes widespread. As many as 80 percent of Native American elders live with diabetes, and the burden of disease extends beyond personal and family hardship to high financial burdens and added stress on the health care system (Henderson 2010). Although extensive research efforts have been dedicated to diabetes prevention, rates continue to increase (Henderson 2010). Approximately 40 percent of AI women are obese, a key risk factor for diabetes (Barnes et al. 2010). Habitual tobacco smoking, limited physical activity, and poor overall health are also elevated in AIs, making them at high risk for developing diabetes (Denny et al. 2005).

CEREBROVASCULAR DISEASE AND STROKE

American Indians have a higher rate of cerebrovascular accident or stroke than non-Hispanic whites and African Americans (Zhang et al. 2008). Fatality from stroke is also higher in AIs than in other racial and ethnic groups in the United States (Zhang et al. 2008). Risk factors for strokes in Native Americans include diabetes mellitus, hypertension, smoking, age, fasting glucose, hemoglobin A1c, and prehypertension (Hsia et al. 2007). Rates for stroke in the general population have been decreasing, but in AIs the rates are more variable and are on the increase in some regions, including Montana (Harwell et al. 2005).

MEMORY/DEMENTIA

In concert with the multiple morbidities experienced by Native American elders includes dementia and related neurologic decline. Vascular damage secondary to hypertension, cardiovascular disease, and diabetes contribute to cognitive decline, among other causes. Although the daily care for an elder with dementia is challenging, many Native cultures see dementia as part of a circular life process in which individuals are seen as returning to the infant stage in the time before death (Hulko et al. 2010; Lanting et al. 2011).

For some tribes, the hallucinations that can accompany dementia are viewed as a window into that person's connection with the next world and are contextualized in their connection with a supernormal presence, accessing life after death (Henderson and Traphagan 2005). In spite of unsteady cognitive function, Native women elders with dementia are still regarded as a rich source of cultural information, including storytelling and continuation of the skilled crafting of traditional artwork (Hulko et al. 2010). When questioned about the cause of cognitive decline late in life, AI research is convergent within tribal communities that the change from the old ways to modernity, the introduction of drugs and alcohol, boarding school experiences, the stresses of modern living, and health conditions such as diabetes are all contributory to dementia (Hulko et al. 2010; Henderson and Traphagan 2005).

RELATED SOCIAL DETERMINANTS OF HEALTH

A common thread throughout the leading causes of chronic illness and death for AI women elders are the social determinants of health that exist from birth. Although the causal relationship between racism and heart disease is disputed, the link between social stress and poor health outcomes is well established. In addition to modifiable risk factors such as physical activity and diet, Native women have additional cultural issues that compound the likelihood of developing these conditions. Fatalism, or the belief that a disease is inevitably fatal, acts as a deterrent to seeking early preventative care and also prevents women from engaging in health-seeking behaviors such as cancer screening (Powe and Finnie 2003). Native women are frequently observed as believing that diabetes is a natural progression associated with aging and that prevention is futile. Likewise, cancer mortality is also seen as inevitable, preventing women from participating in cancer screening and also limiting motivation to adhere to prescribed treatment regimens, even with disease that would be considered curable at early stages (Haozous 2009).

Medical mistrust, or the belief that health care providers or health care systems are inherently untrustworthy, is a pervasive barrier to care-seeking behavior by many AIs (Guadagnolo et al. 2009). Medical mistrust prevents some Native women from participating in preventative care and also prevents women from following medical advice when they believe the health care providers have an ulterior motive that may not be in the patient's best interests. Although a large portion of the medical research implicates medical mistrust in AI participation in clinical research, the effect of medical mistrust on health-seeking behaviors in Native Americans is still poorly understood. In spite of a lack of clinical trials measuring medical mistrust in the literature, there are numerous qualitative studies in which mistrust, trust, or distrust are cited by participants as being a key factor influencing AI decision making about heath-seeking behaviors.

Poverty, nutrition, and food uncertainty all play key roles in determining health for elders. Although scarce literature exists examining the direct effect of poverty on long-term health outcomes in AIs, literature describing food insecurity and poverty and their relationship with immediate health can be extrapolated out to long-term outcomes. For example, poverty and food insecurity have been linked to high-calorie, nutrient-scarce diets. In both urban and rural settings, food availability is limited, and often tribes supplement with commodity foods. Commodity foods, or government-issued foods, are specifically designed to sustain populations during times of difficulty and thus tend to be shelf-stable, canned, or otherwise well preserved. Intended as short-term solutions to food scarcity such as during a natural disaster, commodity foods have become household staples in many Native American homes and provide a large percentage of the basic lifetime caloric needs for many families. As a result of this response to food insecurity, obesity and diseases related to poor diet can be linked to the low availability of fresh foods on reservations.

Racism as a social determinant of health plays out in Native American populations as a subtle but constant stressor. Native American perceptions of health care and their satisfaction with health care are directly related to collective experiences of racism and oppression. Today's elders have survived the civil rights movement and the AI movement, in which AIs made several key political actions that drew attention to the poor living conditions and institutionalized barriers to tribal survival. Many elders were also children during the boarding-school era, in which children were required to attend boarding schools and were subject to systematic assimilative curricula designed to mainstream Native children. The products of the early boarding-school experiences included young families relocated to urban areas, some women being forcibly sterilized without their consent or knowledge, and being taught that practicing traditional ways and speaking their traditional language were dirty and undesirable. The cumulative effect of these destructive state and federal policies has yielded generations of adults who are currently elders and are still reconciling the collective trauma of their lifetimes.

The Indian Health Service (HIS), a treaty-obliged health care system designed to provide basic health care to AIANs, has been dramatically underfunded since its inception (U.S. Civil Rights 2003). Although great progress has been made in reducing death from infectious disease, clinical care for most chronic illnesses is unsupported and in some cases not addressable by the health care providers within the IHS system. AI women with diabetes can receive exceptional treatment within the IHS and tribal clinics, but AI women with cancer are required to seek care through outside care systems because most IHS regional hospitals do not offer oncology services. Delayed care also occurs due to lack of resources, distance, and other barriers (Burhansstipanov and Hollow 2001).

HEALTH CONCERNS IMPACT CULTURE IN AI COMMUNITIES

AI women elders provide important cultural and social services to their communities. They are relied upon for preservation of culture, language, foods, crafts, and ways of living. They also serve as beacons of hope to their families and communities and as representatives of an earlier time.

Although chronic illness, early aging, and other health conditions described here provide obstacles to Native American women elders in meeting their roles and responsibilities, the indefatigable spirit of Native peoples is often most evident in our elders. It is critical that the social determinants of health that dramatically impact the health of Native women are addressed and corrected in response to the growing rates of chronic and terminal disease in this already vulnerable population.

REFERENCES

Administration on Aging (AOA). 2009. "A Statistical Profile of American Indian and Native Alaskan Elderly." *Administration on Aging: Minority Aging.* Accessed July 21, 2011. http://www.aoa.gov/aoaroot/Press.../Stat_Profile_Native_Aged_65.pdf.

Barnes, P. M., P. F. Adams, and E. Power-Griner. 2010. "Health Characteristics of American Indian and Alaska Native Adult Population: United States, 2004–2008." *National Health Statistics Reports* 20, 1–23.

Burhansstipanov, L. and W. Hollow. 2001. "Native American Cultural Aspects of Oncology Nursing Care." *Seminars in Oncology Nursing* 17(3):206–19.

Cross, S. L., A. G. Day, and L. G. Byers. 2010. "American Indian Grand Families: A Qualitative Study Conducted with Grandmothers and Grandfathers Who Provide Sole Care for Their Grandchildren." *Journal of Cross Cultural Gerontology* 25, 371–83.

Denny, C. H., D. Holtzman, R. T. Goins, and J. B.Croft. 2005. "Disparities in Chronic Disease Risk Factors and Health Status between American Indian/ Alaska Native and White Elders: Findings from a Telephone Survey, 2001 and 2002." *American Journal of Public Health* 95(5):825–27.

Goins, R. T. and C. S. Pilkerton. 2010. "Comorbidity among Older American Indians: The Native Elder Care Study." *Journal of Cross Cultural Gerontology* 25, 343–54.

Good, E. 2006. "Grandparents Raising Grandchildren: Supporting Health Generations." *Unified Solutions Tribal Community Development Group, Inc., Training and Technical Assistance Newsletter* 18, 10–11.

Guadagnolo B. A., K. Kristin Cina, Petra Helbig, Kevin Molloy, Mary Reiner, E. Francis Cook, and Daniel G. Petereit. 2009. "Medical Mistrust and Less Satisfaction with Health Care among Native Americans Presenting for Cancer Treatment." *Journal of Health Care for the Poor and Underserved* 20, 210–26.

Haozous, E. A. 2009. *Exploring Cancer Pain in Southwest American Indians.* PhD dissertation, Yale University, New Haven, CT.

Harwell, T. S., C. S. Oser, N. J. Okon, C. C. Fogle, S. D. Helgerson, and D. Gohdes. 2005. "Defining Disparities in Cardiovascular Disease for American Indians: Trends in Heart Disease and Stroke Mortality among American Indians and Whites in Montana, 1991 to 2000." *Circulation* 112, 2263–67.

Henderson, J. N. and J. W. Traphagan. 2005. "Cultural Factors in Dementia: Perspectives from the Anthropology of Aging." *Alzheimer Disease and Associated Disorders* 19(4):272–75.

Henderson, L. C. 2010. "Divergent Models of Diabetes among American Indian Elders." *Journal of Cross Cultural Gerontology* 25, 303–16.

Hsia, J., K. L. Margolis, C. B. Eaton, N. K. Wenger, M. Allison, L. Wu, A. Z. LaCroix, and H. R. Black. 2007. "Prehypertension and Cardiovascular Disease Risk in the Women's Health Initiative." *Circulation* 115(7):855–60.

Hulko, W., E. Camille, E. Antifeau, M. Arnouse, N. Bachnynski, and D. Taylor. 2010. "Views of First Nation Elders on Memory Loss and Memory Care in Later Life." *Journal of Cross Cultural Gerontology* 25(25):317–42.

Indian Health Service (IHS). 2009. *Trends in Indian Health, 2002–2003.* Rockville, MD: U.S. Department of Health and Human Services, Indian Health Service.

Jemal, A., R. Siegal, J. Xu, and E. Ward. 2010. "Cancer Statistics, 2010." *CA, A Cancer Journal for Clinicians* 60, 277–300.

Lanting, S., M. Crossley, D. Morgan, and A. Cammer. 2011. "Aboriginal Experiences of Aging and Dementia in a Context of Sociocultural Change: Qualitative Analysis of Key Informant Group Interviews with Aboriginal Seniors." *Journal of Cross Cultural Gerontology* 26, 103–17.

Lewis, J. P. 2010. "Successful Aging through the Eyes of Alaska Natives: Exploring Generational Differences among Alaska Natives." *Journal of Cross Cultural Gerontology* 25, 385–96.

Palacios, J. F. and C. J. Portillo. (2009). "Understanding Native Women's Health: Historical Legacies." *Journal of Transcultural Nursing* 20, 15–27.

Powe, B. D. and R. Finnie. 2003. "Cancer Fatalism: The State of the Science." *Cancer Nursing* 26(6):454–67.

Rhoades, D. A., T. K. Welty, W. Wang, F. Yeh, R. B. Devereux, R. R. Fabsitz, E. T. Lee, and B. V. Howard. 2007. "Aging and the Prevalence of Cardiovascular Disease Risk Factors in Older American Indians: The Strong Heart Study." *Journal of the National Geriatrics Society* 55(1):87–94.

Storti, K. L., V. C. Arena, M. M. Barmada, C. H. Bunker, R. L. Hanson, S. L. Laston, J. L. Yeh, J. M. Zmuda, B. V. Howard, and A. M. Kriska. 2009. "Physical Activity Levels in American-Indian Adults: The Strong Heart Family Study." *American Journal of Preventative Medicine* 37(6):481–87.

U.S. Civil Rights. 2003. *A Quiet Crisis: Federal Funding and Unmet Needs in Indian Country.* Washington, DC: U.S. Commission on Civil Rights.

Weibel-Orlando, Joan. 1997. "Grandparenting Styles: The contemporary Native American Experiences." http://www.Stpt.usf.edu/-jsokolov/webbook/weibel.pdf.

Wiggins, C. L., D. K. Espey, P. A. Wingo, J. S. Kaur, R. T. Wilson, J. Swan, B. A. Miller, M. A. Jim, J. J. Kelly, and A. P. Lanier. 2008. "Cancer among American Indians and Alaska Natives in the United States, 1999–2004." *Cancer* 113(5):1142–52.

Wilson, K., M. W. Rosenberg, S. Abonyi, and R. Lovelace. 2010. "Aging and Health: An Examination of Differences between Older Aboriginal and Non-Aboriginal People." *Canadian Journal on Aging* 29(3):369–82.

Zhang, Y., James M. Galloway, Thomas K. Welty, David O. Wiebers, Jack P. Whisnant, Richard B. Devereax, Jorge R. Kizer, Betty V. Howard, Linda D. Cowan, Jeunliang Yeh, James Howard, Wenyu Wang, Lyle Best, and Elisa T. Lee. 2008. "Incidence and Risk Factors for Stroke in American Indians: The Strong Heart Study." *Circulation* 118, 1577–84.

CHAPTER 7

Addressing Food Security and Food Sovereignty in Native American Communities

Valarie Blue Bird Jernigan

INTRODUCTION

Many Native American communities experience a lack of access to high-quality and culturally appropriate foods, especially in rural, isolated reservations (Joe and Young 1993; Dixon and Roubideaux 2001; Ferreira and Lang 2006). Food insecurity, defined as "having limited or uncertain availability of nutritionally adequate and safe foods or limited or uncertain ability to acquire acceptable foods in socially acceptable ways" (Anderson 1990:1598), is a result of underlying social, economic, historical, and institutional factors within a community that affect the quantity and quality of available food and its affordability or price relative to the financial resources available to acquire it (Breckwich Vasquez et al. 2007; Cohen 2002). The health consequences of food insecurity are well documented and have numerous implications for the health and welfare of Native Americans.

Food-insecure communities have higher rates of chronic-disease-related outcomes, including obesity, diabetes, and cardiovascular disease (Cade, Calvert, and Greenwood 1999; Morland et al. 2002a; Swinburn et al. 2004). This chapter examines food insecurity, including its causes and associated health disparities, among Native Americans with an emphasis on Native American women. The growing food sovereignty movement is discussed as a systems-level approach to addressing food insecurity in Native American communities.

FOOD INSECURITY AND HEALTH

Nationally, the marked increase in the prevalence of diet-related health conditions, including obesity, diabetes, and cardiovascular disease, has led researchers to examine the food environment. The food environment is typically characterized as the number and types of food stores and food service venues located in the census tract of a particular community or neighborhood (Morland et al. 2002b; Austin et al. 2005; Wang et al. 2006). The high cost of healthy, more nutrient-dense foods, coupled with decreased availability and selection in low-income communities, has been shown to contribute to food insecurity by constraining the ability of consumers to make healthy food choices. Supermarket flight, transportation barriers, the growth of fast-food chains, and a lack of healthy foods sold at corner stores, which instead sell foods high in salt, fat, and sugar, are documented causes of food insecurity (Drewnowski 2004; Hill 2004; Drewnowski and Specter 2004; Galvez, Frieden, and Landrigan 2003; Dannenberg et al. 2003; Morland et al. 2002a). Fluctuations in funding for food assistance and other social safety net programs have also been associated with food insecurity (Cook 2002).

Food insecurity has been studied primarily in urban environments, where it is most prevalent in female-headed households, households with children, and among African Americans and Latinos (Cade et al. 1999; Morland et al. 2002a; Swinburn et al. 2004). Many neighborhoods within these urban areas have been classified as "food deserts," a designation that identifies those places where there are few or no consumer food resources where families can buy healthy and affordable food (Hendrickson, Smith, and Eikenberry 2006; Raja, Ma, and Yadav 2008).

FOOD INSECURITY AND ASSOCIATED HEALTH DISPARITIES

Poor food environments have been associated with a "hunger-obesity paradox" (Townsend et al. 2001), especially among low-income women and children. While individuals with poor food security might be expected to have reduced food intake and thus reduced body fat and less likelihood of being overweight, the prevalence of overweight among women increases as food insecurity increases (Townsend et al. 2001). For example, women reporting food insecurity without hunger were, on the average, 4.5 kilograms (10 pounds) heavier than the comparison group (Townsend et al. 2001; Mokdad et al. 1999). Data from the National Health and Nutrition Examination Survey III also showed that 58 percent of women in food-insufficient households were overweight. Participation in the food stamp program (FSP) was also associated with higher obesity rates among women (Townsend et al. 2001; Mokdad et al. 1999; Kendall, Olson, and Frongillo 1996). It is interesting to note, however, that a comparable relationship between obesity and food insecurity has not been observed among children or among men.

The high rates of diet-related diseases, particularly among Native American women and children, make food insecurity an important public health issue (Power 2008). The prevalence of obesity is approximately 50 percent higher among Native American women than among non-Hispanic white women (Jernigan et al. 2010; Sherwood, Harnack, and Story 2000). One of the key measurements for the degree of obesity is body mass index (BMI), a calculation based on height and weight by gender and by age. In a study on obesity, Caballero and colleagues (2003) found approximately 40 percent of Native American women in their sample had a BMI greater 30 (a BMI greater than 25 classifies one as overweight). In another study that was obtained from a convenience sample of Native American women living in urban and rural areas in Oklahoma, it was found that one-third of the sample had diagnosed diabetes, 90 percent were classified as overweight, and approximately one-third were morbidly obese (with BMI greater than 35) (Taylor, Keim, and Gilmore 2005).

Native Americans have a higher prevalence of diabetes, obesity, and hypertension than other ethnic groups in the United States (Jernigan et al. 2010). Between 1995–1996 and 2005–2006, the adjusted prevalence of diabetes among Native Americans increased by 26.9 percent, from 6.7 percent to 8.5 percent; obesity increased by 25.3 percent, from 24.9 percent to 31.2 percent; and hypertension increased by 5 percent, from 28.1 percent to 29.5 percent (Jernigan et al. 2010). Approximately 40 percent of Native American children have been found to be overweight, and this number continues to increase (Story et al. 2003).

Community-based diabetes prevention and management interventions among Native Americans, as in other communities, have seen limited success (Glasgow et al. 2001; Glasgow, Vogt, and Boles 1999; Green et al. 1995; Green and Glasgow 2006; Kerner 2006; Archer et al. 2002). To address some of these problems, there has been an increased emphasis on the utilization of the community-based participatory research (CBPR) model, a model that is based on community and academic partnership development to facilitate community-directed public health or health-promotion interventions in Native American communities (Davis and Reid 1999; Jernigan 2010; Jernigan and Lorig 2011; Wallerstein and Duran 2006).

Although CBPR models are creative, the interventions proposed or explored often take many years to develop and implement due to the long-term commitment to the capacity-building element of the CBPR orientation and the need to focus on priorities of importance to communities, which may not include public health disease-specific initiatives. While community-based programs are still taking shape and making progress, some of the more recent attention has turned to implementing policy changes that address diet-related health conditions in hopes that systems-level changes may be more successful than traditional health education in addressing these diseases (De Cock and Janssen 2002; Friel, Chopra, and Satcher 2007; Mongeau 2008).

PREVALENCE AND CAUSES OF FOOD INSECURITY AMONG NATIVE AMERICANS

To date, there have been few studies that have assessed the food environments and associated food security among Native Americans (Gittelsohn et al. 2000; Cunningham-Sabo et al. 2003; Curran et al. 2005). One survey among Northern Cheyenne Reservation residents found high levels of food insecurity and diabetes risk (Ward and Whiting 2006). A study examining sociodemographic attributes, food insecurity and environment, and health status among several tribes in the Northern Plains found that 40 percent of the households surveyed ($n = 187$) reported food insecurity, with the prevalence of food insecurity significantly decreasing as household income increased. After adjustment for income, food insecurity was significantly associated with poor general health and bodily pain (Brown, Noonan, and Nord 2007).

A report published by the Food Research and Action Center examining the Women, Infant, and Children (WIC) program in Native American communities found that almost one-fourth of Native American households were food insecure and 1 out of 12 experienced food insecurity coupled with hunger (Henchy, Cheung, and Weill 2000). WIC is a federally subsided nutrition program for low-income pregnant or postpartum women and their young children.

While current instruments measuring the food environment focus on availability, price, and quality of foods at retail food stores and restaurants (Gittelsohn and Sharma 2009), assessment of the food environments and associated food security within Native American communities must also examine several additional factors. The historical factors that have led to the contemporary diets of Native Americans, specifically removal and restriction of Native Americans from their indigenous lands, and the diverse cultural, geographic, and political settings of Native American communities as well as participation in traditional food systems and practices must be considered (Power 2008). In addition, Native American women are central in ensuring the health and survival of families and communities, and their role in health promotion efforts requires special focus and consideration given the uniqueness and vulnerability of the population.

HISTORICAL FACTORS LEADING TO THE CONTEMPORARY DIETS OF NATIVE AMERICANS

Historical factors have significantly impacted the creation of contemporary Native American diets (Lillie-Blanton and Roubideaux 2005; Roubideaux 2002; Roubideaux et al. 2004). In the mid-1800s, Native Americans were forcibly removed from the ecosystems they historically occupied and were confined to reservations, often in areas of harsh, unproductive land. Hunting and food gathering quickly declined with the confinement to reservations. As hunger became critical, the federal government set up a food ration program that introduced white flour, baking powder, and lard, which soon became dietary staples.

Poverty was severe and widespread for most tribal communities, and malnutrition and hunger were the primary health issues facing tribes until the 1950s, when the U.S. government began another form of food distribution program, the food commodities program. Despite the increase in federal food aid, studies have shown Native diets remained nutritionally deficient (Bell-Shetter 2004). By the 1960s, Native American communities were consuming mostly government-provided food commodities, and this pattern largely continues today (Pratley 1998; LaVeist and Wallace 2000; Lillie-Blanton and Roubideaux 2005; Roubideaux 2002; Story et al. 1999).

Of necessity, once removed from their ancestral lands, many Native American women, many of whom were members of matriarchal tribes, had to adopt new foods and agronomical practices in foreign environments modified by European settlers in order to ensure the survival of their children and families. The great knowledge of seasonal variation and availability of plants and animals specific to their ancestral lands was, for many, no longer relevant and was quickly lost within a couple of generations.

DIVERSE CULTURAL, GEOGRAPHIC, AND POLITICAL ENVIRONMENTS OF NATIVE AMERICAN COMMUNITIES

As noted, the cultural, geographic, and political diversity that exists within the Native American population makes assessing the food environments of Native American communities challenging. While few studies have examined food security among Native Americans, several studies have examined the contemporary diets of Native Americans in relation to risk factors for chronic disease, such as diabetes and cardiovascular disease. Across geographic regions in both urban and reservation settings, Native American diets have been found to be high in fat and sodium and low in fiber (Teufel and Dufour 1990; Brown and Brenton 1994; Russell et al. 1994; Story et al. 1986; Story et al. 1998; Story et al. 1999; Ravussin et al. 1994).

A study using cross-sectional data from the 1995–1996 and 2005–2006 Behavioral Risk Factor Surveillance System also found that approximately 85 percent of Native Americans report eating fewer than three servings of vegetables or fruits per day (Jernigan et al. 2010). In another study of the diets of 10 tribes, investigators found the diets to be generally high in fat and low in fiber (Zephier, Himes, and Story 1997; Zephier et al. 1999; Story et al. 1998). The diets of the Hopi, a tribe in the Southwest, also were found to be high in fat and low in calcium, zinc, and vitamin D (Brown and Brenton 1994). Other data, such as a study that examined the Ojibwa-Cree diets, also found deficits—a diet that was also high in fat and low in fiber and containing inadequate amount of vitamin A, calcium, vitamin C, and folate (Harris and Harper 2001). These and other findings also noted that Native Americans on several Montana reservations had diets that were low in greens, fruits, and vegetables (Harris and Harper 2001). Similarly, diet deficiency was also found among the Pimas in the Southwestern United States (Knowler et al. 1993).

Cross-sectional studies of the diets of Native American women in different communities also found that soda, coffee, and white bread are among the foods consumed most often (Taylor et al. 2005; Wharton and Hampl 2004; Vaughan, Benyshek, and Martin 1997). In addition, low-income Native American women in urban environments share many of the problems faced by other low-income residents who experience difficulty accessing healthy and culturally appropriate foods (Dammann and Smith 2010; Sherwood et al. 2000; Story et al. 2003; Jernigan et al. 2011). Some of the contributors to food insecurity Native American families in low-income urban communities cite include transportation barriers, heavy concentrations of fast-food chains in their neighborhoods, and lack of local supermarkets—also referred to as *supermarket flight* or the tendency of supermarkets to prefer suburban locations (Drewnowski 2004; Hill 2004; Drewnowski and Specter 2004; Galvez et al. 2003; Dannenberg et al. 2003; Morland et al. 2002b; Burhansstipanov 2001; Urban Indian Health Commission 2007). Native American women in urban settings have also reported that a lack of knowledge in how to prepare healthy foods and time constraints also contribute to the high consumption of fast food (Jernigan and Salvatore forthcoming; Thompson et al. 2008).

Access to healthy food is also a problem in rural communities. Most reservations are in rural areas and geographically isolated from supermarkets. What are available are often remnants of frontier-style trading posts or convenience stores stocked primarily with unhealthy snacks. In general, most small, reservation-based stores frequently do not stock a full range of food, particularly fresh fruits and vegetables (Cunningham-Sabo et al. 2003; Curran et al. 2005: Gittelsohn et al. 2000). A study of the Navajo Reservation supported this observation; the investigators found that the amount of healthful foods found on the reservation was limited, and most rural convenience stores and trading posts sold primarily high-fat and high-sugar foods (Bell-Shetter 2004). Foods recommended for control of diabetes are therefore either unavailable or too expensive to purchase on a regular basis. Moreover, low-calorie, high-nutrition foods are frequently among the more expensive items in stores accessible to Native populations (Jernigan et al. 2011). The high poverty rates, the limited cash economy, and the geographically remote locations of many communities contribute to the inadequate access (Cook 2002; Gibson 2003).

At the economic level, the majority of foods available in Native American communities are provided by non–Native American owned businesses or the federal government, and there are few successful agricultural enterprises that are locally supported (Bell-Shetter 2004; Jernigan et al. 2011). In Native American communities, as elsewhere in the United States, the ways in which foods are produced, distributed, and consumed have direct implications for local economies and local communities.

PARTICIPATION IN TRADITIONAL FOOD SYSTEMS AND PRACTICES

Traditional food systems and practices of indigenous peoples involved hunting, fishing, and gathering of diverse of foods using dynamic, adaptive knowledge of the local ecosystem and were grounded in indigenous principles of balance and interconnectedness. Traditional food systems and practices were thereby environmentally sustainable and were particularly important in all Native American communities until such resources were completely destroyed or became inaccessible. Today, this type of sustainable food source is rare except in some remote Native Alaskan villages, where approximately 80 percent of the family diet comes from the immediate surroundings (Weinhold 2010). This is an exception, however; consumption of historically traditional Native American foods has declined to peripheral food status with the increased reliance on store-bought food despite the role that traditional foods can play in promoting health.

The potential for historically traditional foods to contribute to contemporary dietary intakes is moderated by several factors, including changes in the natural environment; knowledge, availability, and access to traditional food systems and practices and the value different Native American communities place on these systems; and political and economic factors, such as federal limitations on hunting and gathering practices that restrict the possibility of reliance on fishing and wild game.

CHANGES TO THE NATURAL ENVIRONMENT

Environmental changes are affecting the traditional food systems and practices for Native American communities. Native Alaskans and tribes in the Pacific Northwest are experiencing climate-induced aquatic changes altering the ecosystems that support wild salmon, an economic, cultural, and dietary cornerstone of tribes in this area

(Brubaker et al. 2011; Guyot et al. 2006; Lambden et al. 2006). In the Great Lakes region, decreased water levels and raised water temperatures are threatening some subsistence species and increasing the spread of invasive species introduced by shipping (Weinhold 2010).

In the southeastern part of the United States, rising average temperatures and the resulting soil changes, along with increased coastal flooding, are threatening citrus and sugarcane operations that sustain the Seminole economy (Weinhold 2010). Alaskan coastal villages are subject to increased flooding and erosion due to ice-shelf melting and warmer temperatures that allow the introduction of new disease vectors (Brubaker et al. 2011; Guyot et al. 2006; Lambden, Receveur, and Kuhnlein 2007; Lambden et al. 2006).

A participant observation study with two First Nations communities in Canada was conducted with a goal to record changes in the local environment, harvesting situations, and traditional food species and to explore what impact these changes have on traditional food. The results indicate that both communities in the study are witnessing variable changes in climate that are affecting their traditional food harvest. New species and changes in migration of species being observed by community members had the potential to affect the consumption of traditional food. Similarly, changes in water levels in and around harvesting areas are affecting access to these areas, which in turn affects the traditional food harvest. Community members have been required to change their harvest mechanisms to adapt to changes in climate and to ensure an adequate supply of traditional food. The study concludes that a strong commitment to programs intended to protect traditional food systems is necessary in order for these systems and practices to be sustained (Schuster et al. 2011).

KNOWLEDGE, AVAILABILITY, AND ACCESS TO TRADITIONAL FOOD SYSTEMS AND PRACTICES AND FOOD VALUES

Native American communities differ in their level of knowledge regarding traditional food systems and practices and the value that members of the communities may place on these systems. Results of survey data among First Nations people found convenience, ease, and price rated as more important than the localness or cultural connectedness of food (Stroink and Nelson 2009). Alternatively, surveys of Northwest Coast Swinomish community members reported that seafood represented a symbolic, deeply meaningful food source linked to a multidimensional Swinomish concept of health. Food security, ceremonial use, knowledge transmission, and community cohesion all played primary roles in Swinomish definitions of individual and community health and complemented physical indicators of health (Donatuto, Satterfield, and Gregory 2011).

Native Americans living in urban environments, particularly youth, may have very limited knowledge of the traditional foods of their ancestors (Jernigan and Salvatore forthcoming). However, many gardening and traditional food-harvesting initiatives in urban areas have emerged in recent years, often led by Native American women with a strong history of community organizing and community building (Jernigan and Salvatore forthcoming; Joe 1992). Examples include the community garden at the Indian Health Center of Santa Clara Valley in San Jose, California; the Intertribal Friendship House garden and traditional harvesting initiative in Oakland, California; and the community garden in Minneapolis-St. Paul (Jernigan and Salvatore forthcoming).

POLITICAL AND ECONOMIC FACTORS

Several Native American communities, in response to the high rates of poverty and lack of economic opportunities, have turned to the extraction and production of coal, oil, and natural gas found beneath their lands in order to initiate various forms of economic development. Many of these communities, however, struggle with the conflicting goals of developing economic resources for their tribes while trying to protect their environment, including traditional food systems. Where possible, some Native American tribal governments are working with federal agencies on strategies to address the need for economic development and the impact of climate change, particularly for the communities that are locked into their reservation land, limiting their adaptation options (Weinhold 2010). The federal government, as part of its role as a trustee of natural resources on behalf of tribal lands, is obligated to protect the traditional food harvests of Native Americans. However, the Environmental Protection Agency has been faulted for not protecting the food supply against contamination by waterborne pollutants in the Pacific Northwest and Alaska (Wood 2007).

In the state of Washington, tribes oppose new policies that have that given priority to water for agricultural lands and not the protection of salmon habitat. Salmon has historically been the mainstay of these tribes' food source. The tribes all have special ceremonies to honor salmon as a sacred food source. Many Native American communities in this region, therefore, oppose this expensive new bureaucracy that favors maintaining agricultural viability over the protection of endangered species of salmon.

THE GROWING FOOD SOVEREIGNTY MOVEMENT

Food sovereignty, like community food security, is that state of being in which "all community residents obtain a safe, culturally acceptable, nutritionally adequate diet through a sustainable food system that maximizes community self-reliance and social justice" (Bell-Shetter 2004:4). Food sovereignty is also defined as "the right of peoples, communities, and countries to define their own agricultural, labor, fishing, food, and land policies in ways that are ecologically, socially, economically and culturally appropriate to their unique circumstances" (Bell-Shetter 2004:4). The Indigenous Food Systems Network, a collaborative group of diverse stakeholders including both Native and non-Native activists, academics, and food producers, outlined the following four principles of food sovereignty (Indigenous Food Systems Network 2006):

1. Food, because it sustains life, is considered sacred, a gift from the creator and most Native consider its discovery and use within its claim to indigenous food sovereignty. And like all things considered sacred and received as a gift, food is not only respected but in times of hunger, food cannot be denied to those in need nor can food be controlled by colonial laws, policies, or institutions. Within this context, indigenous food sovereignty also calls for understanding the interdependence that man has with the land, plants, and animals that form the circle of life. Food is life and necessary to help nurture and sustain a healthy population.

2. Individual and group participation is at the heart of the Indigenous food sovereignty. Providing nourishment for the family and others is a responsibility that requires action and engagement by all in the day-to-day care of planting crops and maintaining cultural harvesting strategies to ensure daily healthy food source and subsistence protocol that is to be maintained for each future generation.

3. Indigenous food policies must take into account workable ways to monitor the amount and quality of food that necessary to maintain a healthy population, so reasonable choices are made to decide the amount and quality of food that is hunted, fished, gathered, and eaten. These choices also include the freedom from to decrease dependence on grocery stores or corporately controlled food production, distribution, and consumption common in industrialized economies.

4. Indigenous food sovereignty also responds to applicable policy changes required by changes occurring in other domains such as forestry, fishery, rangeland management and new and innovative strategies in environmental conservation; health; agriculture; and rural and community development.

Some Native American communities have started to use a food sovereignty assessment tool (FSAT) (Bell-Shetter 2004) as an alternative to currently available food security assessments that do not include important factors unique to Native American communities (Gittelsohn and Sharma 2009). An FSAT is a collaborative and participatory process that systematically examines a range of community food assets so as to inform change actions and to make the community food secure; takes a solution-oriented approach that looks at assets and resources as well as problems; and promotes community food security by increasing knowledge about food-related needs and resources and by building collaboration and capacity (Bell-Shetter 2004).

Many Native American communities may not have a reservation land base, such as those living in urban or other small rural communities, but have undertaken unique food sovereignty initiatives. One such example in Oklahoma is the Mvskoke Food Sovereignty Initiative (MFSI), with the mission to "enable the Mvskoke people and their neighbors to provide for their food and health needs that are immediate and maintaining the program for the future through sustainable agriculture, economic development, community involvement, cultural and educational programs" (MFSI 2011). MFSI spans the areas of the Mvskoke (Creek) Nation tribal lands including rural areas, several small towns, and the city of Tulsa, Oklahoma.

The MFSI is producing food for the community from its garden project, a "market basket" program that provides fresh vegetables. The program engages tribal elders and youth through a teaching strategy that promotes group learning to help revive the cultural value of maintaining a healthy, sustainable food source that was important in the history of the tribe. The tribe has also established a seed bank to preserve and restore endangered seeds that are culturally linked to the agricultural legacy of the tribe, including restoring a Mvskoke favorite corn known as Sofkee corn, an indigenous food source that has come close to extinction.

Collaborative effort is also on the agenda for MFSI by partnering with the nearby Okmulgee Main Street Association to jointly establish the first local farmers' market since the 1930s. The market makes available fresh, affordable, locally produced fruits and vegetables to the local and nearby communities.

The tribal program is also working with its own Tribal Elderly Nutrition Services to establish a purchasing policy whereby this program can purchase produce from local growers to enrich the nutrients in the 18,000 meals served to tribal elders each month. Through these various local initiatives, the Creek Nation claims to assert its tribal sovereignty by establishing a policy that protects its indigenous knowledge and biological resources.

Additional food sovereignty initiatives are emerging across tribal communities and urban-based Native organizations in North America. These initiatives include such examples as the Learning Garden program, developed and run with two First Nation communities in northwestern Ontario, a program that uses a holistic and experiential model of learning to rebuild a knowledge base to support a sustainable local food system (Stroink and Nelson 2009). The California Foodway Model, allows individual California tribes to include their specific traditional or regional foods in their basket designs used in brochures and other educational materials for health promotion and to signify their participation in reviving their traditional food systems (Conti 2006).

The Tohono O'odham Community Action (TOCA) in Arizona has a large-scale farm project that is reintroducing traditional food production to their community and using traditional food and its preparation to stimulate a program to improve community health. Their new café in Sells is also helping revitalize a heritage of healthy foods as well as fostering local economic opportunity. Through the successful creation of two farms, TOCA is also able to market traditional foods and has developed an extensive educational program for schools and community. TOCA has helped create educational programs, community gardens, and hands-on workshops on how to harvest and prepare wild foods. Through these efforts, TOCA is helping to increase community self-sufficiency and vitality.

In the Great Lakes region of the United States, the White Earth Land Recovery Project, led by Anishinaabekwe (Ojibwe) activist Winona LaDuke, has as its mission "to continue, revive, and protect the native seeds, heritage crops, naturally grown fruits, animals, wild plants, traditions and knowledge of indigenous and land-based communities; for the purpose of maintaining and continuing indigenous culture and resisting the global, industrialized food system" (LaDuke 2006). One of the central products promoted and protected by the White Earth Land Recovery Project is wild rice.

These various tribal efforts, like the majority of health promotion and wellness initiatives across Native America, are led primarily by women with a strong tradition of community organizing and community building for health promotion. This leadership role for Native American women is not new. Historically, Native American women have always been at the forefront or at the core of indigenous resistance to colonization and understood that the health of their communities depended on them (Walters and Simoni 2002).

SUMMARY

Native American communities are at high risk for food insecurity. Poverty, geographic isolation, and changes in the natural environment are some of the many factors that contribute to diet-related health disparities that exist within the population and make food insecurity an urgent public health priority. The diets of Native American communities have been studied in relationship to cardiovascular disease risk factors, but few studies have examined the overall food environments and associated food insecurity within Native American communities. Current measurements of the food environment and associated food insecurity leave out important variables when examining Native American communities, including the historical factors that have created the modern reservation food environments and participation in traditional food systems and practices.

The food sovereignty movement in tribal communities is growing, and the movement can be described as a holistic approach to addressing current diet-related health conditions while striving for the long-term goal of food security for their Native American communities. Food sovereignty is an appropriate approach to addressing some of the underlying social justice issues at the root of health disparities for Native American communities. The movement is also equally important for the revitalization and continuation of Native American cultural and spiritual traditions. Women play a critical role in the health and well-being of Native American families, and by assuming key leadership roles in the food sovereignty movement, they are regaining their rightful place in protecting and guarding the health of their families and communities.

REFERENCES

Anderson, Sue Ann. 1990. "Core Indicators of Nutritional State for Difficult-to-Sample Populations." *Journal of Nutrition* 120(11, Suppl.):1555–1600.

Archer, Sujata L., Kurt J. Greenlund, Michele L. Casper, Stephen Rith-Najarian, and Janet B. Croft. 2002. "Associations of Community-based Health Education Programs with Food Habits and Cardiovascular Disease Risk Factors among Native Americans with Diabetes: The Inter-Tribal Heart Project, 1992 to 1994." *Journal of the American Dietetic Association* 102(8):1132–35.

Austin, S. Bryn, Steven J. Melly, Brisa N. Sanchez, Aarti Petal, Stephen Buka, and Steve L. Gortmaker. 2005. "Clustering of Fast-Food Restaurants around Schools: A Novel Application of Spatial Statistics to the Study of Food Environments." *American Journal of Public Health* 95(9):1575–81.

Bell-Shetter, Alicia. 2004. *Food Sovereignty Assessment Tool*. Fredericksburg, VA: First Nations Development Institute.

Breckwich Vasquez, Victoria, Dana Lanza, Susana Hennessey-Lavery, Shelley Facente, Helen Ann Halpin, and Meredith Minkler. 2007. "Addressing Food Security through Public Policy Action in a Community-Based Participatory Research Partnership." *Health Promotion Practice* 8(4):342–49.

Brown, A. C. and B. Brenton. 1994. "Dietary Survey of Hopi Native American Elementary Students." *Journal of the American Dietetic Association* 94(5):517–22.

Brown, Blakely, Curtis Noonan, and Mark Nord. 2007. "Prevalence of Food Insecurity and Health-Associated Outcomes and Food Characteristics of Northern Plains Indian Households." *Journal of Hunger and Environmental Nutrition* 1(4):37–53.

Brubaker, M. Y., J. N. Bell, J. E. Berner, and J. A. Warren. 2011. "Climate Change Health Assessment: A Novel Approach for Alaska Native Communities." *International Journal of Circumpolar Health* 70(3):266–73.

Burhansstipanov, L. 2001. "Cancer: A Growing Problem among American Indians and Alaska Natives." Pp. 223–252 in *Promises to Keep*. M. R. Dixon and Y. Roubideaux (Eds.). Washington, DC: American Public Health Association.

Caballero, Benjamin, Theresa Clay, Sally M. Davis, Sally M. Davis, Becky Ethelbah, Bonnie Holy Rock, Tim Lohman, James Norman, Mary Story, Elaine J. Stone, Larry Stephenson, and June Stevens. 2003. "Pathways: A School-Based, Randomized Controlled Trial for the Prevention of Obesity in American Indian Schoolchildren." *American Journal of Clinical Nutrition* 78(5):1030–38.

Cade, J., H. Upmeier, C. Calvert, and D. Greenwood. 1999. "Cost of a Healthy Diet: Analysis from the 1K Women's Cohort Study." *Public Health Nutrition* 2, 505–12.

Cohen, B. 2002. "Community Food Security Assessment Toolkit (E-FAN-02-013)." Washington DC: United States Department of Agriculture, Economic Research Service.

Conti, Kibbe M. 2006. "Diabetes Prevention in Indian Country: Developing Nutrition Models to Tell the Story of Food-System Change." *Journal of Transcultural Nursing* 17(3):234–45.

Cook, J. T. 2002. "Clinical Implications of Household Food Security: Definitions, Monitoring, and Policy." *Nutrition in Clinical Care* 5(4):152–67.

Cunningham-Sabo, Leslie, M. Patricia Snyder, Jean Anliker, Janice Thompson, Judith L. Weber, Olivia Thomas, Kimberly Ring, Dawn Stewart, Harrison Platero, and Linda Nielson. 2003. "Impact of the Pathways Food Service Intervention on Breakfast Served in American-Indian Schools." *Preventive Medicine* 37(Suppl. 1):S46–S54.

Curran, Sarah, Joel Gittelsohn, Jean Anliker, Becky Ethelbah, Kelly Blake, Sangita Sharma, and Benjamin Callabero. 2005. "Process Evaluation of a Store-Based Environmental Obesity Intervention on Two American Indian Reservations." *Health Education Research* 20(6):719–29.

Dammann, Kristen Wiig and Chery Smith. 2010. "Race, Homelessness, and Other Environmental Factors Associated with the Food-Purchasing Behavior of Low-Income Women." *Journal of the American Dietetic Association* 110(9):1351–1356.

Dannenberg, A. L., R. J. Jackson, H. Frumkin, R. A. Schieber, M. Pratt, C. Kochtitzky, and H. H. Tilson. 2003. "The Impact of Community Design and Land-Use Choices on Public Health: A Scientific Research Agenda." *American Journal of Public Health* 93(9):1500–1508.

Davis, Sally M. and Raymond Reid. 1999. "Practicing Participatory Research in American Indian Communities." *The American Journal of Clinical Nutrition* 69(4):755S–759S.

De Cock, K. M. and R. S. Janssen. 2002. "An Unequal Epidemic in an Unequal World." *Journal of the American Medical Association* 288(2):236–8.

Dixon, Mim and Yvette Roubideaux. 2001. *Promises to Keep: Public Health Policy for American Indians and Alaska Natives in the 21st Century*. Washington, DC: American Public Health Association.

Donatuto, Jamie L., Terre A. Satterfield, and Robin Gregory. 2011. "Poisoning the Body to Nourish the Soul: Prioritising Health Risks and Impacts in a Native American Community." *Health, Risk and Society* 13(2):103–27.

Drewnowski, A. 2004. "Obesity and the Food Environment: Dietary Energy Density and Diet Costs." *American Journal of Preventative Medicine* 27(3 Suppl):154–62.

Drewnowski, A. and S. E. Specter. 2004. "Poverty and Obesity: The Role of Energy Density and Energy Costs." *American Journal of Clinical Nutrition* 79(1):6–16.

Ferreira, Mariana K. Leal and Gretchen Chesley Lang. 2006. *Indigenous Peoples and Diabetes: Community Empowerment and Wellness*. Durham, NC: Carolina Academic Press.

Friel, S., M. Chopra, and D. Satcher. 2007. "Unequal Weight: Equity Oriented Policy Responses to the Global Obesity Epidemic." *British Medical Journal* 335 (7632):1241–43.

Galvez, M. P., T. R. Frieden, and P. J. Landrigan. 2003. "Obesity in the 21st Century." *Environmental Health Perspectives* 111(13):A684–85.

Gibson, Diane. 2003. "Food Stamp Program Participation Is Positively Related to Obesity in Low Income Women." *Journal of Nutrition* 133(7):2225–31.

Gittelsohn, Joel and Sangita Sharma. 2009. "Physical, Consumer, and Social Aspects of Measuring the Food Environment among Diverse Low-Income Populations." *American Journal of Preventive Medicine* 36(4, Supplement 1):S161–S165.

Gittelsohn, Joel, Elanah Greer Toporoff, Mary Story, Margurite Evans, Jean Anliker, Sally Davis, Anjali Sharma, and Jean White. 2000. "Food Perceptions and Dietary Behavior of American-Indian Children, Their Caregivers, and Educators: Formative Assessment Findings from Pathways." *Journal of Nutrition Education* 32(1):2–13.

Glasgow, R., G. McKay, J. Piette, and K. Reynolds. 2001. "The RE-AIM Framework for Evaluating Interventions: What Can It Tell Us about Approaches to Chronic Illness Management?" *Patient Education and Counseling* 44, 119–27.

Glasgow, R. E., T. M. Vogt, and S. M. Boles. 1999. "Evaluating the Public Health Impact of Health Promotion Interventions: The RE-AIM Framework." *American Journal of Public Health* 89(9):1322–27.

Green, L. W., M. A. George, M. Daniel, C. J. Frankish, C. P. Herbert, W. R. Bowie, and M. O'Neil. 1995. *Study of Participatory Research in Health Promotion: Review and Recommendations for the Development of Participatory Research in Health Promotion in Canada*. Vancouver, British Columbia: Royal Society of Canada.

Green, Lawrence W. and Russell E. Glasgow. 2006. "Evaluating the Relevance, Generalization, and Applicability of Research: Issues in External Validation and Translation Methodology." *Evaluation and the Health Professions* 29(1):126–53.

Guyot, M., C. Dickson, C. Paci, C. Furqal and H. M. Chan. 2006. "Local Observations of Climate Change and Impacts on Traditional Food Security in Two Northern Aboriginal Communities." *International Journal of Circumpolar Health* 65(5):403–15.

Harris, S. and B. L. Harper. 2001. "Lifestyles, Diets, and Native American Exposure Factors Related to Possible Lead Exposures and Toxicity." *Environmental Research* 86(2):140–48.

Henchy, Geri, Marisa Cheung, and Jim Weill. 2000. "WIC in Native American Communities: Building a Healthier America. Report Summary." Full text available at http://frac.org/reports-and-resources/.

Hendrickson, Deja, Chery Smith, and Nicole Eikenberry. 2006. "Fruit and Vegetable Access in Four Low-Income Food Deserts Communities in Minnesota." *Agriculture and Human Values* 23(3):371–83.

Hill, J. 2004. "Addressing the Environment to Reduce Obesity." Paper presented at Obesity and the Built Environment: Improving Public Health Through Community Design, Washington, DC, May 24–26.

Indigenous Food Systems Network. 2006. *Principles of Food Sovereignty*. Accessed July 15, 2011. http://www.indigenousfoodsystems.org/food-sovereignty.

Jernigan, Valarie Blue Bird. 2010. "Community-Based Participatory Research with Native American Communities: The Chronic Disease Self-Management Program." *Health Promotion Practice* 11(6):888–99.

Jernigan, Valarie Blue Bird, Bonnie Duran, David Ahn, and Marilyn Winkleby. 2010. "Changing Patterns in Health Behaviors and Risk Factors Related to Cardiovascular Disease among American Indians and Alaska Natives." *American Journal of Public Health* 100(4):677–83.

Jernigan, Valarie Blue Bird and Kate Lorig. 2011. "The Internet Diabetes Self-Management Workshop for American Indians and Alaska Natives." *Health Promotion Practice* 12(2):261–70.

Jernigan, Valarie Blue Bird and A. L. Salvatore. Forthcoming. "Native American Food Security and Food Sovereignty in Urban Areas." *Health Education Research*.

Jernigan, Valarie Blue Bird, A. L. Salvatore, D. M. Styne, and M. Winkleby. 2011. "Addressing Food Insecurity among Native Americans Using Community-Based Participatory Research." *Health Education Research [Epub ahead of print]*. *PMID: 21994709*.

Joe, Jennie Rose. 1992. "Cultural Survival and Contemporary American Indian Women in the City." Pp. 136–150 in *Women Transforming Politics: Worldwide Strategies for Empowerment*. J. M. Bystydzienski (Ed.). Bloomington: Indiana University Press.

Joe, Jennie Rose and Robert S. Young. 1993. *Diabetes as a Disease of Civilization: The Impact of Culture Change on Indigenous Peoples*. Berlin and New York: Mouton de Gruyter.

Kendall, A., C. M. Olson, and E. A. Frongillo Jr. 1996. "Relationship of Hunger and Food Insecurity to Food Availability and Consumption." *Journal of the American Dietetic Association* 96(10):1019–24; quiz 1025–26.

Kerner, J. F. 2006. "Knowledge Translation versus Knowledge Integration: A Funder's Perspective." *Journal of Continuing Education in the Health Professions* 26(1):72–80.

Knowler, W. C., M. F. Saad, D. J. Pettitt, R. G. Nelson, and P. H. Bennett. 1993. "Determinants of Diabetes Mellitus in the Pima Indians." *Diabetes Care* 16(1):216–27.

LaDuke, Winona. 2006. *White Earth Land Recovery Project and Native Harvest*. Accessed July 29, 2011. http://nativeharvest.com/.

Lambden, J., O. Receveur, and H. V. Kuhnlein. 2007. "Traditional Food Attributes Must Be Included in Studies of Food Security in the Canadian Arctic." *International Journal of Circumpolar Health* 66(4):308–19.

Lambden, J., O. Receveur, J. Marshall, and H. V. Kuhnlein. 2006. "Traditional and Market Food Access in Arctic Canada Is Affected by Economic Factors." *International Journal of Circumpolar Health* 65(4):331–40.

LaVeist, T. A. and J. M. Wallace Jr. 2000. "Health Risk and Inequitable Distribution of Liquor Stores in African American Neighborhoods." *Social Science and Medicine* 51(4):613–17.

Lillie-Blanton, M. and Y. Roubideaux. 2005. "Understanding and Addressing the Health Care Needs of American Indians and Alaska Natives." *American Journal of Public Health* 95(5):759–61.

Mokdad, Ali H., Mary K. Serdula, William H. Dietz, Barbara A. Bowman, James S. Marks, and Jeffrey P. Koplan. 1999. "The Spread of the Obesity Epidemic in the United States, 1991–1998." *Journal of the American Medical Association* 282(16):1519–1522.

Mongeau, L. 2008. "Curbing the Obesity Epidemic: The Need for Policy Action in a Risk-balanced, Orchestrated, Comprehensive Strategy." *International Journal of Public Health* 53(6):320–21.

Morland, K., S. Wing, A. Diez Roux, and C. Poole. 2002. "Neighborhood Character-istics Associated with the Location of Food Stores and Food Service Places." *American Journal of Preventative Medicine* 22(1):23–29.

Morland, Kimberly, Steve Wing, and Ana Diez Roux. 2002. "The Contextual Effect of the Local Food Environment on Residents' Diets: The Atherosclerosis Risk in Communities Study." *American Journal of Public Health* 92(11):1761–68.

Mvskoke Food Sovereignty Initiative. 2011. *Mvskoke Food Sovereignty Initiative* Accessed July 29, 2011. http://www.mvskokefood.org/.

Power, E. M. 2008. "Conceptualizing Food Security for Aboriginal People in Canada." *Canadian Journal of Public Health* 99(2):95–97.

Pratley, R. E. 1998. "Gene-Environment Interactions in the Pathogenesis of Type 2 Diabetes Mellitus: Lessons Learned from the Pima Indians." *Proceedings of the Nutrition Society* 57(2):175–81.

Raja, Samina, Changxing Ma, and Pavan Yadav. 2008. "Beyond Food Deserts." *Journal of Planning Education and Research* 27(4):469–82.

Ravussin, E., M. E. Valencia, J. Esparza, P. H. Bennett, and L. O. Schulz. 1994. "Effects of a Traditional Lifestyle on Obesity in Pima Indians." *Diabetes Care* 17(9):1067–74.

Roubideaux, Y. 2002. "Perspectives on American Indian Health." *American Journal of Public Health* 92(9):1401–3.

Roubideaux, Y., D. Buchwald, J. Beals, D. Middlebrook D, S. Manson S, B. Muneta, S. Rith-Najarian, R. Shield and K. Acton. 2004. "Measuring the Quality of Diabetes Care for Older American Indians and Alaska Natives." *American Journal of Public Health* 94(1):60–65.

Russell, M. E., K. M. Weiss, A. V. Buchanan, T. D. Etherton, J. H. Moore, and P. M. Kris-Etherton. 1994. "Plasma Lipids and Diet of the Mvskoke Indians." *American Journal of Clinical Nutrition* 59(4):847–52.

Schuster, R. C., E. E. Wein, C. Dickson, and H. M. Chan. 2011. "Importance of Traditional Foods for the Food Security of Two First Nations Communities in the Yukon, Canada." *International Journal of Circumpolar Health* 70(3):286–300.

Sherwood, Nancy E., Lisa Harnack, and Mary Story. 2000. "Weight-loss Practices, Nutrition Beliefs, and Weight-loss Program Preferences of Urban American Indian Women." *Journal of the American Dietetic Association* 100(4):442–46.

Story, M., J. Steven, J. Himes, E. Stone, Rock B. Holy, E. Ethelbah, and S. Davis. 1999. "The Epidemic of Obesity in American Indian Communities and the Need for Childhood Obesity-Prevention Programs." *American Journal of Clinical Nutrition* 69(4 Suppl):747S–754S.

Story, M., K. F. Strauss, E. Zephier, and B. A. Broussard. 1998. "Nutritional Concerns in American Indian and Alaska Native Children: Transitions and Future Directions." *Journal of the American Dietetic Association* 98(2):170–76.

Story, Mary, June Stevens, John Himes, Elaine Stone, Bonnie Holy Rock, Becky Ethelbah, and Sally Davis. 2003. "Obesity in American-Indian Children: Prevalence, Consequences, and Prevention." *Preventive Medicine* 37(Supplement 1):S3–S12.

Story, M., R. A. Tompkins, M. A. Bass, and L. M. Wakefield. 1986. "Anthropometric Measurements and Dietary Intakes of Cherokee Indian Teenagers in North Carolina." *Journal of the American Dietetic Association* 86(11):1555–60.

Stroink, M. L. and C. H. Nelson. 2009. "Aboriginal Health Learning in the Forest and Cultivated Gardens: Building a Nutritious and Sustainable Food System." *Journal of Agromedicine* 14(2):263–69.

Swinburn, B. A., I. Caterson, J. C. Seidell, and W. P. T. James. 2004. "Diet, Nutrition and the Prevention of Excess Weight Gain and Obesity." *Public Health Nutrition* 7(1A):123–46.

Taylor, Christopher A., Kathryn S. Keim, and Alicia C. Gilmore. 2005. "Impact of Core and Secondary Foods on Nutritional Composition of Diets in Native-American Women." *Journal of the American Dietetic Association* 105(3):413–19.

Teufel, N. I. and D. L. Dufour. 1990. "Patterns of Food Use and Nutrient Intake of Obese and Non-obese Hualapai Indian Women of Arizona." *Journal of the American Dietetic Association* 90(9):1229–35.

Thompson, Janice L., Peg Allen, Deborah L. Helitzer, Clifford Qualls, Ayn N. Whyte, Venita K. Wolfe, and Carla J. Herman. 2008. "Reducing Diabetes Risk in American Indian Women." *American Journal of Preventive Medicine* 34(3):192–201.

Townsend, Marilyn S., Janet Peerson, Bradley Love, Cheryl Achterberg, and Suzanne P. Murphy. 2001. "Food Insecurity Is Positively Related to Overweight in Women." *Journal of Nutrition* 131(6):1738–45.

Urban Indian Health Commission. 2007. *Invisible Tribes: Urban Indians and Their Health in a Changing World.* Seattle: Urban Indian Health Commission.

Vaughan, Linda A., Daniel C. Benyshek, and John F. Martin. 1997. "Food Acquisition Habits, Nutrient Intakes, and Anthropometric Data of Havasupai Adults." *Journal of the American Dietetic Association* 97(11):1275–82.

Wallerstein, Nina B. and Bonnie Duran. 2006. "Using Community-Based Participatory Research to Address Health Disparities." *Health Promotion Practice* 7(3):312–23.

Walters, Karina L. and Jane M. Simoni. 2002. "Reconceptualizing Native Women's Health: An 'Indigenist' Stress-Coping Model." *American Journal of Public Health* 92(4):520–24.

Wang, May, Alma Gonzalez, Lorrene Ritchie, and Marilyn Winkleby. 2006. "The Neighborhood Food Environment: Sources of Historical Data on Retail Food Stores." *International Journal of Behavioral Nutrition and Physical Activity* 3(1):15.

Ward, Carol J. and Erin Feinauer Whiting. 2006. "Food Insecurity and Diabetes Risk among the Northern Cheyenne." *Journal of Hunger and Environmental Nutrition* 1(2):63–87.

Weinhold, Bob. 2010. "Climate Change and Health: A Native American Perspective." *Environmental Health Perspectives* 118(2):A64–A65.

Wharton, Christopher M. and Jeffrey S. Hampl. 2004. "Beverage Consumption and Risk of Obesity among Native Americans in Arizona." *Nutrition Reviews* 62(4):153–59.

Wood, Mary Christina. 2007. "EPA's Protection of Tribal Harvests: Braiding the Agency's Mission." *Ecology Law Quarterly* 34(1):175–200.

Zephier, E., J. H. Himes, and M. Story. 1999. "Prevalence of Overweight and Obesity in American Indian School Children and Adolescents in the Aberdeen Area: A Population Study." *International Journal of Obesity and Related Metabolic Disorders* 23(Suppl 2): S28–30.

Zephier, E. M., C. Ballew, A. Mokdad, J. Mendlein, C. Smith, J. L. Yeh, E. Lee, T. K. Welty, and B. Howard. 1997. "Intake of Nutrients Related to Cardiovascular Disease Risk among Three Groups of American Indians: The Strong Heart Dietary Study." *Preventative Medicine* 26(4):508–15.

CHAPTER 8

The Struggle with the Devastation of Diabetes

Jennie R. Joe

In an interview, Mary Thomas, former governor of the Gila River Indian Community and a strong advocate for diabetes prevention in her community, was quoted as saying: "I shock my people by saying that if we don't get this [diabetes] in check now, we'll become an extinct people 75 years from now" (Associated Press, November 1, 1999).

INTRODUCTION: DIABETES, A WORLDWIDE EPIDEMIC

Two members of one research team, Danaei and colleagues (2011) reported in the online journal, *Lancet* (June 25), that the number of adults diagnosed with diabetes worldwide increased to 350 million, a two-fold increase since 1980. The researchers attributed the increase to the global aging population as well as to the rising rates of obesity. Listed elsewhere are other known risk factors for diabetes that include ethnic origin, fetal and early-life nutrition status, quality of diet, and low or lack of physical activity. Danaei and colleagues also noted the recent increase was highest among Pacific Islanders, a population with the highest rates of diabetes in the world. Their data found the presence of diabetes was higher for Pacific Island women, for example, one in three women compared to one in four men (2011:3).

The worldwide epidemic of diabetes mellitus, especially type 2 diabetes mellitus, is rapidly increasing among many indigenous populations, including members of racial and ethnic minority populations in the United States. In 2009, the National Institutes of Health (NIH) reported that 13 percent of adults age 20 and older in the United States have diabetes, but 40 percent of the sample had not yet been diagnosed (NIH News 2009). The data on prediabetics is based on the results from both fasting blood glucose (FBS) tests and oral glucose tolerance tests (OGTT). The FBS test detects the presence of diabetes while the OGTT distinguishes those who have diabetes from those who are pre-diabetic (those on the verge of developing diabetes). The FBS test measures blood glucose after fasting overnight, and the OGTT, a more sensitive test, measures the level of blood glucose two hours after an intake of a strong sugary drink. The significant number of prediabetics is alarming and is reflected in the following statement made by a member of the research team: "We're facing a diabetes epidemic that shows no sign of abating, judging from the number of individuals with pre-diabetes" (NIH News 2009).

Diabetes is marked by high levels of blood glucose due to defects in insulin production, insulin action, or both. If diabetes is not controlled or well managed, it can lead to a number of serious complications, disability, and death. Diabetes is a group of diseases but generally falls into the following three main categories: type 1, type 2, and gestational diabetes. Type 1 diabetes, or juvenile diabetes, is a type of autoimmune disease that occurs when the body's immune system destroys its own insulin-producing beta cells in the pancreas (Laino 2011; National Diabetes Information Clearinghouse (2011), and the patient's survival is dependent on insulin injections. Type 2 diabetes, or adult-onset diabetes, develops when the body cannot make enough insulin or cannot use effectively the insulin produced by the body. Type 2 is the most common form of diabetes. Gestational diabetes occurs during pregnancy, but upon delivery the mother's blood glucose usually returns to a normal range. Mothers who have gestational diabetes, however, as well as babies born to mothers with gestational diabetes, are at high risk for developing type 2 diabetes.

WOMEN AND DIABETES

Because of their lower rates of heart diseases, women generally live longer than men, but the increase of diabetic-related heart diseases for women is diminishing the life expectancy advantage (Gebel 2011). For example, a study that examined mortality rates for men and women with diabetes between 1971 and 2000 found a decrease for men, but the mortality rates remained high and did not change for women (Gebel 2011:47). Differences in physiology and how men and women are treated by health care providers are suggested as some of the reasons for the difference. In particular, heart disease is often suspected more readily in men than in women, but the disease can be more deadly for women because the symptoms of a heart attack, for example, are less pronounced, like nausea or fatigue, than are the acute chest pains often experienced by men. The vague symptoms also keep women from seeking immediate medical attention. Kidney disease, one of the complications of diabetes, is common for males, but the prevalence of kidney diseases increases for women after menopause (Gebel 2011:48).The onset of menopause coincides with a decrease in estrogen for women, a hormonal change that results in an increase in testosterone. Another gender difference noted is that depression is twice as common for women as for men (Lustman et al. 2000; Eaton 2002).

The comorbidity of diabetes and depression for women is more life threatening because the combination accelerates the development of diabetic complications and increases mortality. The biological factors that account for some gender differences have also been linked to the tendency of diabetes in women to increase their triglycerides (blood fat), a situation that lowers the level of good (HDL) cholesterol and thereby increases a woman's risk for heart disease.

AMERICAN INDIANS AND DIABETES

As indicated, ethnic origin is one of the key risk factors for type 2 diabetes. In fact, until recently, one American Indian tribe, the Pima Indians of the Southwest United States, has been described as having the highest rates of type 2 diabetes in United States (Roubideaux et al. 2008: James, Schwartz, and Berndt 2009). Today, the epidemic of type 2 diabetes is prevalent in most tribal communities, although the rate of the disease varies by tribes and by their geographical locations. For example, American Indians, more so than Alaska Natives, have higher rates of type 2 diabetes mellitus (AHRQ 2010; Grim 2003). Health data reports indicate American Indian adults are 2.1 times as likely as white adults to be diagnosed with diabetes, and the morbidity rate among Alaska Natives is 8.1 compared to 27.6 for tribes in southern Arizona (AHRQ 2010:4). The 2006 National Vital Statistic Report, a report issued by the Centers for Disease Control

(CDC 2009), indicates that American Indians are twice as likely as other racial or ethnic minority groups to die from diabetes-related complications. Mortality rates for American Indian women treated for diabetes are also higher than for males. For example, the age-adjusted death rate per 100,000 in 2006 for American Indian women was 40.7 compared to 38 for males. This age-adjusted death rate for American Indian women is three times that reported for non-Hispanic white females (CDC 2009:Tables 16,17).

Because diabetes is now endemic in many other tribal communities, it is not surprising that as these numbers increase, so do the numbers of community members for whom diabetes becomes increasingly seen as a condition that is inevitable and hopeless. For example, one respondent interviewed by Kozak noted: "You can't say that you're not going to get it [diabetes], it can happen at any time. I might have it tomorrow and be diabetic. Or right now" (Kozak 1997:253). The impact the disease has had and continues to have on personal or tribal identity of many Native peoples diagnosed with diabetes is apparent and is verbalized in a number of ways. One Native woman, who has developed end-stage renal disease as a complication of diabetes, laments,

> My life is not normal any more; it is tied to that [dialysis] machine. Diabetes did that to me. They told me that I had diabetes 12 years ago. The doctors tell me that it took my teeth, my foot, and now my kidneys. Old age has already taken the use of my eyes, my hearing. . . . I am not me anymore. (Joe 2003:8)

The personal anguish is also reflected in the ways some patients quietly report that they are ashamed to let others know they have diabetes. They say that for them to acknowledge they have diabetes is to admit personal failure and that getting diabetes is punishment for this failure. One woman said, "I am fat, I know. People think that women like me love to overeat but that is not true" (Joe 2005). She went on to say that she wished she was skinny, but life is so stressful that food had become her comfort zone; now she is ashamed of being overweight as well as having diabetes. Other women, especially those of childbearing age, say they are fearful of diabetes because they are likely to bring a baby into the world who will inherit the dreadful disease. Some health workers also note that frequently some of the newly diagnosed patients are so overcome by fear and anxiety of having the diagnosis that they focus only on the list of possible negative and disabling consequences of diabetes and do not hear the hopeful messages about healthy ways to live with diabetes (Joe 2005).

The American Diabetes Association (ADA) (2011) has for several decades included race, especially American Indian, among its list of leading risk factors for diabetes. Although the list of risk factors is changing, the longstanding message helped promote the idea that that *all* American Indians develop diabetes, an idea that has become ingrained in the consciousness of many tribal members. A new web-based self-administered diabetes risk assessment, for example, has expanded the risk list to include other racial and ethnic groups: http://www.diabetes.org/diabetes-basics/prevention/diabetes-risk -test/risk-test-flyer-2012.pdf. In addition, the negative consequences of diabetes are also well advertised in public health campaigns, where references are made some of these undesirable complications. There are more hopeful messages in some of the prevention literature now, but they have not been around long enough to erase the negative aspects of the disease. Interestingly, the negative messages about diabetes do not appear to convince individuals to change their lifestyle; instead, the negative perception increases anxiety and fear for those already diagnosed with diabetes.

Some of the hopelessness is also invested in the fact that despite considerable resources and time devoted to diabetes research, there is still no cure for the disease. This attitude of frustration is seen in communities where there have been many more years devoted to diabetes research. For example, until recently, members of the Pima tribe of Arizona willingly participated for several decades in a longitudinal study conducted by the NIH on type 2 diabetes. The tribe's frustration over the lack of progress in finding a cure is expressed by one tribal leader, who remarked,

> Thirty years of what? What did we get for all of this? We were human guinea pigs. They've [the investigators] just been watching diabetes take its course, but the people here have been hoping for a cure. (Sevilla 1999:A1)

The community's frustration is understandable as most of the investigation that has occurred in this tribal community has focused on uncovering the pathophysiological process of diabetes. It has only been recently that some attention has turned to examining prevention and intervention strategies. The bench research endeavors have, however, provided some important findings, especially identification of a number of biological factors. Studies of this type, however, are like peeling an onion, a slow process where each layer removed poses more new questions than solutions. The worldwide effort to find a cure, however, is ongoing, especially now that the disease poses a global threat.

The worldwide research on the etiology and prevention of diabetes continues to include genetics. The genetic connection has been one of the key questions explored in the series of longitudinal studies conducted with the Pima tribe. One earlier theory, the notion of a thrifty gene linkage (Neel 1962), has received some attention, but for a variety of reasons, the thrifty gene theory has never been subjected to a rigorous study. The thrifty gene theory speculated that prior to the European contact, most tribes experienced feast or famine, a pattern that conditioned their metabolic response to reserve body fat for lean times. This balanced pattern, however, changed when famine was no longer a problem, when food or access to a food source was no longer the issue. Unfortunately, although the early diet of most tribes was healthy, with the introduction of processed food like flour, lard, and sugar, the accessible and ready food source was mostly unhealthy and contributed significantly to the increase in obesity and subsequently to the increase in diabetes.

The tribal discussion on the thrifty gene theory does acknowledge that such feast and famine was experience by some tribes, mainly hunters and gathers, but they disagree in that the theory overlooks the ability of most tribes to prepare and store food for lean periods (Joe 2005). The tribal researchers note that many coastal and other inland tribes were rarely without a food source; coastal tribes had ready access to fish while some inland tribes engaged in agricultural activities. Tribes knew how to preserve food (Joe 2005): game and fish were preserved, smoked, or dried while those tribes that cultivated plants also prepared and stored food for winter or for anticipated food shortage. Even tribes that were big-game hunters had women who supplemented lean hunting seasons with small game and had storage of dried meat, berries, vegetables, and roots. The discussion in Joe (2005) also makes reference to the possibility of famine. Most agree that famine probably did occur during times of warfare or extreme weather change that prevented hunting or access to foods stored for such emergencies.

Because diabetes was not a disease found among Native peoples until the mid-1950s, most tribal history and existing tribal healing systems have no name or treatment for diabetes (Satterfield et al. 2007). Diabetes is often called the sugar disease because persons diagnosed with diabetes are told they have too much sugar in their blood.

Diabetes is also difficult to place within the traditional categories of illness explanations that explain most sickness as caused by either natural or unnatural sources. The natural causes are those conditions for which there is a natural explanation, that is, a cut, a broken bone from a fall, psychological depression when a person is grieving for deceased relative, and so forth. As in most societies, most conditions were seen to have natural causes and were treated with home remedies or were treated by a specialist with needed expertise, such as an herbalist or a bonesetter, if a joint has been dislocated. Midwives were also plentiful. They were skilled and were utilized in all communities.

The unnatural illnesses are those conditions that have supernatural causes, such as a sickness that might be attributed to breaking a cultural taboo, a spell intended to do harm, or ill health that may be traced back to a series of recurring bad dreams. The traditional tribal healing systems recognize and provide known treatments for these familiar conditions caused by natural and unnatural causes. But because diabetes is not part of this familiar history, it not only posed a problem for patients but also for the tribal traditional practitioners. There was difficulty in treating health problems that came with colonization such as alcoholism, cancer, or chronic health problems such as diabetes.

Western medicine and its process of providing patient care also created some initial difficulties, and some of them continue today. For example, it was customary to have traditional healing ceremonies conducted with involvement of the family and extended kin because it was determined it was a necessary part of the healing process. The traditional practitioners also did not view themselves as curing an illness as much as they saw their role as that of a facilitator or one who guides and helps the patient gain access to spiritual helpers or deities, who empowered the patient to begin the healing process. This type of allopathic intervention is not generally part of Western medicine. In Western medicine, most encounters between the patient and the physician happens in a clinical setting that usually does not accommodate other family members. For most illness, the emphasis is on the medication prescribed or a specific surgical intervention to cure a condition, and the patient and the family have a less active role. It is, therefore, not uncommon for members of a patient's family to have no knowledge of a diagnosis of diabetes because they are not present nor asked to assist the patient in managing his or her diabetes.

For some patients who are newly diagnosed, the idea of having diabetes can be overwhelming, especially the various responsibilities they have to assume, some of which they perceive as being reserved only for skilled health care providers. They are reluctant to stick their finger to get a drop of blood to check their blood glucose level and also uncomfortable having to adjust and self-administer the required units of insulin. Many patients say they have difficulty accepting this responsibility because they don't feel they know enough or have confidence enough to judge insulin units or do a reliable glucose reading.

SELF-EMPOWERMENT AND IMPROVING HEALTH CARE

Today it is understood that many of the persistent health problems that burden the lives of Native peoples and other minority populations cannot be explained by one causal factor. The current discussion has been expanded to include multiple determinants of health. This recognition takes into account not only genetic factors but relevant environmental and other sociocultural factors that contribute to persistent poor health. In an interview for the media series *Unnatural Causes of Health Disparities*, Michael Marmot indicates that data from his longitudinal studies on social class and its hierarchy of health show that access to medical care is not always a key factor in obtaining or maintaining health. He states that there is strong evidence that health status is also impacted by personal autonomy, control, and empowerment. Dr. Marmot's data, drawn from Whitehall studies of British civil servants, indicate that people who are disempowered, lack autonomy, or have little control over their lives are at increased risk for heart disease, mental illness, and other conditions (Unnatural Causes 2006).

Empowerment and self-determination are also key concepts used by most Native peoples in their discussion about health care delivery systems or improving the health of their tribal members. For example, many tribal communities are now managing their own clinics or hospital, a move they see as not only part of self-determination but an opportunity to improve the quality of health care provided to their health care consumers. Many of these health facilities operated by tribes have also placed priority on making the services culturally sensitive and culturally safe. Such additions include ways to improve health literacy or hiring bilingual staff and also involving their traditional healers, either as consultants or hired-on staff, as part of the clinical staff. The inclusion of culture has also gained ground on the national health agenda that calls for developing or improving cultural competency to help close certain health disparity gaps that are found among minority populations who make up the nation's most vulnerable populations.

Because health and health status are influenced and maintained as a part of one's cultural lifestyle, culture is also central to one's identity. Culture helps frame and maintain an individual's or a group's health beliefs, a culture-based belief system that is shaped, changed, or reinforced by individual or group experiences. Within a culturally diverse world, many unexplained illnesses tend to have a cultural as well as a biomedical explanation regarding etiology and treatment. When faced with an illness that cannot be cured by Western medicine, some patients utilize all other alternatives. The tendency to "shop around" is especially common when health problems are either chronic or persistent and are not alleviated or cured by biomedical remedies (Barnes, Moss-Morris, and Kaufusi 2004; Chun and Chesla 2004; Coronado et al. 2004; Hagey 2000; Fleming, Carter, and Pettigrew 2008).

As described elsewhere in this book, many important indigenous health resources for some tribes were destroyed or altered by depopulation and forced removal. Whether the process involved removal or depopulation, those affected lost all or much of their ancestral or traditional health resources, or these resources became inaccessible when former tribal lands were sold and fenced as private property. With little or no health care resources, many tribes became dependent on modern Western medicine. As noted elsewhere, the federal government became the primary health care system for many. That health care delivery system is under the Indian Health Service (IHS), an organization under the U.S. Public Health Services.

The IHS inherited a health care system that was acute-care based and had few resources to address community-based programs that promoted prevention or health maintenance. Today, tribal groups and others like Smith-Morris (2007) advocate for a structural change in the health care delivery system for Native Americans, a change that would include a more holistic approach. Smith-Morris, whose research in diabetes has been conducted with a number of tribes, views a holistic approach as more meaningful than the present acute-care approach that focuses on physiological aspect of a disease or illness without taking into account other important factors such as culture, genetics, environment, and political-economic circumstance (Smith-Morris 2007).

Given the lack of financial resources and related resources, the realization of holistic health care will most likely not happen or, if realized, will come gradually (Soeng and Chinitz 2010). The funds allocated by Congress to support IHS are not an entitlement but are discretionary. As noted in the history of Indian health care, availability of discretionary funds for government-supported programs is not guaranteed, and what is allocated is restricted by budgetary constraints and priorities set by Congress. Each year, the management of the IHS and tribal advocates must present a need-based budget for Congressional consideration, including dollars to cover costs of health services received outside the IHS health care facilities. The latter, called contract care service, ration funds for emergency or medical care that is not available or provided in existing IHS facilities. Once contract care service dollars are depleted, patients who do have life-threatening health needs have to wait until more funds are allocated annually by Congress. The contract care service resource is important because most IHS hospitals are located in small rural communities, have few beds, and are not equipped to do deliveries, medical rehabilitation, or complicated surgery.

CULTURE AND MANAGING DIABETES

Being diagnosed with type 2 diabetes and being willing to live with the disease requires considerable personal adjustment and accommodation. Despite increased public awareness about the disease over the last few decades, many Native patients with the disease believe that diabetes remains a stigmatized health problem. There is no question that not only is diabetes personal and intimate but having the disease also has implications for one's self-image and self-esteem and is a constant reminder that diabetes threatens survival. Because deaths related to diabetic complications are increasingly common in most tribal communities, it is not difficult for a person with diabetes to remember a family member who has died as a result of diabetes-related complications. Because diabetes was not part of the ancestral history of most tribes and because there has been considerable ongoing cultural change, strategies to incorporate a culture-based diabetes prevention or intervention program present challenges for tribal communities as well as for health care providers.

The importance of culture, however, in ways patients perceive or cope with diabetes has not gone unnoticed. For example, several research efforts have examined the role of culture in diabetes self-management (Csordas 1994; Barnes et al. 2004). According to Fleming and colleagues (2008), approaches undertaken in these investigations either view diabetes self-management within the broader dynamics of culture or focus on one or two more narrow cultural interest such as patient's health beliefs. In the dynamic approach, culture is often considered as one of many other influences on health behavior or diabetes self-management. Scholars like Culley (2001), however, posit that when a narrow or reductionist approach is utilized, there is always the danger of emphasizing difference or otherness that can reinforce negative stereotypes and have the tendency to blame the health consequences on the patient. Culley (2001) also notes that the reductionist approach can also fail to acknowledge the complexity of health beliefs and behaviors by portraying culture as a fixed or constraining factor.

To go beyond the biological aspect of diabetes, Scheper-Hughes and Lock (1987) advocate for considering both the "social body" and the "body politic" of diabetes, a consideration that makes physiology and somatic components an interactive experience that can be communicated to others. Scheper-Hughes and Lock define the social body as the symbolic and communicative aspect of an illness experience that is shared and negotiated to express one's illness experience(s). These investigators view the body politic as the regulation or control of bodies. In his study of the Pima community, Kozak (1997) illustrates the latter point by referring to an example of a patient-physician interaction, where the patient is usually a passive recipient of a physician's admonitions (p. 350). In other words, such an example might show a patient being scolded by his or her physician for not keeping the blood glucose level within a prescribed range.

Like all illnesses, diseases like diabetes happen to people who experience the disease differently. The somatic aspect of the diabetes experience helps patients verbalize their hidden emotions of fear, anxiety, and stress, if not to the physician, to a trusted individual (Lyon and Barbalet 1994). For example, in his study of Indian patients with diabetes on one reservation, Kozak (1997) subdivided his respondents according to their sociocultural perception of diabetes: (1) diabetes is inevitable, (2) diabetes is uncontrollable, (3) diabetes is inherited, and (4) diabetes is a "death sentence" (p. 352). All of the four categories illustrate a perception that is marked by hopelessness or powerlessness.

It is important to note, however, that these personal perceptions are not usually captured or recorded by most health care providers caring for Native peoples with diabetes. Understandably, the high volume of patients seen in clinics or hospitals prevents friendly physician-patient chats. Instead the focus is on what the patient needs to do next as a result of his or her recent glucose or other laboratory tests. The unmet need of the emotional or mental health of Native patients with diabetes is widespread. Obviously, some of these unspoken perceptions and fear of diabetes can be decreased if patients are armed with enough useful information on how to manage the disease so that it does not control them. The process of diabetes education, however, is uneven, as confirmed by a study conducted by Moore and colleagues (2006). Moore and colleagues examined the quality of care offered to Indian patients with diabetes at various facilities by conducting a retrospective audit of medical records that covered a 12-month period. The investigators found that urban Indian patients were more likely than rural patients to have received formal diabetes education.

Diabetes education is critical in helping patients manage their diabetes because the more knowledge the patients gain, the more likely it is that they will be empowered and understand why it is necessary for them to manage the disease (Koch, Jenkin, and Kralick 2004; Riley et al. 2009). Such education, however, has to be delivered in such a way that it is culturally sensitive as well as appropriately delivered to meet the needs of the patient. Age, gender, and other important sociodemographic circumstances are also important in targeting the audience as well as providing relevant and culturally appropriate educational materials.

Brown-Riggs (2011) emphasized the importance of cultural competency in her presentation at recent conference by giving this title to her presentation: "When Providers or Diabetes Educators Say They Treat Everyone the Same, That Is the Problem: That Is Not Cultural Competence." This presentation, given at the 2011 annual meeting of the American Association of Diabetes Educators, called on diabetes educators to collaborate with patients to help them set realistic goals and to recognize their personal circumstances, culture, or tastes that may impede them from overhauling their diet or making other changes. Brown-Riggs provides several illustrations of why cultural competency is important with examples of difficulties faced by black patients with diabetes. The examples provided were similar to those of Native Americans who also struggle with diabetes. Some of these difficulties include health literacy, access to care, lack of culturally appropriate diabetes education materials, and the tendency for health care providers to tell patients what to do instead of giving patients enough information and options so they can have an active role in deciding what is workable for them.

THE EMOTIONAL SIDE OF LIVING WITH DIABETES

Pan and colleagues (2011) studied 78,282 women participating in the Nurses' Health Study and reported that where the nurses had both diabetes and depression, the women also had poor glycemic control, were at increased risk for diabetes-related complications, and were less likely to have a social support or a healthy social network. Results from another study, a meta-analysis conducted by Anderson and colleagues (2001), found 15 to 20 percent of patients with diabetes met the criteria for depression, a rate that is more than double the 2 to 9 percent usually found among the general population. The investigators also found that 30 percent of 92,000 adults with diabetes had previous histories of depression, indicating that depression likely accelerated the development of diabetes. The presence of both diabetes and depression has also been found to pose higher risk for major diabetes-related complications as well as changes in quality of life (Lin et al. 2010; Goldney et al. 2004).

Although depression is prevalent among patients with diabetes, mental health has been one of the most neglected areas of health care provided to Native Americans with diabetes. Only recently has there been some effort by health care facilities to do a brief depression inventory of patients attending outpatient clinics. The results are entered into the health record, but it is not clear if these results are acted on. It is likely that many of the unexplained aches and pains that are reported by these patients are substituted for symptoms of depression. The reports of aches and pains are more likely to get some medical attention while symptoms of anxiety are not discussed or addressed. Interestingly, when opportunities are provided, patients are willing to discuss depression. For example, results from one innovative intervention using the Internet to help patients learn diabetes self-management showed that many Native women identified depression as a common problem (Jernigan and Lorig 2010:266).

There are many stressors that impact the health of Native women with diabetes, but because of the needs of their family members they often neglect their own health needs. Those who do well in managing their diabetes often have the support of their adult children, some of whom who make sure the medications are taken and appropriate diet and physical activity or exercise are encouraged or maintained. Familial involvement also becomes more demanding when the mother of the household starts developing complications or other health problems limiting functional abilities, including limitation due to recovery from a cardiac bypass surgery or a limb amputation.

The lack of mental health services for a group of Native women with disabilities underscores this neglect (Joe 2003). The study was conducted on the Navajo Reservation with a sample of 24 Navajo women enrolled in a vocational rehabilitation program who were learning new vocational skills after one or both lower limbs were amputated (half had bilateral below-knee amputation and used wheel-chairs for locomotion while others were wearing or being fitted with prostheses). The average age was 54, and most women had a medical history of diabetes that spanned 14 or more years. Only three of the women had never married while others were divorced, widowed, or married or living with a significant other. The average number of children for women who had children was at least two. In addition to loss of limbs, six of the women were also on dialysis.

When asked what was most challenging when one has to live with diabetes, one respondent replied: "At first, you are neither sick nor well ... but, you are sick inside but looked well on the outside." Another respondent, Sadie, gave her explanation as to why she thought she got diabetes:

> both my husband and son died three years ago. I did not want to live. When I got sick they said I had the sugar disease. All these bad thoughts are probably why I got this problem. (Joe 2003:15)

Sadie also said she lost part of her leg because she and her family could not afford the cost of completing the traditional tribal ceremonies that were recommended. When asked if they thought that their tribal tra-ditional resources were useful in addressing the health problems asso-ciated with diabetes, Alice's father (who was a traditional practitioner/ healer) commented that he was discouraged that his efforts had not cured his daughter's diabetes. He stated: "Our old ways cannot help her, it seems like my prayers and songs are not heard" (Joe 2003:16). Alice elaborated by adding: "I think maybe it is because I am no longer whole ... the deities do not recognize me" (Joe 2003:16). When asked if they discuss some of these cultural concerns with their physicians, Sadie shook her head and states: "the cultural things we keep close ... it is usually misunderstood" (Joe 2003).

As the complications of diabetes become more functionally debili-tating, most of the women also said they become increasingly disengaged by socially isolating themselves. When asked how diabetes has changed their lives, Norma replied: "I don't go many places anymore. . . . I don't want people staring at me or asking me about my health problems" (Joe 2003:19). Alice also commented: "When someone comes to visit, I usually stay in the bedroom" (Joe 2003:19).

In addition to questioning their role as mothers and wives, some also said their amputation made them feel unwhole or too disfigured to have their husbands want to sleep with them. Others resent having others caring for them when they should be the caretakers. One respondent said that because she was no longer physically whole and was in a wheel chair, disciplining her teenage sons had become unmanageable because they didn't listen to her. She attributed her physical disabilities as reasons why she now has a less powerful position in her family. Others said the amputation had made them feel less of a woman, unattractive, and an undesirable marital partner.

Families in some instances also contribute to these women's sense of powerlessness and poor self-image. Because their illness is closely tied to ongoing medical care and attention, some family members attempt to keep them in a "sick role" and expect them to be dependent on others. This type of family situation made it difficult for women to participate in vocational rehabilitation programs where striving for independence is key.

COMMUNITY-BASED EFFORTS
TO PREVENT DIABETES

While most individuals diagnosed with diabetes are under the care of health professionals, increasing numbers of tribal groups are targeting diabetes prevention with an array of community-based programs, programs that include building and operating facilities such as community-based fitness centers and sponsoring community events such as walks and runs. The staff members from these programs are also involved in local schools to help with increasing physical activity for children as well as establishing exercise programs for the elders. Other community activities include collaboration with local supermarkets to promote healthy food or distribution of recipes for preparing healthy meals. While all members of the community are invited, the majority of the audience and participants are women. And it is not surprising that most of these programs are attractive to women as most of these efforts have been proposed and managed by Native women.

Native women, trained or with considerable practical experience, are behind or are the mainstay of these programs. The involvement of Native women in community health efforts has a long history, including the pioneering work started by trained paraprofessionals, the community health representatives (CHRs) in the 1960s. CHRs are valuable because they know their communities, have lived or grown up in those communities, are well acquainted with existing community resources, and are trained to serve as a liaison between their respective communities, their patients, and local health care institutions. They provide patient education and follow-up services and serve as patient advocates when needed. Their employment is usually by the tribal government, but they are trained and utilized by health care staff from clinics or hospitals. Unfortunately, because the CHRs do not specialize in any area of disease prevention or education, they are limited in what they can offer community members who are living with diabetes. An ideal role for some of the CHRs would be to be trained as diabetes support counselors so they can work with those patients who are experiencing depression or other related mental health problems associated with diabetes. In addition, these CHRs should have backup support from a diabetes education team with membership that includes a physician, a mental health professional, and one or two traditional Native practitioners. These trained CHRs should be able to conduct support group meetings as well as work with individual patients.

REFERENCES

Agency for Healthcare Research and Quality (AHRQ). 2010. "AHRQ Research and Other Activities Relevant to American Indians and Alaska Natives." Rockville, MD: USHHS, AHRQ.

American Diabetes Association (ADA). 2011. "Diabetes Basics: Your Risk." Accessed September 12, 2011. http://www.diabetes.org/diabetes-basics/prevention/risk -factors/.

Anderson, R. J., K. Freedland, R. Clouse, and P. J. Lustman. 2001. "Prevalence of Co-morbid Depression in Adults with Diabetes: A Meta-analysis." *Diabetes Care* 24, 1069–78.

Associated Press. 1999, November 1. "Indians Say U.S. Failed to Help in Fight against 'Pima Plague.'"

Barnes, L., R. Moss-Morris, and M. Kaufusi. 2004. "Illness Beliefs and Adherences in Diabetes Mellitus: A Comparison between Tongan and European Patients." *New Zealand Medical Journal* 117, 1–9.

Brown-Riggs, Constance. 2011. "Often People Will Say, 'I Treat Everyone the Same,' but, That's the Problem—That Is Not Cultural Competence." Presented at the American Association of Diabetes Educators Annual Meeting and Exhibition, Las Vegas, NV, August 3–6.

Centers for Disease Control (CDC). 2009. "Summary Health Statistics for U.S. Adults 2008. Table 8." Bethesda, MD: NIH Vital Health Stats.

Chun, K. M., and C. A. Chesla. 2004. "Cultural Issues in Disease Management for Chinese Americans with Type 2 Diabetes." *Psychology and Health* 19(6):767–85.

Coronado, G. D., B. Thompson, S. Tejeda, and R. Godina. 2004. "Attitudes and Beliefs among Mexican-Americans about Type 2 Diabetes." *Journal of Health Care for the Poor and Underserved* 15, 576–88.

Csordas, T. 1994. *Embodiment and Experience: The Existential Ground of Culture and Self.* Cambridge, UK: Cambridge University Press.

Culley, Lorraine. 2001. "Nursing, Culture, and Competence." Pp. 109–28 in *Ethnicity and Nursing Practice.* Lorraine Culley and Simon Dyson (Eds.). Palgrave, NH: Hampshire Press.

Danaei, Goodarz, Mariel M. Finucae, Lu Yuan, M. Singh Gitanjali, M. S. Cowan, C. J. Paciorek, J. K. Lin, F. Farzadfar, Y. H. Khang, G. A. Stevens, M. Rao, M. K. Ali, L. M. Riley, C. A. Robinson, and M. Ezzati. 2011. "National, Regional, and Global Trends in Fasting Plasma Glucose and Diabetes Prevalence since 1980: Systematic Analysis of Health Examination Surveys and Epidemiological Studies with 370 Country-years and 2.7 Million Participants." *Lancet.* Early online publication, June 25. http://www.thelancet.com/journal/lancet/article/PIIS0140-6737(11)606679-X/abstract.

Eaton, W. 2002. "Epidemiologic Evidence on the Comorbidity of Depression and Diabetes." *Journal of Psychosomatic Research* 53, 903–6.

Fleming, Elizabeth, Bernie Carter, and Judith Pettigrew. 2008. "The Influence of Culture on Diabetes Self-Management: Perspectives of Gujarati Muslim Men Who Reside in Northwest England." *Journal of Clinical Nursing* 17(5a):51–59.

Gebel, Erika. 2011, October. "Matter of the Sexes: The Difference between Men and Women with Diabetes." *Diabetes Forecast*, 47–49

Goldney, Robert D., Pat J. Phillips, Laura J. Fisher, and David H. Wilson. 2004. "Diabetes, Depression, and Quality of Life." *Diabetes Care* 27(5):1066–70.

Grim, Charles W. 2003. "The Health of American Indians and Alaska Natives." *British Medical Journal.* Accessed January 11, 2011. http://bmj.com/cgi/content/full/327/7418/E220.

Hagey, R. 2000. "Cultural Safety: Honoring Traditional Way of Life." *Alternative and Complementary Therapies* 6(4):233–36.

James Cara, Karyn Schwartz, and Julia Berndt. 2009. "A Profile of American Indians and Alaska Natives and Their Health Coverage: Race, Ethnicity and Health Care Issue Brief." Menlo Park, CA: Henry J. Kaiser Family Foundation.

Jernigan, Valarie Blue Bird and Kate Lorig. 2011. "The Internet Diabetes Self-Management Workshop for American Indians and Alaska Natives." *Health Promotion Practice* 12(2):261–70.

Joe, Jennie R. 2003. "Behind the Curtain of Words: Diabetic Complications and Re-definition of Self." Pp. 8–21 in *Aboriginal Health, Identity, and Resources.* Oakes et al. (Eds.). Winnipeg: University of Manitoba, Department of Native Studies.

Joe, Jennie R. 2005. "Old Age and Diabetes Are Taking Pieces of Me: Navajo Women and the Redefinition of Self." Unpublished paper presented at the Grand Rounds, University of New Mexico Health Sciences Center, Albuquerque, NM, September 1.

Koch, T., P. Jenkin, and D Kralick. 2004. "Chronic Illness Self-Management: Locating the 'Self.'" *Journal of Advanced Nursing* 48, 484–92.

Kozak, David L. 1997. "Surrendering to Diabetes: An Embodied Response to Perceptions of Diabetes and Death in the Gila River Indian Community." *Omega* 35(4):347–59.

Laino, Charlene. 2011. "Diabetes Rates Double since 1980." Accessed August 22, 2011. http://www.webmed.com.

Lin, Elizabeth, C. M. Rutter, Wayne Katon, S. R. Heckbert, P. Ciechanowski, M. M. Oliver, E. J. Ludman, B. A. Young, L. H. Williams, D. K. McCulloch, and M. von Korff. 2010. "Depression and Advanced Complications of Diabetes." *Diabetes Care* 33(2):264–69.

Lustman, P. J., R. J. Anderson, K. E. Freeland, M. de Groot, R. M. Carney, and R. E. Clouse. 2000. "Depression and Poor Glycaemic Control: A Meta-analysis Review of the Literature." *Diabetes Care* 23, 934–42.

Lyon, M. L. and J. M. Barbalet. 1994. "Society's Body: Emotion and the 'Somatization' of Social Theory." Pp. 48–66 in *Embodiment and Experience*. T. Csordas (Ed.). Cambridge, UK: Cambridge University Press.

Moore, Kelly, Y. Roubideaux, Carolyn Noonan, J. Goldberg, R. Shield, and K. Acton. 2006. "Measuring the Quality of Diabetes Care in Urban and Rural Indian Health Programs." *Ethnicity and Disease* 16(4):772–77.

National Diabetes Information Clearinghouse (NDIC). 2011. "National Diabetes Statistics, 2011." Accessed August 17, 2011. http://diabetes.niddk.nih.gov/DM/PUBS/Statistics/#Racial.

Neel, James V. 1962. "Diabetes Mellitus: A 'Thrifty' Genotype Rendered Detrimental by 'Progress'?" *Journal of Human Genetics* 14, 353–62.

NIH News. 2009. "New Survey Results Show Hugh Burden of Diabetes: Study Includes Sensitive Test of Blood Glucose Abnormalities." Bethesda, MD: National Institute of Diabetes and Digestive and Kidney Diseases (NIDDK).

Pan, A., Q. Lucas, R. M. Sun, R. M. van Darn, O. H. Franco, W. C. Willett, J. E. Manson, K. M. Rexrode, A. Ascherio, and F. B. Hu. 2011. "Increased Mortality Risk in Women with Depression and Diabetes Mellitus." *Archives of General Psychiatry* 68(1):42. DOI: 10.1001/archgenpsychiatry.2010.176.

Riley, Andrea A., Mindy L. Mentee, Linda Gerson, and Cheryl R. Dennison. 2009. "Depression as a Comorbidity to Diabetes: Implications for Management." *Journal for Nurse Practitioners* 5(7):523–35.

Roubideaux, Yvette, Carolyn Noonan, Jack H. Goldberg, S. L. Valdez, T L. Brown, S. M. Manson, and K. Acton. 2008. "Relation between the Level of American Indian and Alaska Native Diabetes Education Program Services and Quality-of-Care Indicators." *American Journal of Public Health* 98(11):2079–84.

Satterfield, Dawn W., John Eagle Shield, John Buckley John, and Sally Taken Alive. 2007. "So That the People May Live (Hecel Lena Oyate Ki Nipi Kte): Lakota and Dakota Elder Women as Reservoirs of Life and Keepers of Knowledge about Health Protection and Diabetes Prevention." *Journal of Health Disparities Research and Practice* 1(2):1–28.

Scheper-Hughes, Nancy and Margaret M. Lock. 1987. "The Mindful Body: A Prolegomenon to Future Work in Medical Anthropology." *Medical Anthropology Quarterly* 1: 6–41.

Sevilla, Graciela. 1999. "Diabetes Ravaging Tribe despite Decades of Study Miscalculations Delayed War for Control of Illness." *Arizona Republic* (Phoenix, AZ), October 31, A.1.

Smith-Morris, Carolyn. 2007. *Diabetes among the Pima: Stories of Survival.* Tucson: University of Arizona Press.

Soeng, Nicole and Julie Chinitz. 2010, August. "Native Health Underfunded and Promises Unfulfilled: The Importance of Investing in the Indian Health Service." Seattle, WA: Northwest Federation of Community Organizations.

Unnatural Causes. 2006. "An Interview with Sir Michael Marmot." Recorded in Cambridge, MA, April 10.

CHAPTER 9

Domestic Violence in American Indian Communities: Background, Culture, and Legal Issues

Mary Rogers and
Jennifer Giroux

INTRODUCTION

Historically, violence against women has always been outside most traditional Native American cultures. The respect for women and gender equality, however, has eroded and continues to do so, a change that was initiated by colonization and reinforced by decades of poverty and lack of resources. The price that women have had to pay has been devastating. For example, according to the U.S. Department of Justice (Tjaden and Thoennes 2000b), one in three Native women is sexually assaulted in her lifetime. Complex systems of law enforcement and legal jurisdictions among federal, state, and tribal governments compound the problem of protecting Native women.

BACKGROUND

Native culture is grounded in the knowledge that we are all related, that the values of respect, compassion and non-violence are integral to our survival, and that women truly are sacred. Historically among Indian people, what we now call "confidentiality" was the practice of honoring an individual's life changes and paths and the right to walk through the world with freedom, safety and respect. We have an alternative to utilizing the hierarchical medical model of dominant society as a basis for the way we do our work. The work in Indian Country to end violence against Native women and their children is powerful when the indigenous culture, beliefs and worldview are used as models.

—Sacred Circle, National Resource Center
to End Violence against Native Women

Domestic violence is defined as a pattern of purposeful coercive behaviors that may include inflicted physical injury, psychological abuse, sexual assault, progressive social isolation, deprivation, and intimidation. These behaviors are perpetrated by someone who is or was involved in an intimate relationship with an adult or adolescent victim with the aim to establish control over the other (Williams 2002). Historically, violence against women was not widespread in indigenous communities, and if it occurred, the traditional response was immediate and harsh. Often the family of the victim provided the first response, integrating the holistic and community intervention.

In most Native American societies, men's and women's roles were delineated in such a way that violence against women among their own groups did not seem to be a common and regular practice (DeBruyn, Wilkins, and Artichoker 1990; Native American Circle 2004). In Indian communities, there is severe economic deprivation and high unemployment accompanied by social problems such as drug and alcohol abuse, assaults, and violent crimes (Williams 2002). Over time, Native women have become increasingly vulnerable to violence in their homes and in their communities.

There is suggestive evidence that domestic violence has become more common, or has become the norm, with estimates suggesting reported domestic violence rates against American Indian women by their partners at a rate 6 percent higher than their white male counterparts. According to the Bureau of Justice Statistics, American Indian women experience 98 violent victimizations per 1,000—higher than Asian males, black males, and white males (Erwin and Vidales 2001). Overall, American Indian and Alaska Native women reported significantly higher rates of intimate partner violence than women of other racial backgrounds (Tjaden and Thoennes 2000a). Results from the National Violence against Women Survey indicated that more than 37 percent of American Indian/Alaska Native women were victimized by their intimate partners, with 15 percent raped, 31 percent physically assaulted, and 10 percent stalked (Tjaden and Thoennes 2000a). In a study of the prevalence of domestic violence among American Indian/Alaska Native women seeking routine care in an Indian Health Service care facility, it was found that 53 percent of women reported at least one episode of domestic violence by a male partner, and 16 percent reported current (past year) domestic violence, with verbal and physical abuse being the most frequently reported types of abuse (Fairchild, Fairchild, and Stoner 1998).

Segal examined the rates of physical and sexual abuse among Alaska Native women entering a residential treatment program. The data indicated that 90 percent of the women had been physically abused at some time in their lives, with 64 percent reporting the abuse happened before the age of 13. Nearly 50 percent of these women were abused by parents and almost 90 percent were beaten while in a relationship. In addition, 78 percent of the women reported having ever been sexually abused, with 76 percent of this abuse happening before the age of 13 (Segal 2001).

American Indian and Alaska Native women and men have led grassroots efforts to address intimate partner violence or sexual assault (IPV/SA) among many tribal nations. During the 1960s and 1970s, these grassroots organizations provided shelter and support to women victims and also began advocating for systemic and policy change, challenging widely held beliefs that domestic violence resulted from stress, marital conflict, or women's provocation (Schechter 1982). Perhaps the most frequently cited association with the high rates of domestic and intimate partner violence, as well as other forms of violence, in American Indian/Alaska Native communities is the historical trauma and resulting historical unresolved grief and intergenerational trauma that have been experienced as a result of European contact and colonization, racism and internalized oppression, boarding schools, and assimilation policies, which may result in the lack of knowledge of gender relations due to family disruption (Brave Heart and DeBruyn 1998). Gray (1998) reported that self-hatred can result from the genocidal assaults that occurred to American Indian/Alaska Native communities, suggesting internalized self-hatred can lead to depression and suicide and, when externalized, it can result in violence against others.

Fortunately, there are model programs in Indian country addressing this public health crisis. Because the authors of this chapter are from the Northern Plains, examples of groundbreaking model programs implemented by the White Buffalo Calf Woman Society, Inc., on the Rosebud Sioux Tribe Reservation, established in 1977, are presented. White Buffalo Calf Woman Society is the oldest shelter for women on an Indian reservation and the first shelter for women of color in the United States, but similar shelters and programs exist in other regions of Indian country. The White Buffalo Calf Woman Society's primary focus has always been to provide safe shelter for victims of violence, 24 hours a day, 7 days a week. In addition, advocacy, emotional support, and referrals to other services are provided for victims of domestic violence and sexual assault. Advocacy for children and for individuals to navigate court systems and initiate protection or restraining orders are additional services provided. Transitional housing or assistance with finding of new and affordable housing for victims is an example of continuity of care and support. White Buffalo Calf Woman Society provides outreach and education for men and assists male victims of domestic violence or sexual assault. Support groups meet on a regular weekly schedule, and education focuses on messages of healthy relationships and respect and teaching that violence is wrong (White Buffalo Calf Woman Society 2011).

HISTORY, CULTURE AND HISTORICAL TRAUMA

It can be said that the world of American Indian people changed following the arrival of western cultures (Easley and Charles 2004). Despite the changes, American Indian/Alaska Natives have held to the tradition of interdependent living, moving away from the "I" mentality of the Western worldview. This unique difference alone establishes the framework for the critical discussion of the values and traditions of indigenous people when developing prevention programs and treatment approaches to address domestic violence and IPV/SA. It can be said that colonization led to a new life for American Indians, fraught with problems that continue to decimate communities even to this day. The erosion of traditional values most dramatically impacted the sense of self and established roles and created a host of problems. The impact of boarding schools, for example, cannot be adequately measured, but through the deliberate policy of removing children from their homes and families prematurely, as youth matured and eventually raised families of their own, many lacked the knowledge and experience needed to provide a stable foundation for their children because they had been removed before having learned how to raise children in a culturally stable manner (Segal et al. 1999). The loss of traditional and spiritual beliefs dramatically affected their ability to maintain their heritage and, more importantly, created a state of cultural dissonance. Many Alaska Natives believe that the problems faced by Native people today are a direct result of their historical experiences (Napoleon 1966).

Current problems such as domestic violence, child abuse and neglect, and alcoholism are a reflection of the stress passed down through families (Alaska Native Commission 1994). This situation has been identified as historical trauma (Brave Heart 1998). Many communities are places where the violence is rampant—places of rage and frustration; such communities, according to one elder, are diseased places to live (Shkilnyk 1985).

Best practices for responding to the needs of American Indian people must begin with the recognition that, for hundreds of years, Native people were capable of successfully coping with their environment and a harsh existence. With survival, Native elders retained their sense of self-worth and dignity. Many of today's generation are impacted by the effects of historical trauma but may or may not be knowledgeable about historical trauma. They have inherited a sense of poor self-worth, along with feelings of powerlessness and helplessness, which leaves them vulnerable to self-condemnation as a way of coping with their sense of distress. Historical trauma is further aggravated by the current economic and social dilemmas impacting Native people (Easley and Charles 2004). Healing efforts by Native people can benefit from creating a common bond across their communities (Ross 1996). Healing from within communities comes from the Native insistence that the whole family be involved, that it be an holistic approach, which recognizes that all must know what each suffers so that all can contribute towards comfort and help instead of unwittingly contribute towards making things worse. Achieving well-being must go far beyond money and program-based solutions. Such well-being involves community and individual empowerment—the ability to take responsibility for one's behavior in order to control one's destiny, and being part of the process that makes decisions affecting individual and community life (Segal et al. 1999). Further, it is important to understand the patterns of violence specific to each Native community, identifying cultural barriers to recognition of domestic violence and traditional methods of prevention and intervention.

CHARACTERISTICS OF COMMUNITY COORDINATED RESPONSE MODEL

Communities offer the most promise for change efforts for a variety of reasons. Community leaders are knowledgeable about and can capitalize on existing governmental and nongovernmental institutions; the social organization of communities is often identified as a source of the problem; and the limits of intervention are bounded by geographical lines that have social and legal meaning. This is especially true of problems involving crime and criminal justice, which involve agencies characterized by practices and customs, and their jurisdictions are clearly bound by city and county lines (O'Connor 1995).

Strategies to reduce violence in Native communities hinge on the grassroots efforts of community members who share a common goal to convey the message that violence is unacceptable. One of the most important ways to effect change and mobilize against domestic violence in Native communities has been community and service provider education. American Indian/Alaska Native women refer to multiple barriers in using standard domestic violence services. Domestic violence agencies historically have been run by white women and are often viewed as connected to the systemic oppression responsible for the violence. White-controlled agencies, unless educated and trained to become culturally competent, often perpetuate issues of racism and discrimination. Sociologists who study the dynamics of different cultural beliefs report that many individuals are not comfortable disclosing personal and intimate information to a counselor or advocate who is outside their culture.

Failure to recognize the life context of the victim is often cited in program approaches that fail. To be recognized as truly responsive to the needs of the woman in a domestic violence case, the "healer" needs an understanding of the experience as the victim experiences it. Without that level of understanding, the advocate or counselor may likely further victimize the woman seeking assistance (Native American Circle 2004). The lack of services for victims of domestic violence remains the most significant barrier for women in Indian country. Shelters, if available, provide short-term support for women for their immediate needs; however, ensuring that long-term support is available is almost nonexistent. Ensuring an economic safety net for victims of violence includes welfare and other public benefit programs, child support, childcare, transportation, housing, and insurance. Without these, the women often cannot leave the abusive relationship.

Researchers note that women stay, return, and decline to leave violent relationships for a variety of reasons, all wrapped within the cycle of violence of power and control. However, Native women share a unique experience, and one that other women of color and white women do not. Communities need to respond to the specific reasons that many American Indian/Alaska Native women stay in an abusive relationship or decline to report:

- Fear that the abuser will not be arrested or prosecuted, particularly in a rural or reservation area where the abuser's friends or relatives are law enforcement officers or criminal justice professionals
- Lack of tribal infrastructure or tribal protection codes
- Tribal programs that can furnish only temporary housing or temporary intervention
- Tribal programs that do not provide any counseling to adequately evaluate her options and resources, her feelings and circumstances, and the potential for violence in her life to continue
- Misperceptions by non-Indian service providers about Native cultures and about services available to Native victims of domestic violence
- Lack of communication between tribal, state, and federal representatives involved in the criminal complaint
- No access to detention or correctional facilities, probation, or aftercare programs, diminishing effective intervention options (Native American Circle 2004).

American Indian and Alaska Native women are battered, raped, and stalked at far greater rates than any other group of women in the United States. While many issues need to be addressed to confront this crisis, it is clear that jurisdictional limitations placed on Indian nations are key factors in creating this disproportionate violence. The U.S. Department of Justice has general jurisdiction over felony crimes by or against Indians, including homicide, rape, and aggravated assault, but perpetrators of such crimes against Indian women are rarely, if at all, prosecuted given the broad caseload faced by U.S. attorneys (Legal Momentum 2005).

If the federal government declines to prosecute, non-Indian rapists, batterers, and stalkers walk free knowing that they can return to commit future crimes in the same or a different Indian nation. Indian nations also face the obstacle that Congress has limited the sentencing authority of tribal courts such that in no event may they impose for conviction of any offense any penalty or punishment greater than imprisonment for one year. As a result, Indian perpetrators not prosecuted by the federal government may not receive a sentence appropriate to the crimes of rape and battery under current law (Legal Momentum 2005). The best practices model for addressing domestic violence in American Indian communities is founded on two basic principles: (1) recognition of the problem, and (2) making a commitment to make the needed changes. It is a difficult process for community members to engage in; often, members of the tribal community will deny the existence of violence for a variety of reasons. It is therefore a critical step for the community to assess its customs and values to determine the value and importance of the woman in the community and to recognize the importance of addressing the endemic violence that Indian women face day to day.

STOP GRANT PROGRAMS

During the period from 1995 to 2000, 123 tribal governments received funding under the Violence against Women Act (VAWA), Title IV of the Violent Crime Control and Law Enforcement Act of 1994, designated as the Service Training Officers Prosecutors (STOP) Grant Programs for Reducing Violence against Indian Women (referred to as STOP grants). Of the 123 tribes receiving STOP grants, 14 tribes were site-visited by the evaluation team supported by funding from the Department of Justice. The following highlights of the evaluation outline the barriers faced in Indian country as well as the interventions implemented to effect change.

Program Activities

Jurisdictional issues, such as the Major Crimes Act, checkerboard coverage (of reservation land that is occupied by both Indians and non-Indians), Public Law 83-280 and the issues of full faith and credit (or comity), overlapping law enforcement agencies working in Indian country, and differences in legal codes and ordinances complicate the development and performance of tribal programs. Programs like STOP VAIW (Violence against Indian Women) play vital roles in empowering tribal governments, thus allowing them to assert and strengthen their sovereignty and consequently deal effectively with surrounding jurisdictions.

CODES AND ORDINANCES

Different jurisdictions with authority in Indian country have codes and ordinances concerning proper law enforcement procedures as they involve violence against Indian women. Often these codes and ordinances vary to such an extent that there are serious complications that arise when the arrest or prosecution of a perpetrator crosses jurisdictional lines. Those jurisdictions, both tribal and nontribal, that seek to coordinate their codes and ordinances greatly enhance their ability to keep Indian women safe.

LAW ENFORCEMENT

Jurisdictional conflicts, issues of mandatory and collateral arrest, victimless prosecution, data collection, and report writing greatly affect the satisfactory apprehension of perpetrators. Adequate funding for fully staffed police forces, training of law enforcement personnel, development of adequate protocols and procedures, appointment of domestic violence enforcement officers, and integration of law enforcement into a community task force and network are essential to a comprehensive community-based approach that deters domestic violence, sexual assault, and stalking and keeps Indian women safe.

THE COURT SYSTEM AND PROSECUTION

The ability of tribal courts to issue effective court orders that are recognized and honored and that are given full faith and credit, or comity, by courts of foreign jurisdiction is essential in keeping women safe. The lack of full faith and credit or comity between tribal and nontribal courts significantly affects the response to violent incidents. One way to remedy this would be for prosecution units to develop innovative systems that will help revise tribal legislative codes and protocols as well as assist with communication between components of the STOP grant. Program evaluators also need to include in their sample users of these services as well as community members to assess women's attitudes and behavior regarding domestic violence and intimate partner violence. In general, program evaluators found that women reported that coordinated services were more helpful and that they were more satisfied with the legal system; additionally, the STOP evaluation helps to illustrate that the multilevel interventions are more effective than interventions at any single level. Interventions implemented in Native communities have to pay close attention to keeping these programs culturally specific (Oetzel and Duran 2004).

Barriers to change exist despite the efforts over the last two decades. A significant barrier is found in the design of federal programs. The federal system imposes one model on all tribes, preempting any opportunity to identify and work with each specific tribe and its needs. The development of culturally appropriate models for domestic violence programs faces an unusual challenge in Oklahoma, for example. The state of Oklahoma has 39 tribes whose diverse origins resulted from Indian removal policies in the 1800s.

Tribes have jurisdiction over their lands and therefore are responsible for developing domestic violence tribal codes. Some tribes have no policies or codes, and some mistakenly think the federal government will assume responsibility. To further complicate legal standing, sexual assault is considered a major crime as defined by law so it will come under the federal government jurisdiction. The FBI will investigate and the U.S. attorney will decide whether or not to prosecute. According to Andrea Smith (2002), the U.S. attorney usually declines to prosecute 70 percent of all cases and rarely prosecutes sexual assault cases. If a case is declined, it may be turned over to the tribe. At this point, the case may be a year old. If the U.S. attorney prosecutes the case, investigators will gear toward winning at the federal level, based on federal standards rather than tribal standards. The federal government limits the extent to which tribes can implement their own remedies in these cases (Smith 2002).

RECIDIVISM

In the early 1990s, policy makers and practitioners recognized the nature and magnitude of violence against women in their communities. Studies reveal that recidivism rates in domestic violence incidents are high regardless of how they are measured. The most conservative measure, rearrest, yields a rate of 20 percent in some studies (Murphy, Musser, and Maton 1998). Victim interview data suggest significantly higher rates of 40 percent or more (Shepard 1992), and in some studies the rate of subsequent assault is as high as 80 percent (Garner, Fagan, and Maxwell 1995). Characterizing findings as "promising," Murphy and colleagues found support for the proposition that coordinated community interventions have a cumulative effect on reducing recidivism (Murphy et al. 1998).With a greater understanding of the responsibility for intervening in violence against women, communities recognize that conventional measures of intervention, such as lenient and casual responses to perpetrators, are ineffective. A more realistic and holistic approach to intervention is through investing resources in safety planning, legal counsel, social services, and protection.

VIOLENCE AGAINST WOMEN ACT (VAWA)

To continue to combat the violence that is now seen as normal, many people are working to restore traditional values and cultural beliefs. One of the most important of those values is that women are sacred. TVAWA, enacted by Congress in 1994 under 18 U.S.C. Section 2265, requires the enforcement of valid protection orders. Congress recognized the unique and extreme violence issues involving families and intimate relationships. This law and related statutes address the need to provide greater protection and enforcement of domestic violence laws. Section 2265, the full faith and credit section of the act, requires states, Indian tribes, and U.S. territories to enforce "foreign" protection orders from any other jurisdiction, including other counties, states, tribes, or U.S. territories (Guerrero 2003).

Full faith and credit as set for 18 U.S.C. Section 2265 permits a victim with a valid protection order in one state, tribe, or U.S. territory to leave and go anywhere in the country, to any U.S. tribe or U.S. territory, and still have that protective order enforced in that new jurisdiction with full force and effect (Guerrero 2003).

There are three types of legal measures that are designed to prevent further domestic violence or intimate partner violence: civil legal sanctions (protection orders), arrests, and domestic violence courts. These measures have mixed success in mainstream settings. For example, protection orders serve as a deterrent for some male perpetrators, but half reabuse and a few even kill their intimate partners (Fagan 1996). These findings have not been established specifically in Indian country.

Some very practical problems exist regarding legal limitations of tribal jurisdiction: often jurisdiction is not clear regarding law enforcement response; one protection order may not cover all jurisdictions; and there is no jurisdiction for criminal law enforcement by tribes against non-Indians. Strategies identified by Melissa Tatum (2002) include:

- Meet with neighboring, shared, or bordering jurisdictions to set procedure for response and enforceability of respective protection orders, take steps to coordinate and educate law enforcement, or change responses.
- Advise petitioner that multiple protection orders may be needed to cover shared jurisdictions.
- Tribes enforce civil sanctions over non-Indians. Tribes may need to create civil sanctions such as fines or banishment. Other ideas include garnishment of wages if employed on the reservation.
- Cross-deputize tribal officers.
- Develop a model code for full faith and credit.
- Develop a model order for protection for full faith and credit.

TITLE IX OF VAWA, 2005

The reauthorization of VAWA in 2005, Title IX, Section 904(a)(1)(2), authorizes the National Institute of Justice (NIJ), in consultation with the U.S. Department of Justice's Office on Violence against Women, to conduct research on violence against American Indian and Alaska Native women in Indian country. The needed research is broad in scope, and NIJ is actively developing a research program for multiple projects over an extended time period to address the issues.

The purposes of the research program are to:

- examine violence against American Indian and Alaska Native women (including domestic violence, dating violence, sexual assault, stalking, and murder) and identify factors that place American Indian and Alaska Native women at risk for victimization,
- evaluate the effectiveness of federal, state, tribal, and local responses to violence against American Indian and Alaska Native women, and
- propose recommendations to improve effectiveness of these responses.

Title IX of the VAWA 2005 requires the attorney general to establish a task force to assist the NIJ. The section 904 task force is to meet semiannually to provide advice and recommendations to NIJ regarding the conduct of the program. The attorney general will submit a report on the program's findings and recommendations to the U.S. Committee on Indian Affairs and to the U.S. House and Senate judiciary committees within two years after the enactment of Title IX.

The landmark American Recovery and Reinvestment Act of 2009 (Recovery Act), signed into law by President Obama, provided the Justice Department's Office on Violence against Women with $20.8 million for the Indian Tribal Governments Program to:

- decrease the number of violent crimes committed against Indian women,
- help Indian tribes use their independent authority to respond to crimes of violence against Indian women, and
- make sure that people who commit violent crimes against Indian women are held responsible for their actions.

Underscoring the legal issues, many tribal jurisdictions continue to struggle with the purpose of full faith and credit. Until recognition and enforcement of valid protection orders across jurisdictional lines is established, the time and efforts for "best" practices in intervention and prevention of violence against women is limited, if not paralyzed. Overall, the research indicates that the model of multilevel interventions (STOP grants), such as those used in mainstream communities and tribal communities, offers universal (education, public information) as well as selected intervention (intervention with perpetrator) strategies. Further, it is critical that specific interventions are designed to be culturally appropriate for each tribe.

IMPLICATIONS FOR THE FUTURE

The law defines domestic violence in very specific ways. Every state and U.S. territory has laws that allow its courts to issue protection orders, as do many Indian tribes. Each state, territory, or tribe decides for itself how to define domestic violence and how its laws will help and protect victims, so the laws are different from one state to another. To effect change, it will be critical to expand education and awareness efforts to increase positive attitudes toward nonviolence and encourage individuals to report family violence. Additional efforts underway include the federal and tribal task forces in place to assess the problem, develop an action plan, and monitor progress. The greatest value is found in the action to advocate laws and judicial procedures at the federal, state, and tribal levels that support and protect battered women.

REFERENCES

Alaska Native Commission. 1994. *Alaska Native Commission Final Report*. Anchorage, AK: Alaska Federation of Natives.

Brave Heart, M. Y. H. 1998. "The Return to the Sacred Path: Healing the Historical Trauma and Historical Unresolved Grief Response among the Lakota through a Psycho-Educational Intervention." *Smith College Studies in Social Work* 68(3): 287–305.

Brave Heart, M. Y. H. and DeBruyn, L. M. 1998. "The American Indian Holocaust: Healing Historical Unresolved Grief." *American Indian and Alaska Native Mental Health Research* 8, 56–78.

DeBruyn, Lemyra, Beverly Wilkins, and Karen Artichoker. 1990. "It's Not Cultural: Violence against Native American Women," paper prepared for the 89th American Anthropological Meeting, New Orleans, Louisiana, 144.

Easley, Cheryl and George P. Charles. 2004. "NRC for American Indian, Alaska Native, and Native Hawaiian Elders." Establishing Best Practices for Alaska Native Elders, University of Alaska, September.

Erwin, P. and G. Vidales. 2001. "Domestic Violence, People of Color and the Criminal Justice System: A Case for Prevention." [Electronic Version]. *Domestic Violence Research for Racial Justice Project*, 1–29.

Fagan, J. 1996. *The Criminalization of Domestic Violence: Promises and Limits*. Washington, DC: National Institute of Justice.

Fairchild, D. G., M. W. Fairchild, and S. Stoner. 1998. "Prevalence of Adult Domestic Violence among Women Seeking Routine Care in a Native American Health Care Facility." *American Journal of Public Health* 88, 1515–17.

Garner, J., J. Fagan, and C. Maxwell. 1995. "Published Findings from the Spouse Assault Replication Program: A Critical Review." *Journal of Quantitative Criminology* 11, 3–28.

Gray, N. 1998. "Addressing Trauma in Substance Abuse Treatment with American Indian Adolescents." *Journal of Substance Abuse Treatment* 15, 393–99.

Guerrero, Eleanor. 2003. "Unpublished Report: Full Faith and Credit: Encourage to Arrest." Boise, MT: Montana Department of Justice and the Montana Coalition against Domestic Violence.

Legal Momentum. 2005. "National Task Force to End Sexual and Domestic Violence against Women. Violence against Women Act 2005: Title IX-Tribal Programs." Washington, DC.

Murphy, C. M., P. H. Musser, and K. I. Maton. 1998. "Coordinated Community Intervention for Domestic Abusers: Intervention, System Involvement, and Criminal Recidivism." *Journal of Family Violence* 13(3): 263–84.

Napoleon, H. 1966. "YU'YA'RAQ: The Way of the Human Being." Unpublished manuscript. Hooper Bay, AK.

Native American Circle. 2004. "Unpublished Report: Reasons Why Indian Women Stay or Decline to Report Intimate Partner Violence." Avery, TX: Native American Circle.

O'Connor, A. 1995. "Evaluating comprehensive community initiatives: A view from history." In J. P. Connell, A. C. Kubisch, L. B. Schorr, and C. H. Weiss (Eds.), *New approaches to evaluating community initiatives: Concepts, methods, and contexts* (pp. 23–63). Washington, DC: Aspen Institute.

Oetzel, J. and B. Duran. 2004. "Intimate Partner Violence in American Indian and/or Alaska Native Communities: A Social Ecological Framework of Determinants and Interventions." *American Indian and Alaska Native Mental Health Research, Journal of the National Center* 11(3).

Ross, R. 1996. *Return to the Teachings*. Toronto, ONT: Penguin Books.

Schechter, S. 1982. "Toward an Analysis of Violence against Women in the Family." In S. Schechter (Ed.), *Women and Male Violence: The Visions and Struggles of the Battered Women's Movement* (pp. 209–240). Boston: South End Press.

Segal, B. 2001. "Responding to Victimized Alaska Native Women in Treatment for Substance Use." *Substance Use and Misuse* 36, 845–65.

Segal, B., et al. 1999. *Alaska Natives Combating Substance Abuse and Related Violence through Self-Healing: A Report to the People.* Anchorage: Alaska Federation of Natives.

Shepard, M. 1992. "Predicting Batterer Recidivism Five Years after Community Intervention." *Journal of Family Violence* 7, 167–78.

Shkilnyk, A. M. 1985. *A Poison Stronger Than Love: The Destruction of an Ojibwa Community.* New Haven, CT: Yale University Press.

Smith, Andrea. 2002. *Color Lines.* Oakland, CA: ARC Publications.

Tatum, Melissa. 2002. "A Jurisdictional Quandary: Challenges Facing Tribal Governments in Implementing the Full Faith and Credit Provisions of the Violence against Women Acts." 90Ky. L. J. 123. University of Kentucky College of Law.

Tjaden, P. and N. Thoennes. 2000a, July. *Extent, Nature, and Consequences of Intimate Partner Violence: Findings from the National Violence Against Women Survey.* National Institute of Justice 1811867.

Tjaden, P. and N. Thoennes. 2000b. *Full Report of the Prevalence, Incidence, and Consequences of Violence Against Women.* US Department of Justice.

White Buffalo Calf Woman Society, Inc. 2011. Brochure.

Williams, L. A. 2002. *Family Violence and American Indians/Alaska Natives: A Report to the Indian Health Service.* Rockville, MD: Indian Health Service.

CHAPTER 10

Native American Women: HIV/AIDS Risk and Activism

Irene S. Vernon

INTRODUCTION

On June 5, 1981, the Centers for Disease Control (CDC) reported in its *Morbidity and Mortality Weekly* (CDC 1981b) a description of a rare and fatal lung infection affecting gay (homosexual) men in Los Angeles, California. This report initiated a 30-year battle against acquired immune deficiency syndrome (AIDS) and the human immunodeficiency virus (HIV). In 1981, little was known about the cause of the disease, how it was transmitted, how it was to be prevented, how to treat it, and who was "really" at risk for contracting it. Because it was initially found predominately in white males, it was first thought that HIV/AIDS was a disease that afflicted mainly white gay men, not heterosexuals, people of color, women, or children. This is no longer the case. HIV/AIDS is a global health problem that is found in every society and among all races and ethnic groups.

AN INTERNATIONAL PROBLEM

Despite progress in diagnosis and treatment, the devastation and fear of HIV/AIDS is found in all societies. When a person develops AIDS, he or she is usually in the late stages of a series of health problems caused by a retrovirus, the human T-cell lymphotrophic virus type 3 (HTLV-3). The decline in an individual's health increases as the virus (HIV) starts to infect a variety of cells in the body and destroys T-cells, the white blood cells that are necessary for defending the body against invading microorganism. Because the HIV invades and becomes integrated into the T-cells, it becomes a source of permanent infection and damages the body's natural immune system (AIDS.gov n.d.).

There are two outcomes when a person becomes infected with HIV: (1) some individuals remain well but carry the virus and are able to infect others; (2) others develop an AIDS-related complex (ARC), which results in fatigue, fever, loss of appetite, and swollen nodes in the neck, armpits, or groin (Sevelius, Carrico, and Johnson 2010). People who develop fatal illness with AIDS have compromised immunity that fails to protect them from either Kaposi's sarcoma, a type of skin cancer, or *Pneumocystis carini* pneumonia, a fatal parasitic infection of the lungs. Prior to the development of highly active medication combinations in the 1990s, many individuals advanced from the HIV stage to the life-threatening stage of AIDS within a couple of years, but today it may take decades, with the CDC "recalculating, revising, and studying" how many people will develop AIDS and how soon (CDC 2008).

Today, mortality due to AIDS is at over 30 million people worldwide, a figure that includes more than 615,000 in the United States. Worldwide, women represent 15.9 million of the 33.3 million people living with HIV/AIDS (AVERT n.d.). And as noted, this is no longer strictly a "gay white male disease" but one that also affects people of color, women, and children. AIDS is also the leading cause of death and morbidity worldwide for women between the ages of 15 and 44 in low- and middle-income countries (Office of Global AIDS Coordinator 2011).

In 2009, 20 percent of all individuals diagnosed with AIDS in the United States were females, and 24 percent of those diagnosed with HIV were females (CDC 2009:18, 21–22). Sadly, every 9-1/2 minutes someone in the United States is infected with HIV. The HIV/AIDS surveillance data indicate that HIV incidence among women in the United States increased slightly during the late 1980s but decreased in the early 1990s and has since remained fairly stable (Hall et al. 2008:520). When the data are examined by race or ethnicity, the overall trend for this group tends to show more increases than decreases.

NATIVE AMERICANS AND THEIR VIEWS ABOUT HIV/AIDS

Most people today have a general understanding of the origins of AIDS, but not all share this understanding. For example, conspiracy theories about the origin of HIV/AIDS are found among many racial and ethnic groups in the United States, including Native Americans. Some Native Americans feel that AIDS was created by the federal government as a form of genocide, others believe it evolved from the misuse of research, while some believe it was created as a means to eliminate gay people (Gilley and Keesee 2007:44). Others refer to it as the "new smallpox." This association recalls earlier attempts by the U.S. military to distribute blankets contaminated with smallpox as a way to help eradicate some tribes. Mortality due to smallpox depopulated many tribes and completely decimated others (Vernon 2001:1–2,81). The perceived connection to smallpox carries with it a strong sense of distrust some Native Americans have against the U.S. government. Conspiracy beliefs aside, HIV/AIDS is a serious concern for Native people and is seen as a threat to the health and survival of Native Americans. The threat is especially urgent for Native women as they are important to reproduction and the ongoing maintenance of the core of tribal traditions and cultures.

HIV/AIDS IN NATIVE COMMUNITIES

The most recent data, reported in 2011, show that the estimated number of Native people diagnosed with AIDS was 3,700 (CDC 2009: 21), a number that represents less than 1 percent of all reported cases. This low percentage may appear to be inconsequential, but there is a problem with the accuracy of the data. Data on Indian health tend to be questioned because of recurring problems of underreporting and racial misclassification. Available data on HIV/AIDS and its impact on the Native American population, however, cannot be dismissed. Between 2006 and 2009, the CDC reported that the annual rate of AIDS diagnoses has been decreasing for African Americans, Hispanics, and whites, but the downward trend is not evident for Native Americans, Asians, and Pacific Islanders. The latter groups do not show a steady decline (CDC 2009:21). This trend over four years is illustrated in Table 10.1.

The data presented for Native Americans, Asians, and Pacific Islanders in Table 10.1 does not explain whether the fluctuation is a reflection of improved screening or whether present prevention

Table 10.1
AIDS Diagnosis by Year and by Race/Ethnicity (rates per 100,000), 2006 to 2009

Race/Ethnicity	2006	2007	2008	2009
American Indian/ Alaska Native	6.4	6.1	7.6	6.6
Asian	3.3	3.5	3.7	3.1
Black/African American	47.4	46.5	45.7	44.4
Hispanic/Latino	16.1	15.2	14.3	13.9
Native Hawaiian/Other Pacific Islander	11.7	12.0	9.2	11.2
White	5.3	5.0	4.8	4.7
Multiple Races	16.5	15.3	13.9	15.1

Source: CDC 2011:21.

strategies are not as effective for these groups as for others. Without more research, it is difficult to determine what accounts for the fluctuation or the uneven trend. Despite the questions the data raise, good ongoing surveillance data is essential to help formulate useful prevention efforts as well as early screening and treatment.

When data for the rates of HIV diagnoses over time are examined, the overall trend indicates Hispanics, Native Hawaiian and other Pacific Islanders, and whites show a steady decline compared to American Indians/Alaska Natives and Asians. Table 10.2 summarizes this observation.

Table 10.2
HIV Diagnosis by Year and by Race/Ethnicity (rates per 100,000), 2006 to 2009

Race/Ethnicity	2006	2007	2008	2009
American Indian/Alaska Native	8.8	9.9	10.2	9.8
Asian	5.5	6.9	6.6	6.4
Black/African American	65.7	65.7	67.4	66.6
Hispanic/Latino	25.1	24.8	23.0	22.8
Native Hawaiian/Other Pacific Islander	31.4	27.1	20.0	21.0
White	7.4	7.5	7.2	7.2
Multiple Races	21.8	21.9	19.0	16.7

Source: CDC 2011:17.

Since public health efforts have established a surveillance of the HIV/AIDS epidemic, it is shown that Native American males, particularly men who have sex with men (MSMs), account for higher rates of HIV/AIDS than Native women. When the rates for Native women are compared to the rate for women from other racial or ethnic groups, the rates for Native women were usually higher. For example, the rates of AIDS diagnosis for Native females in 2009 was 2.9 per 100,000 compared to 1.5 per 100,000 for white women and 1.3 per 100,000 for Asian women (CDC 2009:27). Similarly, the rate of HIV for Native women (6.6 per 100,000) was higher when compared to Asian women (3.4 per 100,000) and white women (2.4 per 100,000) (CDC 2009:25). It is apparent that although Native males are more likely to have higher rates of HIV/AIDS, Native women are at high risk for contracting HIV or AIDS. Their risk factors, however, are not unique but are similar to those found for African American and Hispanic women, the two other groups of minority women with high rates of HIV/AIDS.

PROBLEM WITH NATIVE AMERICAN DATA

According to the federal Indian Health Service (IHS), the systematic collection, analysis, interpretation, and dissemination of HIV/AIDS data on Native Americans are fraught with problems and have led many to question the usefulness of some surveillance information (IHS 1996). This concern over surveillance data began in the late 1960s when it was discovered that racial misclassification was common. Native Americans were often racially misclassified on death certificates although their birth certificates indicate that they were either American Indians or Alaska Natives.

Although IHS, the key federal health care delivery system for tribes residing on federal reservations or rancherias (small homesteads), attempted to correct this problem, it remains a complicated problem to resolve (IHS 1996). In addition to concerns over accuracy of surveillance data, some researchers working with Native communities also report that due to mistrust of state or local governments, some tribes are not always willing to collaborate on data collection, adding another layer to the problems associated with data gaps. In some instances, the distrust may go both ways, where state or local governments do not ask for tribal participation in data collection or other surveillance activities. Epidemiologists and others indicate that this cloud of distrust can weaken surveillance systems and could "result in a failure to recognize or respond effectively to control an outbreak on tribal lands or that involves AI/AN people" (Bertolli et al. 2008:139).

To develop and strengthen their own health surveillance, the Urban Indian Health Institute (UIHI), a epidemiology center located in Seattle, Washington, urges its national coalition of urban Indian health organizations to use health information technology (HIT) to capture more accurate data to compensate for the lack of standardized and accurate primary and secondary health data (UIHI 2010:4–5,25). Another national Indian health organization, the National Indian Health Board (NIHB), echoes a similar need by asking reservation-based tribal health programs to strengthen their data management capacity by using and seeking technical assistance and training made available through the resources of the public health workforce (NIHB 2010:39–41).

The concern with health data also has implications for programs and groups concerned with HIV/AIDS data on Native Americans. In 1991, several scholars questioned data reporting the prevalence of HIV/AIDS for Native Americans and suggested underreporting as one of the major problems in addition to the racial misclassification (Metler, Conway, and Stehr-Green 1991:1470). Metler's research team's position was supported by others familiar with the epidemic of HIV/AIDS for Native Americans (Bertolli, Lee, and Sullivan 2007:388; Bertolli et al. 2004:234; Kelly et al. 1996:92). Understandably, poor quality or lack of quality of HIV/AIDS data not only contributes to the underestimation of infection rates but can potentially lead to the "under-allocation of resources and lack of support for services and programs tailored to American Indians/Alaska Natives (AI/AN) needs" (Bertolli et al. 2007:388). The data collection process and data accuracy, however, remains a complex problem that tribes, states, and governmental agencies need to address in order to have a more reliable accounting of Native health status and to effectively allocate resources where needed.

Another reason why many question the accuracy of HIV/AIDS data for Native Americans is related to the opposition held by many tribal members to testing for HIV/AIDS. This opposition is also sometimes rooted in their lack of trust for Western medicine and the medical system. For some tribes, the introduction of Western medicine to Native Americans has a long history of mistrust, some of it due to high mortality rates in these facilities during the early reservation period. Another factor that adds to the mistrust is the concern of community members over patient confidentiality, a real concern when one lives in small rural communities where there are usually few secrets. The other concern often reported is that of a cultural barrier, a belief that to volunteer to be tested or screened for HIV/AIDS is like wishing for the presence of the disease.

An additional reason given, especially by Native women, is the distrust they have of the medical system because of the history of forced sterilization received by some Native women while under the medical care of the IHS (Lawrence 2000:400). Reluctance expressed by some health care providers is another barrier to HIV/AIDS screening. Some health professionals who provide health care to Native Americans say they do not suggest or encourage screening because they have difficulty discussing sexuality (IHS 2007:17).

There is no question that getting individuals tested is vital for determining the "true" number of HIV/AIDS infections. In many cases, some communities do not initiate HIV/AIDS screening until health statistics prove alarming. In many tribal reservation communities where the census is low, even a couple cases of HIV/AIDS can quickly become a public concern. For example, the Navajo Area IHS did not expand their HIV/AIDS screening until epidemiological data showed an increase in the number of cases. In 2000, there were 15 people diagnosed with HIV on the Navajo reservation. In 2009, there were 40 new cases, and before the year 2010 ended 35 new cases were reported (Calvin 2011). In discussing this increase, Mr. Melvin Harrison, the executive director of the Navajo AIDS Network, expressed a special concern about the "increasing number of women being diagnosed with HIV" and advocated for expanding the testing program (Calvin 2011).

The expansion of the screening program, however, is not easy to implement due to cost and the distance people have to travel to access health care. For example, not all rural clinics on the Navajo Reservation offer screening, and if offered, the service targets only those deemed at high risk. Currently, most of the testing on the Navajo Reservation is conducted as part of patient care in either outpatient or inpatient services of the hospital and is available to individuals between the ages 13 and 64. Priority for testing, however, is given to patients receiving urgent care or women receiving prenatal care.

NATIVE WOMEN AT RISK

The incidence and prevalence of HIV/AIDS as well as resource allocation for prevention and treatment cannot be driven by the numbers alone and must also take into account other key social determinants of health such as income, health services, and social environment. A comprehensive approach is especially necessary to obtain a greater understanding of the impact of HIV/AIDS on Native women who are increasingly at greater risk for HIV/AIDS. When the book *Women, Poverty and AIDS: Sex, Drugs and Structural Violence* by Farmer and colleagues was released a decade ago, Farmer persuasively argued that poverty and social inequality were main drivers of the HIV/AIDS epidemic for men and women (Farmer et al. 1996). This position remains true today.

It is well known now that women of color in the United States. are disproportionately impacted by this disease. African American women 13 years and older account for 64 percent the estimated number of individuals diagnosed with AIDS, although they represent only 12 percent of the U.S. female population. Hispanic women, too, represent only 14 percent of the U.S. female population but account for 18 percent of the estimated cases of individuals with AIDS (Kaiser 2011a; Kaiser 2011b). Statistics on Native American women are more difficult to capture, but Native Americans represent less than 1 percent of the United States population, and therefore it is not surprising that Native women have lower rates than other racial or ethnic women diagnosed with HIV/AIDS. All of these women of color, however, share similar risks for HIV/AIDS, namely low income, often as single heads of household with greater family responsibilities, and limited access to health care because of poverty (Kaiser 2011a).

Research findings indicate that some of the key risks for HIV infection for women include unprotected heterosexual sex with a partner who has HIV or AIDS. Unprotected sex places all women at risk because men have higher levels of HIV in their semen than women's vaginal fluids; thus a male-to-female transmission is approximately eight times more efficient than female-to-male transmission (Padian et al. 1997:354).

Although HIV infection diagnosis is lower for Native women than other racial or ethnic women, their risk for HIV/AIDS is greater because of the high prevalence of sexually transmitted disease (STD) in this population (Vernon 2001:46; Vernon 2000). Having had or having an active case of STD increases the woman's risk for getting infected with HIV because the STD infection provides a convenient entry point for the virus through the infected broken tissues such as open sores or other microscopic breaks in the tissue. Individuals who are infected with both HIV and STD are also more infectious and are more likely to shed HIV in the genital secretions (Wasserheit 1999:549).

According to a national 2009 surveillance report, STD remains a serious public health problem, especially for members of racial or ethnic minority populations. The rate of STD for Native Americans is high. For example, the chlamydia rate for Native Americans is 776.5 per 100,000 and the rate for gonorrhea is 113.3 per 100,000, or 4.3 times and 4.2 times higher, respectively, than rates reported for whites (CDC 2009:8,18). Between 2008 and 2009, the rates of reported syphilis increased 4.3 percent for Native Americans while they decreased 4.5 percent for whites (CDC 2009:34).

It should be noted that the chlamydia rate for Native women is four times the rate reported for Native men, that is, 1,214.9 per 100,000 compared to 323.8 per 100,000, respectively. The gonorrhea rate for Native women is also twice that of Native men, 147.3 per 100,000 and 78.2 per 100,000, respectively (CDC 2009:72,73). One of the reasons for this glaring gender difference may be the fact that women are more likely to seek medical care and therefore can be tested for STD.

STD rates vary regionally among Native communities. The highest rates are found in three Indian Service geographic areas: Aberdeen (Plains states), Alaska, and Tucson (in southern Arizona). According to the IHS, the chlamydia rate in Alaska is highest for women between the ages of 15 and 24: 11,483 per 100,000 in 2007 (CDC/IHS 2007:14,18,20). Compared to the rest of the state's population, Alaska Natives represent the highest rate of that state's prevalence of STD. In 2009, 67 percent of Alaska's reported gonorrhea cases and 50 percent of the chlamydia cases were Alaska Natives (Simons and Jessen 2011:70). The high rate of STD obviously places these women at greater risk for HIV infection.

In an examination of data on Native Americans infected with HIV in three different metropolitan areas in the western United States, researchers found HIV rates higher among younger Native Americans than among non-Natives. The study also reported that those with HIV were more likely to be female and to have other existing comorbidity including STD and tuberculosis. Women who have been "diagnosed with psychiatric illnesses and alcoholism" are also at greater risk (Diamond et al. 2001:639; Baldwin et al. 2000). By all indications, for this population as well as for others, STD was identified as a key risk factor for HIV, a finding that calls for increased public health interventions that include funding for more aggressive STD testing and treatment.

As mentioned before, poor socioeconomic circumstances place individuals at greater risk for STD and HIV/AIDS. Numerous sources, including reports issued by the Substance Abuse and Mental Health Services Administration on findings of the National Survey on Drug Use and Health (NSDUH), cite poverty as an important risk factor for HIV/AIDS, a situation that threatens many Native American communities where poverty is endemic (NSDUH 2010a). The most recent census placed a higher percentage of Native people than whites below the poverty line (25.7% versus 12.4%, respectively). The role of poverty and its impact on health is also illustrated in the report by IHS, a report which presents Indian health data by different geographical regions. The IHS regions with the highest STD rates also had the highest rates of poverty for Native women. These regions included the Tohono O'odham reservation, located in south-central Arizona, where two in five or 40.8 percent of Native women live in poverty. And in South Dakota, Native women with high rates of STD were also those who were most impoverished (Caiazza, Shaw, and Werschkul 2004:11,12).

When economic circumstances for Native women are compared to those of white women, the disparity is alarming. For example, the median household income for Native women is $24,000 versus $54,536 for white women. Moreover, 32.9 percent of Native females are heads of household compared to 17.4 percent of white women (Grant Makers Health 2009:7,8). It is well known that most Native women who are single heads of household generally have expanded personal and financial responsibilities beyond the immediate family that include other members of the extended family such as grandparents, aunts, uncles, and other children in need.

Because poverty is often associated with the lack of quality health care, poverty is integrally tied to a greater risk for HIV infection. Poverty also indirectly speeds up the progression of HIV to full-blown AIDS, a situation resulting in higher rates of morbidity and premature mortality. Results from one study conducted with a tribe in the western United States found that the most common barrier to quality health care for persons with HIV/AIDS included the "lack of knowledge about what service were or were not available, lack of money, lack of transportation, and long waits for appointments and/or inconvenient clinic hours" (Duran et al. 2000:29).

A Native woman who was diagnosed with AIDS spoke of her challenges in accessing health care as a result of poverty. She states, "I live on a very limited income. I have to be very careful about my budget and try to make sure that I have enough money set aside so I will have gas money to get to my doctor appointments" (Seasons 1997/1998:5).

Lack of transportation has been cited by several Native women as a serious barrier to accessing health care. Transportation is especially difficult for families living in rural communities where public transportation is lacking and where cost of gas is expensive and available health care facilities miles away. A Native woman with HIV said she had to travel "as far as 300 miles one way to a health clinic," and another woman described how, when the weather made the road to her home difficult, she said she "traveled on foot to a main road . . . then hitchhiked to her doctor appointments" (Vernon 2001:50). More than half of tribal health organizations surveyed by the NIHB reported a distance of over 50 miles to access health care services with the average distance reported as "123 miles, one way" (NIHB 2010:33).

Native women who rely primarily on IHS for prevention and treatment services indicate that the availability of these services varied from one facility to the next. Prevention services such as testing may be offered in all 12 IHS geographic regions, but not all facilities offer treatment, so most patients who are being treated for HIV/AIDS are referred to other facilities (IHS 2007:16,18). The IHS cites a number of reasons why their health care delivery system lacks resources to treat patients with HIV/AIDS. Some of their reasons given include that there were few patients with AIDS within their service areas or that their staff have little or limited experience in delivering AIDS treatments. IHS also cites the need for their facilities to respond to other urgent health priorities (IHS 2007:20).

Understandably, poverty creates many barriers for patients to maintain healthy living, and poverty is also a major contributor to the lack of resources to help those with HIV/AIDS. These circumstances make it difficult for many Native families to overcome the health challenges they face. Poverty puts them at risk for HIV infection, especially when it is combined with problems of substance abuse and violence. A recent study of individuals with HIV found that those living in poverty and who are between the ages of 18 and 25 had the greatest need for HIV/AIDS treatment but received the lowest rate of treatment. In this study, 21.6 percent of Natives Americans needed treatment compared to 15.3 percent of whites (NSDUH 2010b:1).

The importance of addressing the comorbidity issue of substance abuse is clear: when one is under the influence of alcohol or drugs, one's inhibitions are decreased, perceptions altered, and the ability to make healthy sexual choices limited. A number of Native Americans who have a drinking problem report blacking out while drinking, engaging in unprotected sex, and having multiple partners while under the influence of alcohol or drugs (Baldwin et al. 2000). It is not surprising that approximately a quarter of individuals diagnosed with HIV/AIDS are also in need of substance use treatment (NSDUH 2010a).

These high-risk behaviors create an ideal climate for transmission of HIV infection. Another recent survey found that individuals who used an illicit drug intravenously sometime in their life were 30 times more likely to have HIV/AIDS than those who never used illicit drugs (NSDUH 2010a). A number of studies have provided some insight into Native women's substance use or misuse and HIV/AIDS. One Native woman who tested positive for HIV spoke about how she and others with HIV have been victims of abuse. She said she and others "all had experienced sexual and/or physical abuse, all have substance abuse issues, and have engaged in unsafe sex" (Sailors and Daliparthy 2005:275). Other researchers note that Native female drug users report having engaged in more high-risk behaviors than Native men. These women reported higher numbers of sex partners and using contaminated or used drug paraphernalia (Stevens, Estrada, and Estrada 2000:39).

Another study discusses the experiences of Native women who used drugs and often deferred to their male partners in the relationship, especially if the sex partner happened to be a white male. For example, some Native Alaskan women in one study with white male partners were reluctant to ask their partner to use a condom (Fenaughty et al. 1998:275–76). Another Native female drug user who lives in Arizona commented about the lack of concern about HIV/AIDS risk behavior when she said: "Y'know, when you're using your drugs, you're not worrying about... protecting yourself for sex, y'know. You're worrying about your drug" (Baldwin et al. 1999:286).

The complex web of substance abuse and risky sexual behavior is difficult to untangle for women in any society. Some Native women say they use alcohol and drugs to cope with violence and trauma in their lives even though the substance use places them at greater risk for HIV (Fisher et al. 2000). Other Native women who are in abusive relationships say they fear for their lives, fear abandonment, fear for the safety of their children, and are forced to make unhealthy choices about sex. One Native woman, for example, lamented, "In fact, the person that infected me turned out to be very abusive.... He gave me the virus.... He knew he had it, but he did not tell me" (Sailors and Daliparthy 2005:276).

Women who have experienced violence in relationships often engage in risky sexual behaviors, and sadly, Native women who encounter violence regularly are also at a higher risk of being murdered. Bachman and colleagues (2008:20,33,36) report that Native women in these types of relationships are three times more likely to experience rape or sexual assault than white women and more likely to acquire injuries that need medical attention.

HISTORICAL TRAUMA AND RISK BEHAVIORS

Risk for HIV/AIDS, however, must be contextualized in order to understand why Native women take these risks. One theory that is frequently cited involves the unresolved historic or intergenerational trauma. Historical intergenerational trauma is defined as traumatic experiences or events that leave deep negative emotional impacts that are passed down from one generation to the next. The basis for some of this lingering trauma includes the loss of lives, land, and vital aspects of Native culture. Brave Heart, Yellow Horse, and Debruyne (1998) define historical trauma as events that continue to "contribute to the current social pathology" of Native peoples" (p. 60).

The experiences of childhood physical, sexual, and psychological trauma for women add other avenues for HIV risk and other abnormal behaviors or situations that result in arrested personal development, low self-esteem, high alcohol and drug use, poor parenting skills, and failure in sustaining relationships, all behaviors that result in destructive sexual relationships, acceptance of multiple sexual partners, and even prostitution. When examining risk behaviors for HIV among a sample of urban Native women, Walters and Simoni (1999) found that "trauma and AOD (alcohol and other drug use) played a key role in risk-taking sexual behaviors" (p. 244). Walters states that "for American Indian women, non-partner sexual trauma was associated with IDU (intravenous drug use), which, in turn, accounted for a significant part of the relationship between non-partner sexual trauma and high-risk sex" (Simoni, Sehgal, and Walters 2004:42).

Historical trauma has also been found to impact family relationships, particularly parenting. Policies that were part of colonizing Native Americans impaired parenting skills by forcibly removing children from their families and placing them in boarding schools. This practice severed these children from their natural world where generations before them learned parenting skills through caring for their younger siblings or other children (Bigfoot 2008:54). Until the early 1950s, Native children were forcibly placed in boarding schools operated by the federal government or designated missionary organizations. Most of the schools were strategically and purposefully located many miles away from the home community of the children, and therefore the boarding school robbed them of learning their language, cultural traditions, and their adult roles.

BEING A RESPONSIBLE PARENT

Native women who struggle with addictions say they find it extremely hard to manage their lives and to adequately care for their children. One Native woman, pregnant after she exchanged sex for drugs and got infected with HIV, voiced the difficulties she has in accepting motherhood. She stated: "I don't want to be responsible. I want to keep drinking; I want to keep drugging," and adds: "This baby is in the way; I was too messed up" (Fernandez, Keigher, and Stevens 2005:72–73). Drug and alcohol addiction aside, HIV-positive women, generally, encounter a great deal of stress over the demands of family responsibilities and the disruption of their relationships with others, including their children.

Stress is a major concern for many women who are HIV positive and who must balance their own health care needs as well as the needs of their family and particularly their children. Those who are single heads of household have additional burdens, indicating that their individual health is usually neglected for the sake of their family (Hartman et al. 2006). Many mothers who care for, protect, and nurture their children while living with HIV/AIDS also worry about how their children will be treated if and when their health status becomes publicly known. Some say they do not want to burden their children with their diagnosis for fear of discrimination that might target their children.

Not all women, however, see motherhood as a burden. Some of them, although they have considerable parenting responsibilities and encounter "good and bad" sick days, refer to their children or their child as "a gift," "a miracle," or a "blessing" and describe how being a mother motivates them to survive and that their children make their lives worthwhile (Vernon 2001:4; Fernandez et al. 2005:73; Seasons 1997/1998:7; POZ 2011; Project Positive 2011).

THE YOUNG GIRLS

When examining issues related to Native women and HIV/AIDS, attention must also be paid to young Native girls as they are also at great risk for HIV/AIDS. According to CDC (2008), young people (between the ages of 15 and 25) worldwide accounted for 45 percent of all new HIV infections in 2007. In the United States, this epidemic remained concentrated among minority youth and especially young MSMs. Risk factors most often reported for female adolescents in the United States include substance use, initiation of sex at an early age, lack of recognition of possible risk that would come from the partners, having sex with older men, and lack of awareness (CDC 2008).

The potential for being infected with HIV for the young is especially worrisome because in comparison to the rest of the U.S. population, the Native Americans population is younger; specifically, 33 percent of Native Americans are under the age of 18 years compared to 26 percent of the total U.S. population of all races (U.S. Census 2006). Adolescents and young adults also tend to increase their risk for HIV/AIDS when they are also engaged in other risk behaviors such as drug use and abuse.

Barlow and colleagues (2010) found that Native adolescents report higher lifetime as well as recent use of illicit drugs than any other racial or ethnic group. Between 2006 and 2008, Native youth over age 12 were three times more likely to use methamphetamines (meth) than other racial or ethnic groups, 1.4 percent versus 0.54 percent, respectively (p. 1). Of grave concern, however, is high drug use found among female teens. Barlow's team of researchers found, in their sample of pregnant Native teens, the lifetime meth use rate was three times more than that reported for non-Native teens in other previous national studies. These teens' use of meth in the past month was twice that reported by other racial or ethnic youth. The reported meth use during pregnancy by these Native teens was five times higher than found in a national sample of pregnant women (p. 16).

The teen birth rate for Native Americans is higher than the national average. According to the NSDUH, when teen mothers (ages 15–19) are compared by race, Native mothers far outnumber white teen mothers, 9.4 percent versus 3.4 percent, respectively (NSDUH 2011). While teen pregnancy is often discouraged and stigmatized, some culture groups do not see this situation as a problem. The acceptance of teen motherhood as the norm tends to be found among culture groups that highly value babies. In most Native American communities, teen mothers are not stigmatized (Kaufman et al. 2007:2160).

Although data on sexual behavior for Native adolescents is sparse, some efforts have been made to get a better understanding through surveys. The UIHI found in their survey that Native youth living in urban communities do engage in high-risk sexual behavior; for instance, compared to white peers, a higher percentage of them report having had sexual intercourse, and some reported having had multiple sex partners or recently had sex with at least one partner (UIHI 2010). What is most alarming from the data reported by the UIHI is that many of the youth reported their "initiation of sexual intercourse before the age 13," and that many of these sexual behaviors resulted in pregnancy for Native females, a rate that was nearly three times that for white female youth (UIHI 2010:17). Native youth also reported that compared to white youth they were "less likely to have been taught about AIDS or HIV infection in school" (UIHI 2010:17).

Another common risk factor for HIV/AIDS for young Native females is having sex with older men, mainly because they are not mature enough to make healthy choices or know enough to engage in safe sex, especially with older men. The UIHI (2010) study found that urban Native women between the ages 15 and 24 "were more likely to have had their first sexual experience with a partner who was 4–6 years older," a finding that is higher than reported for their white peers. UIHI also found that compared to whites Native American youth were twice as likely to have a nonvoluntary first sexual encounter (UIHI 2010:26–27). This study also notes that urban Native women who reported forced sexual intercourse were often raped before the age of 15, another unhealthy situation that places them at risk for STD, HIV, and teen pregnancy. Although the numbers who are raped are alarming, it is not clear how many of these cases were reported to law enforcement.

SURVIVING AND LIVING TO TELL THE STORY

In listening to and reading the stories of Native women with HIV/ AIDS, their routes to the infection include drug use, sleeping with a drug user, and heterosexual contact. Their stories tell of relationships that were riddled with lies, abuse, violence, denial, and a sustained state of powerlessness. The strength of their stories is not, however, how they contracted their disease but how they continued to survive and live with the infection. As one woman stated: "There were no holidays off from this disease, no waking up one day to just have a free day or time apart from it" (Vernon 2011). Many of these women struggle with living with their disease while battling poverty, substance abuse, unresolved grief, and violence.

Other Native women have been able to find a healthy way to live, and many women choose the path of activism. Bonnie Blackwolf, for example, who died of AIDS in December 1997, understood that once she was diagnosed with HIV her new role was to educate others. One of her messages was, "AIDS is clearly a tool of genocide . . . knowing what we know, we've got to be responsible about choices that we make, and make choices that don't endanger ourselves and our own people" (Caldwell 1999:47).

Tori, a Native woman who was exposed to many of the risk factors for HIV, including being raised by a poor single mother, child maltreatment, neglect, and rape at the age of nine by four boys, was able to cope with her HIV/AIDS diagnosis by reconnecting with her traditional tribal roots and developing a strong and protective relationship with her son (Fernandez et al. 2005). Her desire is to educate young Native Americans about the dangers of HIV/AIDS. She focuses on what she sees as misinformation and says that, "Native youth see any STD out there as a white man's disease. Used to be the gay disease . . . so to talk to the Native youth, you have to be real and honest" (Fernandez et al. 2005:79).

Shana Cozad, who did not use drugs and had very little sexual experience, contracted the disease in college from an older man. Although, prior to the sexual encounter, she had asked if he ever had an STD or HIV test, he told her, "I don't have any STDs. I have tested for everything. I don't have anything. . . . There's no reason why we would have to bring condoms into this relationship" (Ford 2011). Shana was lied to and was placed in danger partly through her own misconceptions or misperceptions she had about a person with AIDS or HIV. She describes such a person as

People who have AIDS, they look sick, they are sick; they are not going to university, they're somewhere dying and they're in wheelchairs and they're hooked up to IVs and they're hooked up to oxygen tanks and that certainly wasn't what he looked like. He was completely healthy looking. And he never got sick and never went to the doctor. And we lived together. Of course he wasn't 'that way.' (Ford 2011)

Shana's partner did have HIV, a virus that he gave to Shana. Shana has now been living with HIV for 18 years but says she made a commitment to not "sit quietly at home and just not do anything about it." So her activism is to make sure that there will not be "another single person to be infected because of lack of education or lack of resources" (Ford 2011). Her goal is to work with Native people so they can have better access to HIV/AIDS education, and she says she feels that she has done her job when individuals know where to get tested and know the true facts about the disease (Ford 2011).

Lisa Tiger, a Muscogee Creek woman who has been HIV positive for 23 years, is another outspoken advocate (woman warrior). Since her diagnosis in 1992, she has crisscrossed the country sharing her story with others. She never shies away from discussing her disease or tries to hide behind the shame of having HIV. She tells how from the time of her diagnosis she has openly disclosed her health status with her family, friends, and others. Her strength is to be admired. She is raising a daughter and is a foster mother to four Native children who were abused. She took in all of these children so they would not be separated and placed in different foster homes. She not only cares for others but makes sure to take care of herself. She says she eats well and exercises often by walking or running a mile "every day for over four years" and tracks her activities on Facebook (POZ 2011). Today, despite her demanding parenting role, with full-blown AIDS and Parkinson's disease, she continues to travel and give presentations about HIV/AIDS prevention.

Tiger tells her story mainly to Native audiences to help heal and to prevent what happened to her from happening to someone else. She speaks with conviction, compassion, and love. For example, when talking to those who are infected, she generally closes her presentation with words of wisdom: "Don't waste your time blaming yourself or others for your diagnosis. Time is precious. Spend it making plans for your fabulous future" (POZ 2011), and to those who are not infected, to be beware and get tested to know your status. Although Native women are at risk for HIV/AIDS, there are other Native women who are there to nurture and care for their health and safety. Many Native women who have HIV have taken the traditional road of generosity and love for their sisters along with a commitment to the survival of Native women, children, tribes, and communities.

There is no question that many of the lives of these women who have HIV or AIDS have been shaped by historical forces as well as varying circumstances that have led not only to their contemporary health conditions but also to their commitment to activism to help others. Many of these women continue to enrich their own lives through their work on behalf of others and continue to help shape the future of their people.

REFERENCES

AIDS.gov. n.d. "HIV/AIDS Basics–Immune System 101." Accessed August 24, 2011. http://www.aids.gov/hiv-aids-basics/diagnosed-with-hiv-aids/hiv-in-your-body/immune-system-101/.

AIDS Info Website. n.d. "National Women and Girls HIV/AIDS Awareness Day." Accessed March 17, 2011. http://aidsinfor.ni.gov/other/specialityPage.aspx?pageID-30.

AVERT. n.d. "Worldwide HIV and AIDS Statistics." Accessed July 27, 2011. http://www.avert.org/worldstats.htm.

Bachman, Ronet, Heather Zaykowski, Rachel Kallmyer, Margarita Poteyeva, and Christina Lanier. 2008. *Violence against American Indian and Alaska Native Women and the Criminal Justice Response: What Is Known*. NCJ 22369). Washington, DC: U.S. Department of Justice.

Baldwin, Julie A., Carol J. C. Maxwell, Andrea M. Fenaughty, Robert T. Trotter, and Sally J. Stevens. 2000. "Alcohol as a Risk Factor for HIV Transmission among American Indian and Alaska Native Drug Users." *Journal of the National Center* 9, 1–14.

Baldwin, Julie A., Robert T. Trotter, Dina Martinez, Sally J. Stevens, Debbie John, and Christiane Brems. 1999. "HIV/AIDS Risks among Native American Drug Users: Key Findings from Focus Group Interviews and Implications for Intervention Strategies." *AIDS Education and Prevention* 11, 279–92.

Barlow, Allison, Britta C. Mullany, Nicole Neault, Yvonne Davis, Trudy Billy, Ranelda Hastings, Valerie Coho-Mescal, Kristin Lake, Julia Powers, Emily Clouse, Raymond Reid, and John T. Walkup. 2010. "Examining Correlates of Methamphetamine and Other Drug Use in Pregnant American Indian Adolescents." *Journal of the National Center* 17, 1–24.

Bertolli, Jeanne, Lisa M. Lee, and Patrick S. Sullivan. 2007. "Racial Misidentification of American Indians/Alaska Natives in the HIV/AIDS Reporting Systems of Five States and One Urban Health Jurisdiction, U.S., 1984–2002." *Public Health Reports* 122, 382–92.

Bertolli, J., A. D. McNaghten, M. Campsmith, L. Lee, R. Leman., R. Bryan, and J. Buehler. 2004. "Surveillance Systems Monitoring HIV/AIDS and HIV Risk Behaviors among American Indians and Alaskan Natives." *AIDS Education and Prevention* 16, 218–37.

Bertolli, Jeanne, Amy Roussel, Jennie Harris, Dan Lentine, Julia Gable, Ron Fichtner, JoAnn Kauffman, Michael Landen, Ralph T. Bryan. 2008.

"Surveillance of Infectious Diseases among American Indians and Alaska Natives." *Journal of Health Disparities Research and Practice* 2, 121–44.

Bigfoot, Dolores Subia. 2008. "Violence and the Effects of Trauma on American Indian and Alaska Native Populations." *Journal of Emotional Abuse* 8, 51–66.

Brave Heart, Maria Yellow Horse, and Lemyra M. DeBruyn. 1998. "The American Indian Holocaust: Healing Historical Unresolved Grief." *Journal of the National Center* 8, 60–82.

Caiazza, Amy, April Shaw, and Misha Werschkul. 2004. *Women's Economic Status in the States: Wide Disparities by Race, Ethnicity, and Region.* Washington, DC: Institute for Women's Policy Research.

Caldwell, E. K. 1999. *Dreaming the Dawn: Conversations with Native Artists and Activists.* Lincoln: University of Nebraska Press.

Calvin, Carolyn. 2011. "Rise in HIV Cases 'Alarming,' IHS Says." *Navajo Times,* June 2.

Centers for Disease Control (CDC). 1981a. "HIV/AIDS Basics—How Long Does It Take for HIV to Cause AIDS?" Accessed August 8, 2011. http://www.cdc.gov/hiv/resources/qa/definitions.htm.

Centers for Disease Control (CDC). 1981b. "Pneumocystis pneumonia—Los Angeles." *MMWR* 1981(30):250–52.

Centers for Disease Control (CDC). 2008, August. "HIV/AIDS among Youth." *HIV/AIDS Fact Sheet,* Revised.

Centers for Disease Control (CDC). 2009. *HIV Surveillance Report, 2009.* Accessed May 8, 2011. http://www.cdc.gov/hiv/topics/surveillance/resources/reports/.

Centers for Disease Control and Prevention and Indian Health Service (CDC/IHS). 2007. *Indian Health Surveillance Report—Sexually Transmitted Diseases 2007.* Atlanta: U.S. Department of Health and Human Services.

Diamond, Catherine, Arthur Davidson, Frank Sorvillo, and Susan Buskin. 2001. "HIV-infected American Indians/Alaska Natives in the Western United States." *Ethnicity and Disease* 11, 633–44.

Duran, Bonnie, Marc Bulterys, Jon Iralu, Cheryl Graham, Ahmed Edwards, and Melvin Harrison. 2000. "American Indians with HIV/AIDS: Health and Social Service Needs, Barriers to Care, and Satisfaction with Services among a Western Tribe." *Journal of the National Center* 9, 22–35.

Farmer, Paul, Margaret Connors, and Janie Simmons, eds. 1966. *Women, Poverty and AIDS: Sex, Drugs and Structural Violence.* Monroe, ME: Common Courage Press.

Fenaughty, Andrea M., Dennis G. Fisher, Henry H. Cagle, Sally Stevens, Julie A. Baldwin, and Robert Booth. 1998. "Sex Partners of Native American Drug Users." *Journal of Acquired Immune Deficiency Syndromes and Human Retrovirology* 17, 275–82.

Fernandez, Angela R., Sharon M. Keigher, and Patricia E. Stevens. 2005. "Risk Factors for HIV/AIDS among American Indian/Alaska Native Women: One Woman's Story." *Journal of HIV/AIDS and Social Services* 4, 63–86.

Fisher, Dennis G., Andrea M. Fenaughty, David M. Paschane, and Henry H. Cagle. 2000. "Alaska Native Drug Users and Sexually Transmitted Disease: Results of a Five-Year Study." *Journal of the National Center* 9, 47–57.

Ford, Olivia, 2011. "This Positive Life: Interview with Shana Cozad." The Body: The Complete HIV/AIDS Resource Website. Accessed June 7, 2011. http://www.thebody.com/content/art61045.html?ts=pf.

Gilley, Brian Joseph, and Marguerite Keesee. 2007. "Linking "'White Oppression' and HIV/AIDS in American Indian Etiology: Conspiracy Beliefs among AI MSMs and Their Peers." *Journal of the National Center* 14, 34–51.

Grant Makers Health. 2009, October 1. "Changing the Conversation: Taking a Social Determinants of Health Approach to Addressing HIV/ADS among Women of Color." Washington, DC. http://www.gih.org/Publications/MeetingReports Detail.cfm?ItemNumber=4074.

Hall, Irene, Ruiguang Song, Philip Rhodes, Joseph Prejean, Qian An, Lisa M. Lee, John Karon, Ron Brookmeyer, Edward H. Kaplan, Matthew T. McKenna, and Robert S. Janssen. 2008. "Estimation of HIV Incidence in the United States." *Journal of the American Medical Association* 300, 520–29.

Hartmann, Heidi, Olga Sorokina, and Erica Williams, with the assistance of Vicky Lovell, Tori Finkle, Ashley English and Amy Caiazza. 2006, December. "The Best and Worst State Economies for Women." Briefing Paper. Washington, DC: Institute for Women's Policy Research.

Indian Health Services (IHS). 1996, November. *Adjusting for Miscoding of Indian Race on State Death Certificates.* Washington, DC: Indian Health Services.

Indian Health Services (IHS). 2007, December. *HIV/AIDS Prevention and Treatment Services for American Indians and Alaska Natives.* GOA-08-09. Washington, DC.

Kaiser Family Foundation. 2011a, March. *HIV/AIDS Policy Fact Sheet: The HIV/AIDS Epidemic in the United States.*

Kaiser Family Foundation. 2011b, March. *HIV/AIDS Policy Fact Sheet: Women and HIV/AIDS in the United States.*

Kaufman, C. E., J. Desserich, C. K. Big Crow, B. Holy Rock, E. Keane, and C. M Mitchell. 2007. "Culture, Context, and Sexual Risk among Northern Plains American Indian Youth." *Social Science and Medicine* 64, 2152–64.

Kelly, J. J., S. Y. Chu, T. Diaz, L. S. Leary, and J. W. Buehler. 1996. "Race/Ethnicity Misclassification of Persons Reported with AIDS." *Ethnicity and Health* 1, 87–94.

Lawrence, Jane. 2000. *The Indian Health Service and the Sterilization of Native American Women* 24, 400–503.

Metler, Russ, George A. Conway, and Jeanette Stehr-Green. 1991. "AIDS Surveillance among American Indians and Alaska Natives." *American Journal of Public Health* 81, 1469–71.

National Indian Health Board (NIHB). 2010. *2010 Tribal Health Public Health Profile: Exploring Public Health Capacity in Indian Country.* Washington, DC: National Indian Health Board.

National Survey of Drug Use and Health (NSDUH). 2010a, December 1. *The NSDUH Report: HIV/AIDS and Substance Use.* Rockville, MD: Center for Behavioral Health Statistics and Quality.

National Survey of Drug Use and Health (NSDUH). 2010b, January 14. *The NSDUH Report: Substance Use Treatment Need and Receipt among People Living in Poverty.* Rockville, MD: Office of Applied Studies.

Office of Global AIDS Coordinator and the Bureau of Public Affairs Website. 2011. "PEPFAR: Addressing Gender and HIV/AIDS." Accessed March 17, 2011. http://www.pepfar.gov/press/2011/157860.htm.

Padian, Nancy S, Stephen C. Shiboski, Sarah O. Glass, and Eric Vittinghoff. 1997. Heterosexual Transmission of Human Immunodeficiency Virus (HIV) in

Northern California: Results from a Ten-year Study. *American Journal of Epidemiology* 146, 350–357.

POZ. 2011, May 2. "POZ Profiles: 31 at 30: Lisa Tiger." POZ website. Accessed June 9, 2011. http://www.poz.com/articles/lisa_tiger_HIV_2601_20251.shtml.

Project Positive. 2011. Lisa Paririe and Sharon Videos. HIV Stories for the Greater Good Website. Accessed June 8, 2011. http://thepositiveproject.org.

Sailors, Karen and Nalini Daliparthy. 2005. "Native Women, Violence, Substance Abuse and HIV Risk." *Journal of Psychoactive Drugs* 37, 273–80.

Seasons. 1997/1998, Winter. "Interview with Cordelia Thomas." *Native American Women and HIV/AIDS,* 4–11.

Sevelius, Jae, Adam Carrico, and Mallory Johnson. 2010. "Antiretroviral Therapy Adherence among Transgender Women." *Journal of the Association of Nurses in AIDS Care* 12, 256–64.

Simoni, Jane M., Shalini Sehgal, and Karina L. Walters. 2004, March. "Triangle of Risk: Urban American Indian Women's Sexual Trauma, Injection Drug Use, and HIV Sexual Risk Behaviors." *AIDS and Behavior* 8, 33–45.

Simons, Brenna and Connie Jessen. 2011, April. "A Road Map to Implementing At-home Gonorrhea and Chlamydia Testing in Alaska: Logistical Aspects and Adaptation." *IHS Primary Care Provider* 36, 70–72.

Stevens, Sally J., Antonio L. Estrada, and Barbara D. Estrada. 2000. "HIV Drug and Sex Risk Behaviors among American Indians and Alaska Native Drug Users: Gender and Site Differences." *Journal of the National Center* 9, 33–46.

United States Census Bureau. 2006, February. *We the People: American Indians and Alaska Natives in the United States, Census 2000 Special Reports.*

Urban Indian Health Institute (UIHI). 2010. *Reproductive Health of Urban American Indian and Alaska Native Women: Examining Unintended Pregnancy, Contraception, Sexual History and Behavior, and Non-Voluntary Sexual Intercourse.* Seattle: Urban Indian Health Institute.

Vernon, Irene S. 2000. "Facts and Myths of AIDS and Native American Women." *American Indian Culture and Research Journal* 24, 93–110.

Vernon, Irene S. 2001. *Killing Us Quietly: Native Americans and HIV/AIDS.* Lincoln: University of Nebraska Press.

Vernon, Irene S. 2011. "2010 Native Women HIV/AIDS Self Care Survey." Unpublished raw data.

Walters, Karina L. and Jane M. Simoni. 1999, August. "Trauma, Substance Use, and HIV Risk among Urban American Indian Women." *Cultural Diversity and Ethnic Minority Psychology* 5, 236–48.

Wasserheit, Judith N. 1999, November. "HIV Infection and Other STDs: So Close and Yet So Far." *Sexually Transmitted Diseases* 26, 549–50.

CHAPTER 11

Differences in Cancer Patterns in American Indian and Alaska Native Women across the United States

Teshia G. Arambula Solomon
and Carol Goldtooth-Begay

INTRODUCTION

Cancer is now the second leading cause of death among women in the United States and is expected to double between 2010 and 2030 (Leffall and Kripke 2011), and while American Indian and Alaska Native (AIAN) women are reported to experience less cancer than non-Hispanic white (NHW) women, they were the only racial or ethnic group that did not experience a decline in cancer mortality from 1975 to 2004, and they experienced higher incidence and mortality rates for specific cancers (Espey et al. 2007). Incidence and mortality rates for AIAN kidney and gallbladder cancer are higher than rates for NHWs, and stomach and liver cancer rates are approximately double. Mortality rates for cervix cancer are higher, and Native Americans have the poorest five-year survival rate for lung cancer (Horner et al. 2009). This chapter reviews the cancer burden among AIAN women in the United States with particular attention to regional differences.

CANCER TRENDS AND AMERICAN
INDIAN WOMEN

Cancer was rarely reported among American Indians in the early twentieth century as compared to the white population (Levin 1910; Hrdlicka 1905). The Surveillance, Epidemiology, and End Results (SEER) program of the National Cancer Institute (NCI) began in 1973 to track cancer incidence and survival in the states of Connecticut, Iowa, New Mexico, Utah, and Hawaii and the metropolitan areas of Detroit and San Francisco–Oakland. In 1980, Arizona was added in order to track American Indian cases. Subsequently, when cancer in AIANs was reported in the latter part of the century, findings were based on the SEER data from Arizona and New Mexico and were not representative of AIANs living in other parts of the country. In addition, problems in racial misclassification and coding errors led to inaccurate interpretations of data and patterns of cancer in the AIAN population (Burhansstipanov, Hampton, and Tenney 1999).

In 1998, the first *Report to the Nation* documented the first sustained decrease in cancer death rates since the 1930s (Kohler et al. 2011). Each year the report provides an update on trends in cancer incidence and death rates. Data from 1992 to 2007 were analyzed for trends and showed that overall cancer incidence rates for all racial and ethnic groups combined decreased by 0.8 percent per year. During the most recent period, 2003 to 2007, a statistically significant decrease of 0.6 percent was reported. For women of all races and ethnicities, the trend analysis of breast cancer showed a marked decrease in 2002 and 2003, but rates stabilized thereafter. Seven cancers showed statistically significant decreasing trends—cancers of the breast, lung, colon and rectum, corpus uteri (uterus), cervix uteri (cervix), bladder, and oral cavity—but kidney, pancreas, melanoma of the skin, leukemia, and thyroid cancers showed increasing trends. Death rates from liver and pancreatic cancers in women continued to show increases. Following a period of increase in lung cancer, death rates among women decreased, and cervical cancer death rates evened out after a period of decreasing.

While the incidence of overall cancer rates for AIAN women are lower than for other racial and ethnic groups, the decline in mortality rates have not kept pace with declines for other populations. Analysis of current trends in cancer indicate that overall incidence rates decreased by 0.5 percent each year from 1998 to 2006, with decreases in two major cancer sites in women: breast and colorectum. This decrease occurred in all racial and ethnic groups, in both men and women, with the exception of AIAN women, for whom rates were stable. White women continue to have the highest overall cancer incidence rates compared to other racial or ethnic groups, and breast cancer is the most commonly diagnosed cancer among women. For women of all races combined, lung and colorectal cancers rank second and third (for AIAN women as well), and cancer of the uterus ranks fourth. While incidence rates for all cancer sites combined decreased between 1998 and 2007 in all populations, the decrease is not statistically significant for AIAN women.

THE CANCER BURDEN AND AMERICAN INDIAN WOMEN

Reporting health data on AIAN is problematic for multiple reasons and may not fully represent the patterns of health and disease among the AIAN population. Five major problems include (1) racial misclassification, (2) underreporting, (3) coding errors, (4) inclusion of insufficient population numbers, and (5) regional limitations for data collection (Burhansstipanov, Hampton, and Tenney, 1999). Racial misclassification occurs when a patient's racial or ethnic category is reported incorrectly, and misclassification rates for AIAN have been found to be as high as 40 to 50 percent in some areas (Hampton and Henderson 1999). Examples of how misclassification of coding occurs include using Spanish surnames to determine race, or a provider or data collector selecting the wrong racial category (white) for a patient based on physical appearance, or omitting AIAN as an option on data collection forms (Burhansstipanov and Satter 2000).

Underreporting data continues to be a problem as AIANs are often not included in studies because the population of specific tribes, as well as the overall population, is too small to find significant differences when compared with other, larger populations. This is especially true when the disease or issue of concern is relatively rare, such as some childhood cancers. Combining AIANs with other racial categories or into a single "other" category is comparable to having no data or being excluded from a study or study findings (Burhansstipanov, Hampton, and Wiggins 1999; Burhansstipanov and Satter 2000). This takes away the power of the population to advocate for their health and health care and makes them invisible and their problems invisible.

International Classification of Diseases (ICD) codes classify morbidity and mortality information for statistical purposes as well as for reimbursement, administration, epidemiology, and health services research. Patterns in cancer morbidity, care, and outcomes can be studied by grouping patients according to their ICD diagnoses. Coding errors can occur in diagnostic and procedure coding and have been found to range from 0 to 70 percent (Benesch et al. 1997; Faciszewski, Broste, and Fardon 1997; Goldstein 1998). Coding errors occur when the diagnosis is unclear, or the documentation by the physician is difficult to understand, or if coders are inexperienced and unfamiliar with new codes (O'Malley et al. 2005). Coding errors are particularly problematic in analytical interpretation when the data sets are small.

Studies that do not include a large enough sample of AIANs will not be able to show significant differences in cancer statistics. Such studies generally combine the AIAN population with other groups, or omit AIANs from analyses altogether. Clustering and omission both lead to underreporting and are a disservice to the AIAN community. Also, data that is collected in one region of the country (e.g., the Southwest) is not necessarily generalizable to other regions (e.g., the Northern Plains). Errors such as these can provide an incomplete picture of the patterns of cancer among the AIAN population.

The supplement to the *Report to the Nation on Cancer, An Update on Cancer in American Indians and Alaska Natives* (Edwards 2010) provides one of the most complete pictures of cancer incidence among AIANs to date. In order to improve classification of race for AIAN cancer cases, Espey and colleagues(2008) linked cancer registry records to the Indian Health Service (IHS) records and reported information by geographic region. Even this data, however, is limited by the record-linkage methodology (Espey et al. 2008) used to reduce misclassification. The process linked IHS records with cancer registry data and was restricted to residents of contract health services delivery area (CHSDA)[1] counties; therefore AIANs who were not users of the IHS system or not residents in CHSDA counties were not likely

---

1. CHSDA counties, in general, "contain federally recognized tribal lands or are adjacent to tribal lands. Unpublished data indicate less race misclassification for AIAN in these counties than in non-CHSDA counties. Also, the proportions of AI/AN in relation to total population are higher in CHSDA counties than in non-CHSDA counties; 57% of the U.S. AI/AN population resides in the 624 counties designated as CHSDA (AIAN population by region and residence in CHSDA county, is available at www.seer.cancer.gov/report_to_nation/)" (Espey et al. 2008).

included and it represents only 56 percent of the AIAN census-reported population. Presenting a clear picture of the impact of cancer on the AIAN population is difficult and requires reviewing multiple data sources and consideration of the limitations of the data available.

INCIDENCE

There is wide variance in the cancer incidence rates among AIANs across regions of the United States, sometimes more than a five-fold difference (Espey et al. 2008; Cobb, Wingo, and Edwards 2008). Wiggins, Espey, and colleagues (2008) in "Cancer among American Indians and Alaska Natives in the U.S." explored these differences by comparing AIAN and NHW women. When considering all types of cancer, AIAN rates were higher than the NHW rates in the Northern and Southern Plains regions but lower in Alaska. The incidence rates from all sites combined ranged from a low of 219.3[2] in the Southwest to 500.7 in Alaska as compared to 398.9 (Southwest) and 437.9 (Pacific Coast and East) among NHWs. Breast cancer was found to be the most common cancer site in both AIAN and NHW women in all regions, and three cancer sites—breast, colorectal, and uterine—were the most common among AIAN women in all regions. Lung, non-Hodgkin's lymphoma, kidney, and ovarian cancers round out the top five cancer sites for AIAN women across the country. Table 11.1 compares rates between AIAN and NHW women for all regions.

Regional variations in age-adjusted cancer incidence rates were also found among young AIAN women age 20 to 44 (Weir et al. 2008). Compared to their NHW counterparts, the overall cancer rate for AIAN young women was lower (83.8 compared to 111.2); however, there was variation across regions for AIAN women with a low of 76.2 in the East and high of 155.7 in the Southern Plains. Among this age group of women, four cancers were found to account for nearly 75 percent of all diagnoses: breast cancer (29%), cancers of the female genital system (21%), cancers of the endocrine system (12%), and cancers of the digestive system (10%). Table 11.2 compares the incidence and mortality rates for select cancers between AIANs and women from other racial and ethnic groups, and Table 11.3 shows the regional differences.

---

2. All rates reported are per 100,000 unless otherwise noted.

Table 11.1

Comparison of Incidence Rates by Race for Select Women's Cancer Sites, All Regions Combined, 1999–2004

	Rank among AIANs	Cancer Site	AIAN Rate	NHW Rate	AIAN: NHW RR
		All sites combined	337.6	424.0	0.80
Higher than NHW	5	Kidney	14.2	8.7	1.62
	8	Pancreas	9.8	9.4	1.04
	9	Cervix uteri	9.4	7.4	1.28
	11	Stomach	7.9	3.6	2.18
	13	Liver/HBD	5.8	2.5	2.36
	14	Myeloma	5.8	3.7	1.56
	18	Gallbladder	3.9	1.1	3.50
Lower than NHW	1	Breast	85.3	134.4	0.63
	2	Lung/bronchus	48.5	58.6	0.83
	3	Colorectal	41.6	43.6	.95
	4	Corpus/uterus	18.1	23.6	0.77
	6	Non-Hodgkin's lymphoma	13.1	16.4	.80
	7	Ovary	11.5	14.4	.80
	10	Thyroid	8.5	12.1	0.70
	12	Leukemia	7.6	9.7	.78

Data source: Wiggins et al. (2008).

Table 11.2

U.S. Female Cancer Incidence and Mortality Rates per 100,000 by Site and Race/Ethnicity, 2002–2006

	American Indian/ Alaska Native	White	African American	Asian American/ Pacific Islander	Hispanic/ Latina[*]
INCIDENCE					
All sites	265.1	420.0	389.5	276.3	326.8
Breast	67.2	123.5	113.0	81.6	90.2

Table 11.2   (Continued)

	American Indian/ Alaska Native	White	African American	Asian American/ Pacific Islander	Hispanic/ Latina*
Colorectum	30.7	42.6	51.7	33.1	35.1
Kidney and renal pelvis	10.6	10.3	10.6	4.5	10.3
Liver and bile duct	4.6	2.8	3.8	8.1	6.2
Lung and bronchus	41.3	57.1	50.7	27.6	26.5
Stomach	4.7	4.2	8.5	9.8	8.6
Uterine cervix	6.6	7.9	11.1	7.6	12.7
MORTALITY					
All sites	140.1	157.3	183.7	95.1	103.9
Breast	17.6	23.9	33.0	12.5	15.5
Colorectum	13.7	14.9	21.6	10.0	10.7
Kidney and renal pelvis	4.2	2.8	2.7	1.2	2.4
Liver and bile duct	6.5	2.9	3.9	6.6	5.1
Lung and bronchus	33.5	41.9	40.0	18.2	14.4
Stomach	4.6	2.4	5.3	5.8	4.8
Uterine cervix	3.4	2.2	4.6	2.2	3.1

*Persons of Hispanic/Latina origin may be of any race.
Data source: Edwards et al. 2010.

Table 11.3
Regional Differences in Age-adjusted Incidence of Cancers Rates among AIAN Women, 1999–2004

Region	Highest	Rate	Lowest	Rate
Alaska	Breast	134.9	Melanoma	1.1+
East	Uterine	15.2	Breast	71.4
			Thyroid	6.6
Northern Plains	Stomach	9.2	Melanoma	5.3
	Colorectal	59.8		

(*continued*)

Table 11.3　(Continued)

Region	Highest	Rate	Lowest	Rate
Pacific Coast	Kaposi sarcoma	NA	Melanoma	4.0
			Breast	74.7
			Thyroid	6.3
Southern Plains	Cervix	14.1	Melanoma	7.8
	Colorectal	53.8		
Southwest	Stomach	8.6	Breast	50.8
	Uterine	16.7	Cervix	7.8
			Melanoma	1.8
			Thyroid	8.9
			Lung	10.4

Data source: Wiggins, Espey, Wingo et al. 2008.

MORTALITY RATES

Data from 1998 to 2007 (Espey et al. 2008) show a decrease in overall cancer death rates for all racial and ethnic groups except AIAN women. Death rates for the three major cancers in women, lung, colorectal, and breast, decreased for each racial and ethnic group except that lung cancer rates among women of all races were not statistically significant. Liver cancer and pancreatic cancer death rates both increased for white women over this period. AIAN women have low five-year survival rates (60%), second only to African American women (55.8%) and 5 percent lower than NHW women (Jemal et al. 2010).

The overall age-adjusted rate of death from cancer for AIAN women from 2002 to 2006 was 140.1, which is lower than the white death rate of 157.3; however the annual percent change for the period of 1997 to 2006 was significantly lower for the white female population (–0.9) but not for AIAN females (–0.3) (Horner et al. 2009). AIAN women are more likely to die from cancer of the kidney, stomach, liver and gallbladder, and cervix uteri than other racial or ethnic groups. However, death rates, like incidence rates, vary regionally.

CANCER SITES AND REGIONAL VARIATION

Due to the limitations of cancer data collection as previously discussed, differences in cancer among AIAN people were previously masked (Wiggins, Espey, Wingo, et al. 2008). Looking at linked-incidence data by geographical region allows for consideration of the social, cultural, environmental, and behavioral factors influencing the variation that exists among the 564 federally recognized tribes.

LUNG CANCER INCIDENCE RATES

Nutting and colleagues (1993), in utilizing 1980–1987 IHS records and SEER data, found lower lung cancer incidence rates in the female population of three Southwestern tribes as compared to Alaska Natives and Northern Plains tribes [Apache (8.3), Navajo (4.6), and Tohono O'odham (17.9); Alaska Aleut (101.7) and Alaska Athabaskan (111.3) and Northern Plains (34.1)]. Bliss and colleagues (2008), in looking at the CHSDA linked data set, found comparable regional variation, but with a lower rate for Alaska (75.4), a much higher rate for the Northern Plains (93.8), and a rate for the Southwest of 10.4. They also found higher rates in the Southern Plains (69.9) and lower rates in the Pacific Coast (48.0) and the East (43.5).

Compared to the NHW female population in the same regions, the lung cancer incidence rates for AIAN women are lower in the East, the Pacific Coast, and the Southwest but significantly higher in the Southern plains, and Alaska and almost double in the Northern Plains. The variation between the lowest rates in the Southwest and the highest rates in the Northern Plains is a seven-fold difference and may reflect the differences in cigarette smoking between these two regions. Behavioral risk surveys report smoking rates for the AIAN female population (27.2%) exceed those of NHW women (22.1%) and are considerably higher in the Northern Plains (37.7), Alaska (36.7%), and the Southern Plains (32.7%) and lower in the Pacific Coast (18.4%) and the Southwest (17.3%). Historically, women in general took up smoking about 10 years after men took up the habit, and recent decreases in lung cancer rates in women also follow the decreases in lung cancer incidence and death rates for men (Espey et al. 2007). While AIAN women's overall lung cancer rates are lower than those of NHW women (48.5 and 58.6 respectively), AIAN regional differences show lung cancer incidence rates are almost double the AIAN U.S. rates in the Northern Plains (93.8) and higher in Alaska (75.4) and the Southern Plains (69.9) (Bliss et al. 2008).

COLORECTAL CANCER INCIDENCE RATES

Using CHSDA data, Alaska Natives have the highest colorectal cancer incidence rate (106.2) for AIAN women, 2.6 times that of the

NHW female population (40.6) and higher than any other region (Perdue et al. 2008). Women in the Northern Plains (59.8) and the Southern Plains (53.8) also experience a higher rate while women in other regions experience lower rates than their NHW counterparts (Perdue et al. 2008; (Perdue et al. 2008). The rate for Alaska Native women is five times the rate for AIAN women in the Southwest (106.2 and 17.3 respectively). Colorectal cancer risk factors include diabetes, obesity, smoking, and binge alcohol consumption (Steele 2008). While the smoking behavior is consistent with this regional variation, the other risk factors are not. These differences may be attributed to differences in colorectal screening rates or other access-to-care issues. AIANs in the Southwest and Northern Plains have been found to underutilize screening (Chao 1998), and screening rates in Alaska range between 7.2 percent and 64 percent at different facilities (ANEC/ANTHC 2009).

Breast Cancer Incidence Rates

Regional patterns in female AIAN breast cancer incidence rates mirror those of lung and colorectal cancer with the highest rates in Alaska (134.8) and the Northern and Southern Plains (115.9 and 115.7, respectively) and the lowest rates in the Southwest (50.8), a significant, almost threefold difference (Wingo et al. 2008). These rates are lower than the rates for NHW women.

Invasive female breast cancer rates, however, show a different picture with rates that are either comparable to or higher than those for NHW women. Alaska Native women of all ages experience higher rates than NHW women in Alaska, while women in the Pacific Coast, East, and Southwest all have significantly lower rates (Wingo et al. 2008). AIAN women are diagnosed with breast cancer at a younger age than NHW women (30% compared to 19% for women younger than 50 years), presumably indicative of the differences in age distribution of the two populations (Wingo et al. 2008).

Kidney Parenchyma and Bladder Cancer Incidence Rates

Incidence rates for kidney cancer among AIAN women (13.9) exceed those for NHW women (8.1) in all regions and are more than double in the Northern (19.2) and Southern Plains (17.9). Rates for other regions include Alaska (12.0), Pacific Coast (9.4), East (13.3), and Southwest

(12.4 (Wilson et al. 2008). Conversely, bladder cancer rates are lower than for NHW women and up to seven times lower in the Southwest (Wilson et al. 2008). Regional differences in kidney cancer incidence among AIAN women range from a low of 9.4 in the CHSDA counties in the Pacific Coast to a high of 19.2 in those of the Northern Plains.

Bladder cancer rates were lowest in the Southwest (1.4) and highest in the Southern Plains (7.3) (Wilson et al. 2008). Wilson and colleagues (2008) note multiple possibilities for urinary tract cancer incidence rates including smoking, obesity, hypertension, use of diuretics, infection, diet, occupational exposures, family history, and diabetes, and they suggest that a relationship with regional tobacco-smoking patterns may explain the regional differences.

GASTRIC CANCER INCIDENCE RATES

Gastric (stomach) cancer incidence rates are high among AIAN women compared with NHW women (7.9 compared to 3.6) (Wiggins, Perdue, Henderson, et al. 2008). There is also dramatic regional variation for AIAN women with the highest rates in Alaska (17.7) being almost six times higher than their NHW counterparts (3.0) (Wiggins, Perdue, Henderson, et al. 2008). The incidence rates in the Northern Plains (9.2) and in the Southwest (8.6) were approximately three times higher than the comparable NHW rates of 3.4 and 3.0, and the rates in the Southern Plains (7.6) were more than double the rates for NHW women (3.4). The regions with the lowest rates among AIAN women were the Pacific Cost (4.7) and the East (4.8), and these rates were also higher than the NHW women's rates of 3.5 and 4.8, respectively, but with a less dramatic differential (Wiggins, Perdue, Henderson, et al. 2008). Risk factors found to influence differing forms of gastric cancer include consumption of fresh fruits and vegetables, micronutrient consumption (vitamins E and C, carotenoids, selenium), high salt and nitrate consumption, cigarette smoking, family history of the disease, and *Heliobacter pylori* infection. Explanations for the high rates among AIAN women are unclear, but this unique correlation with *H. pylori* infection suggests an area for further investigation (Wiggins, Perdue, Henderson, et al. 2008).

CERVICAL CANCER INCIDENCE RATES

Invasive cervical cancer incidence rates are significantly higher among AIAN women (9.4), and the disease is more likely to be diagnosed at later stages when compared with NHW women (7.4), AIAN women in the Southern (14.1) and Northern (12.5) Plains have higher cervical cancer incidence than do women in other regions, an almost two-fold difference from AIAN women in the Pacific Coast (6.9) and the East (7.1) (Becker, Espey, et al. 2008). Age-specific incidence rates show a statistically significant difference between AIAN and NHW women overall in the 30- to 49-year and 50- to 64-year groups and rates that are double among women 65 and older (30–49: AIAN 7.6, NHW 6.3; 50–64: AIAN 7.4, NHW 5.7; 65+: AIAN 10.0, NHW 5.4) (Becker, Espey, et al. 2008).

When comparing stage at diagnosis between AIAN and NHW women, AIAN women had lower rates of localized disease (3.6 vs. 3.9) but higher rates in regional (3.2 vs. 2.0) and distal (1.1 vs. 0.6) disease (Becker, Espey, et al. 2008). While rates for AIAN women were higher, they were lower than previously documented rates due in part to aggressive screening programs developed by the CDC and IHS (Becker, Espey, et al. 2008; Becker et al. 1992). Known risk factors for cervical cancer include smoking and human papilloma virus (HPV) infection. In addition, delays in diagnosis are reflected in the disparities in screening at late stage of diagnosis.

Gallbladder Cancer Incidence Rates

Lemrow and colleagues (2008) found astounding disparities in gallbladder cancer incidence rates among AIAN females (3.9) compared to NHW females (1.1). Gallbladder cancer is approximately three times more likely to occur in an AIAN woman than in a white woman, with women in the Southwest and Alaska experiencing rates seven to eight times greater than their NHW counterparts (6.6 and 6.9 vs. 0.6 and 0.9, respectively). For women 50 and over, gallbladder cancer is almost four times more likely to occur in a Native person than in a white person, and rates for gallbladder cancer are higher among women than men (Lemrow et al. 2008). These high rates in AIANs may be explained in part by chronic inflammation due to the gallstone formation found to occur more frequently among AIANs than NHWs (Bartlett, Ramanathan, and Deutsch 2005; Everhart et al. 2002; Lowenfels et al. 1985; Randi, Franceschi, and La Vecchia 2006). Other studies have also found disparities in gallbladder disease between AIAN (64.1%) and NHW women (16.6%) (Everhart et al. 1999; Everhart et al. 2002).

FACTORS THAT INFLUENCE THE CANCER BURDEN

Several factors have been found to be related to cancer incidence and mortality, including behavioral factors such as tobacco use, obesity, a lack of physical activity, infectious agents such as *H. pylori* and HPV, and access to screening and treatment. Larger socioecological issues may also influence the variation of cancer incidence among the AIAN population, including geographical residence, quality of care, and poverty (Wiggins, Espey, Wingo, et al. 2008; Von Wagner et al. 2009; Marmot et al. 2008).

COMMERCIAL TOBACCO SMOKE

Tobacco smoke has been linked to approximately 90 percent of all lung cancers (Peto et al. 1992), and Native communities that experience the greatest smoking rates—the Plains states and Alaska—experience higher cancer rates than those that have less smoking, such as the Southwest (Wingo et al. 2008). Cigarette smoking rates among American Indians in the Southwest (21.1%) are comparable to the percentage of the U.S. population that smokes (19.3%) and about half that of the Plains states (42%) (Steele 2008). Evidence shows that those who quit smoking can lower the risk of lung cancer, but it is still higher than the risk for people who have never smoked (IARC 2007). Cancer rates lag behind smoking rates by 20 to 30 years; therefore, as smoking among youth in the Southwest increases, changing the historical smoking patterns of their parents, we can expect to see changes in cancer incidence as well (Alberg and Samet 2003). Cigar and pipe smoking is also associated with lung cancer but less so than for cigarette smoking, due primarily to differences in smoking frequency and the depth of inhalation (NCI 1998). Epidemiologic evidence also shows a relationship between secondhand smoke, also called environmental tobacco smoke, and lung cancer (Bofetta 2002; Taylor et al. 2001).

THE INFLUENCE OF INFECTIONS

Over 20 percent of cancers have been causally linked to infectious agents (Zur Hausen 2009). Hepatitis B increases risk of liver cancer

100 times, and HPV is linked to 70% of cervical cancers (Stein 2011). Epstein-Barr has been linked to nasopharyngeal carcinoma, Burkitt lymphoma, Hodgkin disease, and lymphoproliferative tumors (Stein 2011). *H. pylori* is linked to stomach cancer and HIV.

Hepatitis B (HBV) or hepatitis C (HCV) can cause liver cancer after many years of infection (NCI 2009). Virus transmission occurs from person to person through blood (such as by sharing needles) or sexual contact, and mothers can also pass the viruses to their infants (NCI 2009). AIANs are almost twice as likely to develop a case of HCV, and AIANs 40 and over are 2.5 times more likely to have HBV, than NHWs (CDC 2008). Stomach and liver cancer incidence and death rates are also associated with HBV and HCV.

H. pylori is a bacterium commonly found in the stomach that can attach to cells of the stomach, causing gastritis and excess stomach acid. Over time, infection with the bacteria can increase the risk of stomach cancer. *H. pylori* may be contracted through food and water. According to the NIH, approximately 20 percent of people under 40 and 50 percent of the population over 60 carry *H. pylori* (NCI 2011).

HPV is a group of more than 150 viruses that can cause abnormal tissue growth and cellular changes such as benign genital warts. More than 40 sexually transmitted types are easily spread, and long-term infection with oncogenic or carcinogenic types can cause cervical cancer and anal cancer (NCI 2011). Genital HPV infection also causes some cancers of the vulva, vagina, and penis (Parkin 2006), and oral infection can cause cancers of the throat (Parkin 2006; D'Souza et al. 2007). At least 15 types have been identified as high risk, including HPV 16 and 18. Together, these two types cause about 70 percent of all cervical cancer cases (Munoz et al. 2004; Schiffman et al. 2007) and about 85 percent of anal cancers (Abbas, Yang, and Fakih 2010).

Two HPV vaccines approved by the Food and Drug Administration (FDA), Gardasil and Cervarix, have been found to be highly effective in preventing infections with HPV types 16 and 18. Gardasil also prevents infection with HPV types 6 and 11, which cause 90 percent of genital warts (Koutsky et al. 2002). There is some evidence that AIAN women may experience a different distribution of high-risk viral types that may include lower levels of expression (Schiffman et al. 2007), a higher prevalence of mixed infections, and a higher percentage of infections not preventable by the vaccines. Higher prevalence rates for AIAN women have been found for HPV types 26, 31, 33, 35, 40, 45, 51, 52, 55, 56, 58, 61, 66, 68, 71, 72, 73, 81, 82, 83, 84 and lower rates for 16, 18, 39, 53, 54, and 59

(Schmidt-Grimminger et al. 2011). These differences in prevalence and infection patterns may explain the disparities in cervical cancer experienced by AIAN women, although these studies were conducted with small community samples, which limit generalizability to other AIAN women. Schiffman and colleagues (2007) also note that the a majority of infections with high-risk HPV types resolve on their own and do not cause cancer, warranting even further exploration in this area specific to AIAN women. Understanding why some infections turn cells into cancer would lead to new prevention and treatment strategies.

NUTRITION AND OBESITY

Obesity increases the risk of cancers of the breast (in postmenopausal women), endometrium, colon, kidney, and esophagus, and regular physical activity has been found to lower the risk of colon and breast cancer. Between 25 and 30 percent of these cancers may be attributed to obesity and lack of physical activity (Vainio and Bianchini 2002). Calle and colleagues (2003) found that 14 percent of women who died from cancer were overweight or obese. The rates of obesity and overweight among a sample of AIAN women has been found to range between 48.5 and 65 percent with differences due to regional and tribal variation (Welty et al. 2002). In a study of the Behavioral Risk Factor Surveillance System data, Denny, Holtzman, and Cobb (2003) found that Alaska Natives experience the highest prevalence of obesity, with an BMI of 29.0.

Few AIAN communities have managed to hang on to their traditional practice of hunting and gathering fresh foods; like the rest of the United States, diet trends in Native communities have changed. Diets that were historically high in nutrients have been replaced by commercially developed foods high in refined sugars, fat, and sodium (IHS 2001). Fast-food restaurants and convenience stores are increasingly available to both urban and reservation communities and, when these are coupled with government commodities, high-fat, high-sugar foods are prevalent, leading to high rates of obesity (Broussard et al. 1995; Michel 2004; Sugarman et al. 1990).

Physical activity is a key component of the energy balance equation. Like the situation in diet, the traditional lifestyle with natural activity has been replaced with a sedentary one. Barnes and colleagues (2005) found that 50.3 percent of AIANs never engages in regular physical activity, as compared to 36.6 percent of white adults. Barriers to physical activity among AIANs include lack of childcare, lack of time, safety issues, lack of willpower or motivation, lack of fitness equipment and facilities, medical conditions and disabilities, and a lack of outdoor facilities such as parks or sports facilities (Harnack, Story, and Rock 1999; Giuliano et al. 1998; Phillips and Finn 2000; Powell, Slater, and Chaloupka 2004).

ALCOHOL

Heavy alcohol use has been found to increase risk for mouth and esophagus, prostate, colorectal, breast, stomach, and liver cancer (Coughlin, Uhler, and Blackman 1999; El-Serag, Tran, and Everhart 2004; Gammon et al. 1997; McMahon et al. 1985; Sasazuki et al. 2002). Variation in cancer rates may be attributed to variation in alcohol consumption across regions.

Both binge and chronic drinking have been found to be high among AIAN women with variation across regions; reservation women reported a low rate of 2.6 percent, with higher rates in the West (11.3%) and in the Plains (27.0%) (Spicer 2003). However, rates among women in urban communities have been found to be three times the U.S. NHW rates (Risendal et al. 1999; Castor et al. 2006). Women 50 and over and married women are less likely to report alcohol consumption. The National Health Interview Survey for the period 2004 through 2008 reports much lower rates, however, for "current moderate or heavier"[3] drinking for AIAN females as 11.6 percent, as compared to NHW females at 14.7 percent.

SOCIOECONOMIC STATUS

Twenty-eight percent of AIANs live in poverty, more than double the national average, with a median income of just over $37,000 (U.S. Census Bureau 2008). AIAN cancer patients from low-income families are less likely to have access to employer-sponsored coverage (29.2% compared with 12% of NHWs) (U.S. Census Bureau 2009) and even with coverage have difficulty making copayments and deductibles for testing and treatment.

---

3. Current moderate or heavier drinker is at least 12 drinks in lifetime, at least 12 drinks in past year, and drank more than 3 drinks per week on average.

While the relationship between socioeconomic status (SES) and health has not been fully explained, health status decreases relative to decreases in income. This differential health pattern between the rich and the poor holds across the economic continuum, with those in the middle income range less healthy than their wealthier counterparts (Marmot et al. 2008; Schootman et al. 2006; Von Wagner et al. 2011). It is expected that income differentials inhibit access to care, thereby limiting cancer prevention screening and timely diagnosis and treatment for those who must pay for treatment, but the same disparities have been found in countries where screening is provided free (Marmot et al. 2008). It is also important to remember that SES is not only related to health outcomes but also to risk-related behaviors such as smoking, alcohol use, nutrition, and physical activity further, confounding our understanding of the risk relationships.

These socioeconomic influences affect the health of AIANs through living conditions, lack of employment and safe employment, the availability and quality of food, and lack of exercise and recreational resources, placing them at greater risk for cancer.

Lack of Access to Culturally Acceptable Cancer Services

Health care access for the AIAN population is a complex mix of care provided by the IHS, tribally owned and operated clinics and hospitals, private insurance, and other public sources such as the Veterans Administration that provide services. Access also includes proximity of services, availability of childcare, transportation, and culturally competent providers (Misra-Herbert 2003). The IHS is severely underfunded, leaving "over half of the health needs of AI/AN beneficiaries unmet" (National IHS Tribal Budget Formulation Workgroup 2010). The 2012 budget recommendation for IHS requested a 16.6 percent increase in funding to meet the current need and a plan to achieve parity with the general American population within seven years.

Eligibility for care is dependent on multiple issues. For example, Houston, Texas, has an AIAN population of 8,184 (U.S. Census Bureau 2008), but no IHS facility exists, nor any AIAN urban health center. There are only 40 urban programs to meet the needs of the approximately 605,000 AIANs living in urban communities (IHS 2011). These programs primarily provide only basic family and community medicine and behavioral health services. When an IHS or tribal facility cannot provide a service, care through contract agencies is available, but only as long as funding is available. Care is therefore rationed based on the seriousness of the diagnosis.

Medical services are not always available to AIAN patients because many live in rural areas and often struggle to get to health care facilities, and those living in remote areas may have to traverse through extreme weather, hazardous roads, and long distances to get care. Those living in urban communities may not have access to Native-specific services or have to travel hundreds of miles to access them. There are many ways to measure access to health care, and each method yields different results. Approximately 28 percent of AIANs are uninsured, and another 30 percent use public health care sources; approximately 16 percent utilize IHS services and 49 percent have private insurance, as compared to the NHW population, of whom 12.9 percent are uninsured, 5 percent use public health care, and 83 percent have private insurance (Zuckerman et al. 2004). The figures for AIAN women who are uninsured is higher (34%) and for NHW is lower (11%) (Office of Research on Women's Health 2006).

The quality of care can influence patient outcomes in cancer care. Patients need to accept and follow provider advice and instructions requiring a culturally competent relationship between the provider and the patient that may include using traditional Indian medicine. Culturally competent care requires asking about patient beliefs and respecting these beliefs (Kitzes and Domer 2003). Health care providers need to ask about and be informed if patients are using herbal or other traditional medicine and to appreciate the importance of integrating it with their Western medicine cancer treatment. Integration of traditional medicine varies across communities; some, like the Chinle Comprehensive Health Care Facility, have an Office of Native Medicine within their clinics. Traditional medicine generally includes a spiritual component. But Native American beliefs mirror the variability of religions practiced across the country and the world; patients may practice one of many faiths and not believe in traditional medicine, and some may practice both.

Some communities still speak their Native language with English as their second language; coupled with medical terminology, difficulties in understanding instructions and directions can influence health outcomes. This can be a particular problem with elders.

MEDICAL DISCRIMINATION

According to the Institute of Medicine (Smedley, Stith, and Nelson 2003), discrimination can occur during the provider-patient interaction and may harm the health care process, including patient health care decisions and provider's medical decisions and recommendations (Smedley et al. 2003). When a patient perceives discrimination, she will negatively engage with that provider and the system, thereby negatively affecting future health care encounters and her health. Gonzales (2010) found that women perceived they were discriminated against based on race but also based on their income and their weight. They also felt that their drug or alcohol use, or a reputation of such use by a family member, influenced the quality of care they received. Of the women who reported discrimination, 82.9 percent reported their health-seeking behaviors were negatively affected with almost 70 percent postponing seeking care or treatment.

SUMMARY

Looking at cancer among AIANs is like looking at a puzzle picture. While an image is visible, like a puzzle there are gaps between pieces, and some of the pieces may well be missing. National data indicate cancer rates are decreasing in other racial and ethnic groups but mortality rates for AIAN women are not, and AIAN women experience higher rates in certain cancers. But because of the complexity in collecting health data on the AIAN population, the picture of the cancer experience among AIAN women is incomplete. The data linkage project by Espey and others (2008) provides a new perspective on the patterns of cancer incidence across the country, presenting a view of differences between regions not previously visible. Evidence supports the idea that these differences are likely related to differences in health behavior patterns between regions, differences in smoking rates, and the prevalence of *H. pylori*, for example, but more work is needed to confirm these theories.

The picture of cancer among AIANs is incomplete. There are signs of progress but also signs of significant burden. Data is a powerful tool in the advocacy for resources needed to provide quality health care in a system that rations care like the IHS, Medicaid, Medicare, and the U.S. public health system. Communities that lack accurate, timely, and complete data cannot adequately describe the pictures and patterns of health they experience. They lack the evidence necessary to tell the stories of their community and to advocate for much-needed health and health care resources. Innovative data collection and analysis methods like the data linkage project are needed to fill in the gaps in the puzzle or the missing pieces of information that complete the picture. Including AIAN people in national studies, analyzing data, and providing results and findings back to the more than 580 AIAN nations allows them to tell their stories and pursue solutions through cancer prevention, treatment, and control. These stories that describe how AIAN women experience cancer helps give voice to an otherwise invisible cancer patient, her family and community and those that provide her treatment and care. The unique challenges faced by AIAN cancer patients, such as financial resources, access to care, and discrimination, effect survivorship and quality of care.

REFERENCES

Abbas, A., G. Yang, and M. Fakih. 2010. "Management of Anal Cancer in 2010. Part 1: Overview, Screening, and Diagnosis." *Oncology* 24(4):364–69.

Alaska Native Epidemiology Center and Alaska Native Tribal Health Consortium (ANEC/ANTHC). 2009. "Alaska Native Health Status Report" p. 78. Accessed September 24, 2011. http://www.anthc.org/chs/epicenter/pubs.cfm.

Alberg, A. J. and J. M. Samet. 2003. "Epidemiology of Lung Cancer." *CHEST* 123(1):215–495.

Barnes, P. M., E. Powell-Griner, P. F. Adams, and Centers for Disease Control and Prevention. 2005. *Health Characteristics of the American Indian and Alaska Native Adult Population, United States, 1999–2003.* Washington, DC: U.S. Department of Health and Human Services, Centers for Disease Control and Prevention, National Center for Health Statistics.

Bartlett, D. L., R. K. Ramanathan, and M. Deutsch. 2005. "Cancer of the Biliary Tree." Pp. 1009–031 in *Cancer: Principles and Practice of Oncology* (7th ed). Vincent T. DeVita, Samuel Hellman, and Steven A. Rosenberg (Eds.). Philadelphia: Lippincott Williams & Wilkins.

Becker, T. M., J. Bettles, J. Lapidus, J. Campo, C. J. Johnson, D. Shipley, and L. D. Robertson. 2002. "Improving Cancer Incidence Estimates for American Indians and Alaska Natives in the Pacific Northwest." *American Journal of Public Health* 92(9):1469–71.

Becker, T. M., D. K. Espey, H. W. Lawson, M. Saraiya, M. A. Jim, and A. G. Waxman. 2008. "Regional Differences in Cervical Cancer Incidence among American Indians and Alaska Natives, 1999–2004." *Cancer* 113(S Suppl):1234–43.

Becker, T. M., C. M. Wheeler, C. R. Key, and J. M. Samet. 2008. "Cervical Cancer Incidence and Mortality in New Mexico's Hispanics, American Indians, and Non-Hispanic Whites." *Western Journal of Medicine* 156(4):376–79.

Benesch, C., D. M. Witter, A. L. Wilder, P. W. Duncan, G. P. Samsa, and D. B. Matchar. 1997. "Inaccuracy of the International Classification of Diseases (ICD-9-CM) in Identifying the Diagnosis of Ischemic Cerebrovascular Disease." *Neurology* 49(3):660.

Bliss, A., N. Cobb, T. Solomon, K. Cravatt, M. A. Jim, L. Marshall, and J. Campbell. 2008. "Lung Cancer Incidence among American Indians and Alaska Natives in the United States, 1999–2004." *Cancer* 113(5 Suppl):1168–78.

Boffetta, P. 2002. "Involuntary Smoking and Lung Cancer." *Scandinavian Journal of Work, Environment and Health* 28(Suppl 2):30–40.

Broussard, B. A., J. R. Sugarman, K. Bachman-Carter, K. Booth, L. Stephenson, K. Strauss, and D. Gohdes. 1995. "Toward Comprehensive Obesity Prevention Programs in Native American Communities." *Obesity Research* 3(Suppl 2): 289s–297s.

Burhansstipanov, L., J. W. Hampton, and M. J. Tenney. 1999. "American Indian and Alaska Native Cancer Data Issues." *American Indian Culture and Research Journal* 23(3):217–41.

Burhansstipanov, L., J. W. Hampton, and C. L. Wiggins. 1999. "Issues in Cancer Data and Surveillance for American Indians and Alaska Native Populations." *Journal of Registry Management* 26(4):153–57.

Burhansstipanov, L. and D. E. Satter. 2000. "Office of Management and Budget Racial Categories and Implications for American Indians and Alaska Natives." *American Journal of Public Health* 90(11):1720.

Calle, E. E., C. Rodriguez, K. Walker-Thurmond, and M. J. Thun. 2003. "Overweight, Obesity, and Mortality from Cancer in a Prospectively Studied Cohort of U.S. Adults." *New England Journal of Medicine* 348(17):1625–38.

Castor, M. L., M. S. Smyser, M. M. Taualii, A. N. Park, S. A. Lawson, and R. A. Forquera. 2006. "A Nationwide Population-Based Study Identifying Health Disparities between American Indians/Alaska Natives and the General Populations Living in Select Urban Counties." *American Journal of Public Health* 96(8):1478–84.

Centers for Disease Control and Prevention (CDC). 2008. "Surveillance for Acute Viral Hepatitis—United States, 2006." Accessed January 15, 2011. http://www .cdc.gov/mmwr/PDF/ss/ss5702.pdf.

Chao, A., F. D. Gilliland, W. C. Hunt, M. Bulterys, T. M. Becker, and C. R. Key. 1998. "Increasing Incidence of Colon and Rectal Cancer among Hispanics and American Indians in New Mexico (United States), 1969-94." *Cancer Causes & Control: CCC* 9 (2): 137–144.

Cobb, N., P. A. Wingo, and B. K. Edwards. 2008. "Introduction to the Supplement on Cancer in the American Indian and Alaska Native Populations in the United States." *Cancer* 113(5 Suppl):1113–16.

Coughlin, S. S., R. J. Uhler, and D. K. Blackman. 1999. "Breast and Cervical Cancer Screening Practices among American Indian and Alaska Native Women in the United States, 1992–1997." *Preventive Medicine* 29(4):287–95.

Denny, C. H., D. Holtzman, and N. Cobb. 2003. "Surveillance for Health Behaviors of American Indians and Alaska Natives. Findings from the Behavioral Risk Factor Surveillance System, 1997–2000." *Morbidity and Mortality Weekly Report* 52(7):1–13.

D'Souza, G., A. R. Kreimer, R. Viscidi, M. Pawlita, C. Fakhry, W. M. Koch, W. H. Westra, and M. L. Gillison. 2007. "Case-Control Study of Human Papillomavirus and Oropharyngeal Cancer." *New England Journal of Medicine* 356(19):1944–56.

Edwards, B. K., E. Ward, B. A. Kohler, C. Eheman, A. G. Zauber, R. N. Anderson, A. Jemal, M. J. Schymura, I. Lansdorp-Vogelaar, and L. C. Seeff. 2010. "Annual Report to the Nation on the Status of Cancer, 1975–2006, Featuring Colorectal Cancer Trends and Impact of Interventions (Risk Factors, Screening, and Treatment) to Reduce Future Rates." *Cancer* 116:544–73.

El-Serag, H. B., T. Tran, and J. E. Everhart. 2004. "Diabetes Increases the Risk of Chronic Liver Disease and Hepatocellular Carcinoma." *Gastroenterology* 126(2):460–68.

Espey, D. K., C. L. Wiggins, M. A. Jim, B. A. Miller, C. J. Johnson, and T. M. Becker. 2008. "Methods for Improving Cancer Surveillance Data in American Indian and Alaska Native Populations." *Cancer* 113(S5):1120–30.

Espey, D. K., X. C. Wu, J. Swan, C. Wiggins, M. A. Jim, E. Ward, P. A. Wingo, H. L. Howe, L. A. G. Ries, B. A. Miller, A. Jemal, F. Ahmed, N. Cobb, J. S. Kaur, and B. K. Edwards. 2007. "Annual Report to the Nation on the Status of Cancer, 1975–2004, Featuring Cancer in American Indians and Alaska Natives." *Cancer* 110(10):2119–52.

Everhart, J. E., M. Khare, M. Hill, and K. R. Maurer. 1999. "Prevalence and Ethnic Differences in Gallbladder Disease in the United States." *Gastroenterology* 117(3):632–39.

Everhart, J. E., F. Yeh, E. T. Lee, M. C. Hill, R. Fabsitz, B. V. Howard, and T. K. Welty. 2002. "Prevalence of Gallbladder Disease in American Indian Populations: Findings from the Strong Heart Study." *Hepatology* 35(6):1507–12.

Faciszewski, T., S. K. Broste, and D. Fardon. 1997. "Quality of Data Regarding Diagnoses of Spinal Disorders in Administrative Databases: A Multicenter Study." *Journal of Bone and Joint Surgery, American Volume* 79(10):1481–88.

Gammon, M. D., H. Ahsan, J. B. Schoenberg, A. Brian West, H. Rotterdam, S. Niwa, J. Blot, H. A. Risch, R. Dubrow, S. T. Mayne, T. L. Vaughn, J. L. Stanford, D. C. Farrow, W. Chow, J. F. Fraumeni Jr. 1997. "Tobacco, Alcohol, and Socioeconomic Status and Adenocarcinomas of the Esophagus and Gastric Cardia." *Journal of the National Cancer Institute* 89(17):1277–84.

Giuliano, A., M. Papenfuss, J. Guernsey De Zapien, S. Tilousi, and L. Nuvayestewa. 1998. "Prevalence of Chronic Disease Risk and Protective Behaviors among American Indian Women Living on the Hopi Reservation." *Annals of Epidemiology* 8(3):160–67.

Goldstein, L. B. 1998. "Accuracy of ICD-9-CM Coding for the Identification of Patients with Acute Ischemic Stroke: Effect of Modifier Codes." *Stroke* 29(8):1602.

Gonzales, K. L. 2010. "Perceived Medical Discrimination in American Indian Women: Effect on Health Care Decisions, Cancer Screening, Diabetes Services and Diabetes Management." PhD Diss., Oregon State.

Hampton, J. and J. Henderson J. 1999. "Report of the Data Working Group Meeting: Issues for American Indian and Alaska Native Populations." Intercultural Cancer Council Report.

Harnack, L., M. Story, and B. H. Rock. 1999. "Diet and Physical Activity Patterns of Lakota Indian Adults." *Journal of the American Dietetic Association* 99(7):829–35.

Horner, M. J., L. A. G. Ries, M. Krapcho, N. Neyman, R. Aminou, N. Howlader, S. F. Altekruse, E. J. Feuer, L. Huang, and A. Mariotto. 2009. "SEER Cancer Statistics Review, 1975–2006." Bethesda, MD: National Cancer Institute.

Hrdlicka, A. 1905. *Diseases of the Indians: More Especially of the Southwest United States and Northern Mexico* 4(6).

Indian Health Service (IHS). 2011. "IHS Fact Sheets Rx: Urban Indian Health Program." Accessed January 16, 2012. http://www.ihs.gov/PublicAffairs/IHSBrochure/UrbnInds.asp.

Indian Health Service (IHS). 2001. *IHS Report to Congress: Obesity Prevention and Control for American Indians and Alaska Natives* http://www.ihs.gov/hpdp/documents/obesitypreventionreport.doc.

International Agency for Research on Cancer (IARC). 2007. *IARC Handbooks of Cancer Prevention*. Vol. 11: *Tobacco Control: Reversal of Risk after Quitting Smoking*. Lyon, France: International Agency for Research on Cancer.

Jemal, A., R. Siegel, J. Xu, and E. Ward. 2010. "Cancer Statistics, 2010." *CA: A Cancer Journal for Clinicians*. 60 (5): 277–300.

Kitzes, J. A. and T. Domer. 2003. "Palliative Care: An Emerging Issue for American Indians and Alaskan Natives." *Journal of Pain and Palliative Care Pharmacotherapy* 17, 201–10.

Kohler, B. A., E. Ward, B. J. McCarthy, M. J. Schymura, L. A. Ries, C. Eheman, A. Jemal, R. N. Anderson, U. A. Ajani, and B. K. Edwards. 2011. "Annual Report to the Nation on the Status of Cancer, 1975–2007, Featuring Tumors of the Brain and Other Nervous System." *Journal of the National Cancer Institute* 103(9):714–36.

Koutsky, L. A., K. A. Ault, C. M. Wheeler, D. R. Brown, E. Barr, F. B. Alvarez, L. M. Chiacchierini, K. U. Jansen, and Proof of Principle Study Investigators. 2002. "A Controlled Trial of a Human Papillomavirus Type 16 Vaccine." *New England Journal of Medicine* 347(21):1645–51.

Leffall, L. D. and M. L. Kripke. 2011. *America's Demographic and Cultural Transformation: Implications in Cancer. President's Cancer Panel 2009–2010 Annual Report*. Bethesda, MD: National Cancer Institute.

Lemrow, S. M., D. G. Perdue, S. L. Stewart, L. C. Richardson, M. A. Jim, H. T. French, J. Swan, B. K. Edwards, C. Wiggins, L. Dickie and D. K. Espey. 2008. "Gallbladder Cancer Incidence among American Indians and Alaska Natives, US, 1999–2004." *Cancer* 113(5 Suppl):1266–73.

Levin, I. 1910. "Cancer among the American Indians and Its Bearing upon the Ethnological Distribution of the Disease." *Journal of Cancer Research and Clinical Oncology* 9(3):422–35.

Lowenfels, A. B., C. G. Lindstrom, M. J. Conway, and P. R. Hastings. 1985. "Gallstones and Risk of Gallbladder Cancer." *Journal of the National Cancer Institute* 75(1):77–80.

Marmot, M., S. Friel, R. Bell, T. A. Houweling, S. Taylor, and Commission on Social Determinants of Health. 2008. "Closing the Gap in a Generation: Health Equity through Action on the Social Determinants of Health." *Lancet* 372(9650): 1661–69.

McMahon, B. J., W. L. Alward, D. B. Hall, W. L. Heyward, T. R. Bender, D. P. Francis, and J. E. Maynard. 1985. "Acute Hepatitis B Virus Infection: Relation of Age to the Clinical Expression of Disease and Subsequent Development of the Carrier State." *Journal of Infectious Diseases* 151(4):599–603.

Michel, K. L. 2004. "The New Focus on Native American Cooking." *Washington Post*, September 22. http://www.washingtonpost.com/wp-dyn/articles/A38390 -2004Sep21.html.

Misra-Hebert A. 2003. "Physician Cultural Competence: Cross-cultural Communication Improves Care." *Cleveland Clinical Journal of Medicine* 70, 289–303.

Munoz, N., F. X. Bosch, X. Castellsague, M. Diaz, S. de Sanjose, D. Hammouda, K. V. Shah, and C. J. Meijer. 2004. "Against which Human Papillomavirus Types Shall We Vaccinate and Screen? The International Perspective." *International Journal of Cancer* 111(2):278–85.

National IHS Tribal Budget Formulation Workgroup. 2010, March 4. "FY2012 Tribal Budget Recommendations to the U.S. Department of Health & Human Services. Advancing a New Tribal and Federal Government Partnership: Investing in Indian Health to Achieve a Sustainable Model for National Health Care Reform." Accessed November 14, 2011. http://www.nihb.org/docs/030102010/ IHS%20Budget%20Testimony%20_2_.pdf.

National Cancer Institute. 1998. "Smoking and Tobacco Control Monograph 9. Cigars: Health Effects and Trends." Publication 98–4302. Bethesda, MD: National Cancer Institute.

National Cancer Institute. 2009, April 29. "What You Need to Know about Liver Cancer. Risk Factors." Accessed December 28, 2011. http://www.cancer.gov/ cancertopics/wyntk/liver/page4.

National Cancer Institute (NCI). 2011. "Helicobacter Pylori and Cancer. 2/14/ 2011." Accessed November 6, 2011. http://www.cancer.gov/cancertopics/ factsheet/Risk/h-pylori-cancer.

Nutting, P. A., W. L. Freeman, D. R. Risser, S. D. Helgerson, R. Paisano, J. Hisnanick, S. K. Beaver, I. Peters, J. P. Carney, and M. A. Speers. 1993. "Cancer Incidence among American Indians and Alaska Natives, 1980 through 1987." *American Journal of Public Health* 83(11):1589–98.

Office of Research on Women's Health. 2006. "Women of Color Health Data Book: Adolescents to Seniors." Accessed November 13, 2011. http://orwh.od.nih.gov/ pubs/WomenofColor2006.pdf.

O'Malley, K. J., K. F. Cook, M. D. Price, K. R. Wildes, J. F. Hurdle, and C. M. Ashton. 2005. "Measuring Diagnoses: ICD Code Accuracy." *Health Services Research* 40 (5p2):1620–39.

Parkin, D. M. 2006. "The Global Health Burden of Infection-Associated Cancers in the Year 2002." *International Journal of Cancer* 118(12):3030–44.

Perdue, D. G., C. Perkins, J. Jackson-Thompson, S. S. Coughlin, F. Ahmed, D. S. Haverkamp, and M. A. Jim. 2008. "Regional Differences in Colorectal Cancer Incidence, Stage, and Subsite among American Indians and Alaska Natives, 1999–2004." *Cancer* 113(S5):1179–90.

Peto, R., J. Boreham, A. D. Lopez, M. Thun, and C. Heath. 1992. "Mortality from Tobacco in Developed Countries: Indirect Estimation from National Vital Statistics." *Lancet* 339(8804):1268–78.

Phillips and Finn. 2000. "Dietary Choices and Weight Loss Practices among Cheyenne River Lakota Households." http://www.nptao.arizona.edu/pdf/DietaryChoicesandWeightLossPracticesAmongCheyenne12.pdf.

Powell, L., S. Slater, and F. J. Chaloupka. 2004. "The Relationship between Community Physical Activity Settings and Race, Ethnicity, and Socioeconomic Status." *Evidence-Based Preventive Medicine* 1(2):135–44.

Randi, G., S. Franceschi, and C. La Vecchia. 2006. "Gallbladder Cancer Worldwide: Geographical Distribution and Risk Factors." *International Journal of Cancer* 118(7):1591–1602.

Risendal, B., J. Dezapien, B. Fowler, M. Papenfuss, and A. Giuliano. 1999. "Cancer Prevention among Urban Southwestern American Indian Women: Comparison to Selected Year 2000 National Health Objectives." *Annals of Epidemiology* 9(6):383–90.

Sasazuki, S., S. Sasaki, S. Tsugane, and Japan Public Health Center Study Group. 2002. "Cigarette Smoking, Alcohol Consumption and Subsequent Gastric Cancer Risk by Subsite and Histologic Type." *International Journal of Cancer* 101(6):560–66.

Schiffman, M., P. E. Castle, J. Jeronimo, A. C. Rodriguez, and S. Wacholder. 2007. "Human Papillomavirus and Cervical Cancer." *Lancet* 370(9590):890–907.

Schmidt-Grimminger, D. C., M. C. Bell, C. J. Muller, D. M. Maher, S. C. Chauhan, and D. S. Buchwald. 2011. "HPV Infection among Rural American Indian Women and Urban White Women in South Dakota: An HPV Prevalence Study." *BMC Infectious Diseases* 11, 252.

Schootman, M., D. B. Jeffe, E. A. Baker, and M. S. Walker. 2006. "Effect of Area Poverty Rate on Cancer Screening across US Communities." *Journal of Epidemiology and Community Health* 60(3):202–7.

Smedley, B. D., A. Y. Stith, and A. R. Nelson. 2003. *Institute of Medicine (U.S.). Committee on Understanding and Eliminating Racial and Ethnic Disparities in Health Care. Unequal Treatment: Confronting Racial and Ethnic Disparities in Health Care.* Washington, DC: National Academy Press.

Spicer, P., J. Beals, C. D. Croy, C. M. Mitchell, D. K. Novins, L. Moore, S. M. Manson, and American Indian Service Utilization, Psychiatric Epidemiology, Risk and Protective Factors Project Team. 2003. "The Prevalence of DSM-III-R Alcohol Dependence in Two American Indian Populations." *Alcoholism, Clinical and Experimental Research* 27 (11): 1785–1797.

Steele, C. B., C. J. Cardinez, L. C. Richardson, L. TomOrme, and K. M. Shaw. 2008. "Surveillance for Health Behaviors of American Indians and Alaska Natives: Findings from the Behavioral Risk Factor Surveillance System, 2000–2006." *Cancer* 113(S5):1131–41.

Stein, R. A. 2011. "Epigenetics: The Link between Infectious Diseases and Cancer." *Journal of the American Medical Association* 305, 14.

Sugarman, J. R., M. Hickey, T. Hall, and D. Gohdes. 1990. "The Changing Epidemiology of Diabetes Mellitus among Navajo Indians." *Western Journal of Medicine* 153(2):140.

Taylor, R., R. Cumming, A. Woodward, and M. Black. 2001. "Passive Smoking and Lung Cancer: A Cumulative Meta-Analysis." *Australian and New Zealand Journal of Public Health* 25(3):203–11.

U.S. Census Bureau, 2008. "Small Area Income and Poverty Estimates (SAIPE), State and County Estimates for 2008." Accessed May 8, 2010. http://www.census.gov/did/www/saipe/index.html.

U.S. Census Bureau. 2009. "2009 American Community Survey One-Year Estimates." Washington, DC: U.S. Census Bureau.

Vainio, H. and F. Bianchini. 2002. *Weight Control and Physical Activity*, Vol. 6. World Health Organization.

Von Wagner, C., A. Good, K. L. Whitaker, and J. Wardle. 2011. "Psychosocial Determinants of Socioeconomic Inequalities in Cancer Screening Participation: A Conceptual Framework." *Epidemiologic Reviews* 33(1):135.

Von Wagner, C., A. Good, D.Wright, B. Rachet, A. Obichere, S. Bloom, and J. Wardle. 2009. "Inequalities in Colorectal Cancer Screening Participation in the First Round of the National Screening Programme in England." *British Journal of Cancer* 101(Suppl 2):S60–S63.

Weir, H. K., M. A. Jim, L. D. Marrett, and T. Fairley. 2008. "Cancer in American Indian and Alaska Native Young Adults (Ages 20–44 Years): US, 1999–2004." *Cancer* 113(S5):1153–67.

Welty, T. K., D. A. Rhoades, F. Yeh, E. T. Lee, L. D. Cowan, R. R. Fabsitz, D. C. Robbins, R. B. Devereux, J. A. Henderson, and B. V. Howard. 2002. "Changes in Cardiovascular Disease Risk Factors among American Indians: The Strong Heart Study." *Annals of Epidemiology* 12(2):97–106.

Wiggins, C. L., D. K. Espey, P. A. Wingo, J. S. Kaur, R. Wilson, J. Swan, B. A. Miller, M. A. Jim, J. J. Kelly, and A. P. Lanier. 2008. "Cancer among American Indians and Alaska Natives, 1999–2004." *Cancer* 113(S5):1142–52.

Wiggins, C. L., D. G. Perdue, J. A. Henderson, M. G. Bruce, A. P. Lanier, J. J. Kelley, B. F. Seals, and D. K. Espey. 2008. "Gastric Cancer among American Indians and Alaska Natives in the United States, 1999–2004." *Cancer* 113(S5):1225–33.

Wilson, R. T., L. C. Richardson, J. J. Kelly, J. Kaur, M. A. Jim, and A. P. Lanier. 2008. "Cancers of the Urinary Tract among American Indians and Alaska Natives in the United States, 1999–2004." *Cancer* 113(S5):1213–24.

Wingo, P. A., J. King, J. Swan, S. S. Coughlin, J. S. Kaur, J. A. Erb-Alvarez, J. Jackson-Thompson, and T. G. Arambula Solomon. 2008. "Breast Cancer Incidence among American Indian and Alaska Native Women: US, 1999–2004." *Cancer* 113 (S5):1191–202.

Zuckerman, S., J. Haley, Y. Roubideaux, and M. Lillie-Blanton. 2004. "Health Service Access, Use, and Insurance Coverage among American Indians/Alaska Natives and Whites: What Role Does the Indian Health Service Play?" *American Journal of Public Health* 94(1):53–59.

Zur Hausen, H. 2009. "The Search for Infectious Causes of Human Cancers: Where and Why." *Virology* 392(1):1–10.

CHAPTER 12

Three Native Sisters: Being Young and the Need to Fit In

Nina S. Wampler and
Lorenda Belone

INTRODUCTION

American Indians and Alaska Natives (AIANs) comprise a young population, and 49 percent are females under 18 years of age (U.S. Census Bureau 2011). Because this is a young population, it also means significant numbers are also in a high risk-taking group. In fact, much of what is written about high-risk behaviors among AIAN adolescent girls focuses on those that result in poor health or early death, for instance from suicide. It is important to note, however, that while there are many AIAN youth caught in the web of negative lifestyle behaviors, many more are well adjusted and utilize parental and other resources as protective factors.

The high-risk profile of AIAN youth is not unique. Young people in all cultures have to navigate a transition from childhood to adulthood, a transition that may be smooth or troublesome. In some cultural groups, societies have ways to help with a smooth transition. For example, many tribal communities mark the transition with special puberty ceremonies, which helps lessen the uncertainties for young people entering adulthood. The public puberty ceremonies are celebrated as formal initiation of a young person into an adult role. Culture change and acculturation, however, have displaced these celebrations so that only few tribes still maintain these traditions.

Native youth, like most of their non-Native peers, now live in a larger society where periods of childhood and adolescence have been prolonged. The extension of the period of adolescence not only gives youth more time with their peers, but as youth begin to assert their independence, their relationships with their parents or other adults can result in conflicts with parents, especially when the youth's home situation is not stable or parental guidance and support is lacking or weak. These and other types of conflict are a common thread in the stories of the three sisters presented in this chapter. Their stories are presented in an honored tradition of storytelling, an approach commonly used by most tribal groups.

Each of their stories reflects some of the common problems faced by many others like them and who are also caught under the influence of peer pressures, some resulting in negative outcomes. Positive relationships, however, can help youth develop healthy friendships and positive self-identity, and increase self-esteem and independence. Negative peer influences usually encourage youth to take risk-taking behaviors that can result in substance abuse, school performance problems, gang activity, and similar outcomes.

PREVALENCE OF RISK

According to the 2010 census, the total population of the United States was over 308 million with 5.2 million individuals identifying themselves as AIAN alone or in combination with other races (U.S. Census Bureau 2011). And as noted before, this demographic information places 31 percent of the AIAN population under age 18 compared to 26 percent for the total U.S. population (U.S. Census Bureau 2011).

The high proportion of risky behaviors that is characteristic of a young population presents a significant problem for this population. This problem, in particular, was noted by Jones and colleagues (2011) when they examined youth and risk factors reported by the Centers for Disease Control and Prevention (CDC) in its *Morbidity and Mortality Weekly Report* (MMWR), a data source that identified high rates of risky behavior from aggregated sets of data collected in 2001, 2003, 2005, 2007, and 2009. The primary data source examined by Jones and colleagues (2011) is based on the CDC's national Youth Risk Behaviors Survey (YRBS). In particular, the data examined from the MMWR focus on the following six risk behavior categories: (1) behaviors that contribute to unintentional injuries and violence;

(2) tobacco use; (3) alcohol and other drug use; (4) sexual behaviors that contribute to unintended pregnancy and sexually transmitted disease, including human immunodeficiency virus (HIV) infection; (5) unhealthy dietary behaviors; and (6) physical inactivity.

The six areas examined are the risk behaviors that are sometimes motivated by youth wanting to fit in with their peers, behaviors that might be adopted in response to peer pressure or as coping mechanism in dealing with other forms of stress. Fitting in or wanting to be accepted can be particularly stressful if the youth is an outsider and wants to be accepted by peers in a new school or a new environment. If her efforts to fit in are not met, the stresses she encounters can lead to depression, or she may seek other outlets, including self-medicating or use of alcohol or drugs. Some adolescent girls are also tempted to engage in risky sexual behaviors as another way to cope with the stresses of adolescence or to find acceptance.

THE THREE NATIVE SISTERS

This is a story about three sisters: Rosaline, Carla, and Laura. They are not sisters in the conventional sense in that they all have different parents. Rather, they are Native sisters who grew from childhood to adolescence to adulthood in different family situations and different cultural backgrounds. These women are now all in their late twenties and have experienced life in different ways. Their lives have been shaped by their family circumstances and by the cultures in which they have been raised. Their experiences during their adolescent years are examples of some of the risky behaviors that contribute to an overall health profile of adolescent American Indian females.

TOBACCO USE

Laura was born in a town near her mother's reservation. Laura's white father worked for the federal Bureau of Indian Affairs (BIA), and he saw to it that Laura received the best education available. Laura felt pressured by her father to get good grades and do well in school. She worked hard on her schoolwork and did her best academically but was unhappy most of the time because she was overweight, a problem she had had since she was a young girl in elementary school. In eighth grade, Laura started hanging out with some popular girls, who told her that smoking cigarettes was a way to be thin. Despite the academic excellence expected of her by her parents, Laura found acceptance among her new eighth-grade friends, and her behavior was greatly influenced by them. In fact, she felt cool being with her new friends who smoked and who scoffed at the idea of doing homework. As a result, Laura's schoolwork was no longer a priority.

Instead, Laura was happy to be part of a hip group. Smoking also helped her feel less nervous in the day-to-day drama of life at home. Laura could escape the pressures of home to be with her friends, who accepted her now. Cigarettes were easy to get on the reservation, and Laura told herself that smoking may not be healthy or acceptable but it was worth it because she was losing weight and was more popular than she had ever been.

The CDC annually monitors health risks for youth through surveys that target different grade levels. The YRBS collects data from youth and serves as an important resource for schools and health care providers in observing trends of certain risk factors among this population. For example, Jones and colleagues (2011) utilized YRBS to report that the prevalence of ever having smoked cigarettes and of current cigarette use was higher among AIAN students (71%) than non-Hispanic white (55%), black (53%), and Hispanic (58%) students. Interestingly, cigarette use by gender was similar among AIAN girls (70%) and AIAN boys (72%). In comparison with other racial or ethnic groups, the prevalence of current frequent cigarette use was significantly higher among AIAN students (14%) than among black (4%) and Hispanic (5%) students. Jones and colleagues (2011) also report that this prevalence was also slightly higher among AIAN boys (15%) than AIAN girls (12%).

Public health indicators show that early initiation of cigarette use can result in continued use of this highly addictive substance, an addiction that can result in a number of health problems, including lung cancer.

ALCOHOL AND OTHER SUBSTANCE USE

The second Native sister, Carla, was born the youngest of four children on a large reservation in the Southwest. Her father left when Carla was an infant, leaving her mother to raise the children in extreme poverty. Unable to cope, Carla's mother turned to drinking to escape the stresses of her life and subsequently gave up caring about herself and her children. Left without a mother in the household, Carla's older siblings went out on their own, and because she was only

10 years old, Carla was adopted by a couple who were friends of her father's family. Carla's adoptive parents were religious and were very active in the local church, and they were not supportive of Carla learning or maintaining her connection to her tribal heritage. Her adoptive parents were kind but strict, but by age 13, Carla began to rebel against the strict rules of home life and started to pick up the habits of her friends who encouraged her to smoke, drink alcohol and use drugs, and engage in other unhealthy behaviors. In the midst of this unhappy home life and peer pressure, Carla soon lost herself in a fog of booze and drugs and unaware that the addictive nature of these substances held a potential death trap for her.

According to Jones and colleagues (2011), their examination of the YRBS showed prevalence of ever drinking among high school students in the United States was higher among AIAN students (79%) than black student (69%). The prevalence rate for AIAN youth, however, was close to that reported for white (76%) and Hispanic students (78%). Interestingly, the rate of alcohol use by gender for AIAN girls was 79 percent, and the same for AIAN boys, 79 percent. Many youth, however reported that they were current drinkers; the prevalence of current alcohol use was higher among AIAN students (48%) than black students (34%) but nearly the same as that reported for white (47%) and Hispanic students (46%).

Jones and colleagues (2011) also indicate that the prevalence of binge drinking was also significantly higher among AIAN students (31%) than black students (13%); however, the prevalence for AIANs was similar to that of the white students (31%). The prevalence of current alcohol use by gender was higher among AIAN boys (53%) than AIAN girls (43%), but binge drinking was the same for both · AIAN boys and girls (26%).

It should be noted that there is a paucity of current population-based information on the use and abuse of other substances among AIAN youth. In a report from the National Institutes of Health (NIH 1998) on the 1996 National Household Survey on Drug Abuse conducted by the federal Substance Abuse and Mental Health Services Administration (SAMSHA), AIAN youth between the ages of 12 and 17 years were found to have the highest prevalence of self-reported illicit drug use (18%) compared to other races and ethnicities (9% for non-Hispanic white youth; 9% for African American youth; 6% for Asian/Pacific Islanders). The report did not contain data on teens' drug use by gender, but in general, self-reported illicit drug use among AIAN males was nearly twice as high as that reported by AIAN females.

While more recent population-based data on drug use among AIAN teens are also not available, the alarmingly high rates of reported drug use among AIAN youth in the previous decade may mean that the rates may even be higher today. Due to the significance of this problem, Carla and other young Native women deserve to receive fact-based information delivered through culturally driven drug education programs and treatment services.

TEEN PREGNANCY

Rosaline, the third of the three Native sisters, was one of four daughters of an American Indian mother and a Mexican farmer, and until Rosaline was 10 years old, they lived just over the border in Mexico. Her mother, who is from the Cocopah Tribe in the Southwestern United States, was a nurse's aide. Both of Rosaline's parents had limited formal school but were hard-working. Rosaline's father therefore wanted more education for his daughters, so when Rosaline was 10, he moved his family to Tucson in southern Arizona.

Life in Tucson was different from the small Mexican village—it took some getting used to for Rosaline. She spoke little English and found it difficult to keep up with the coursework in her new school. Not only was she not accepted as an "American," but because she had not been raised in her mother's tribal culture, she did not have this particular cultural grounding to be considered an American Indian by her schoolmates. Thus, Rosaline's identity with her mother's Cocopah culture was weak and prevented her being accepted as an American Indian by her American Indian peers. The situation was difficult for her; Rosaline not only was experiencing a cultural shock of being in a new place, but she was also an outsider. What did it mean to be an American? Where did Rosaline fit into American society?

Through her preteen years, Rosaline resisted using drugs or other substances, but as she entered adolescence, she became more vulnerable in other ways, especially when she became attentive to the attentions of young men. When a boy who was a year older asked her out, Rosaline was flattered and wanted to spend time with the young man because she felt that he understood her situation. The mutual attraction eventually led to a more intimate relationship, a relationship that left her pregnant. Dealing with pregnancy at age 15 was not something for which Rosaline and her family had been prepared. Her pregnancy consequently meant that she had to drop out of school, a decision that ultimately led to a cascade of events that dramatically changed the life of this hopeful teenager.

Teen pregnancy is not unique to Indian country, and in most instances, pregnancies are accepted. In the history of many tribes, it was acceptable for women to marry early and to have children in their younger years. For example, a puberty ceremony that marks coming of age in many tribes was celebrated publically and used to announce to the community that the young woman was eligible for marriage. Having children was also considered an important role for women, so much so that a barren woman was often gifted with a child by her relatives to rear as her own. These earlier cultural practices, however, are no longer encouraged, especially when there is not a lot of support for teen mothers to continue their education or to have the means to support a child.

Needless to say, life caught in the cycle of poverty is strong and persistent for many teens, and having a child may be seen by some young women as a way to escape parental control as well as to find a male companion outside the home. Because of high rates of teen pregnancies, Rosaline's pregnancy was probably not considered unusual and may have been expected by some members of her family, her peers, and her community. The high rates of teen pregnancy are not unique to AIANs; similar situations confront many teens and their families in all societies.

According to a CDC 2010 report, teen birth rates are the lowest in U.S. history, but the U.S. rates remain significantly higher than those in other industrialized nations (CDC 2010). In the United States, the live birth rate among women between the ages of 15 and 19 years has declined since 1991, except for a brief increase between 2005 and 2007. While the 2009 live birth rate among AIAN teens dropped from 58 births per 1,000 births to 56 per 1,000 in 2008, this rate was more than twice the rates for non-Hispanic white teens: 27 teen births among 1,000 teens in 2008 and 26 per 1,000 in 2009. It should, however, be noted that AIAN teen birth rates continue to be lower than the rates for Hispanic teens: 78 Hispanic teen births per 1,000 in 2008 and 70 per 1,000 in 2009 (CDC 2010). The underlying causes for the decreases in teen birth rates are not yet known, and the rates may very well level off with minimal declines over the coming years.

Factors that are associated with teen pregnancy in all societies, especially those living in low-income communities, include a lack of access to contraception, poverty, poor performance in school, growing up in a single-parent family, or having parents with low levels of education (CDC 2010). The culture, community, family, and peer group in which a young girl grows up are big factors in whether teen pregnancies are accepted. Acceptance and a supportive environment often are more likely to occur for teen mothers in cultures that have had a long history of encouraging early marriages and place a high value on having children early.

DIETARY BEHAVIORS, OVERWEIGHT, AND OBESITY

Because of the increasing numbers of chronic diseases like type 2 diabetes and cancer worldwide, most countries are now taking aggressive action to prevent or decrease the rates of childhood and adult obesity. One of the leading causes of obesity has been linked to diets that are high in fat and sugar. Like many teenage girls, Laura, Carla, and Rosaline tended to eat a lot of fast food because it was convenient and inexpensive. In general, their routine diet included foods high in fat and low in protein. According to Jones and colleagues (2011), risks to nutritional health among AIAN high school students show that only a few reported consuming the recommended daily amount of milk. For example, the prevalence of drinking three glasses of milk was lower among AIAN students (83%) than among black (90%) and Hispanic students (87%). However, the prevalence of drinking three glasses of milk was higher among AIAN girls (90%) than AIAN boys (77%).

Nutritional deficits, however, are not reflected in rates of obesity. The prevalence of overweight and obesity is higher among AIAN students (20% overweight and 16% obese) than among white students (14% overweight and 10% obese). The prevalence of being overweight by gender was slight higher among AIAN girls (21%) than among AIAN boys (19%). The prevalence of obesity, however, was significantly higher among AIAN boys (20%) than among AIAN girls (10%) (Jones et al. 2011).

PHYSICAL ACTIVITY

Laura, Carla, and Rosaline were all physically inactive and did not participate in organized sports in their schools. Without the structure of organized programs, the physical fitness level of these girls was quite low. The schools that the three sisters attended were not sufficiently funded to offer physical education, a situation that is also common for AIAN students enrolled in many of the rural reservation schools. The lack of physical activity among this age group is also confirmed by CDC data. For example, Jones and colleagues (2011) found the prevalence of insufficient vigorous physical activity was higher among AIAN students (38) than among non-Hispanic white students (33%) but was similar to Hispanic students (37%).

Jones and colleagues (2011) also examined the rates of sedentary lifestyle or insufficient vigorous physical activity by gender. They found that lack of physical activity was significantly higher among AIAN girls (45%) than among AIAN boys (31%). However, certain sedentary activities such as hours of watching television (three or more hours per day) was lower among AIAN students (39%) than among black (63%) and Hispanic students (44%). Interestingly, the rate of watching television three or more hours per day was higher among AIAN boys (42%) than among AIAN girls (35%).

Compared to their peers, AIAN students are more likely not to participate in organized sports in school, specifically, 49 percent compared to 41 percent of non-Hispanic students. Fifty-three percent of AIAN girls, compared to 45 percent of AIAN boys, report they do not participate in school sports (Jones et al. 2011). This disparity is not particularly surprising for AIAN adolescent girls because many of them have demands to help or assist with childcare or in preparing meals. In general, many AIAN girls have a more difficult time working in physical activity as well as maintaining a healthy diet than their peers from other races and ethnicities.

EXPLANATORY FACTORS

In their recent exhaustive review of the literature on mental health of youth, Goodkind and colleagues (2010) cite a number of governmental reports on the needs of mental health service for youth by key agencies, namely, the Institute of Medicine, the Surgeon General's Office, the National Institute of Mental Health, and so forth. These reports contain recommendations for action that give special attention to mental health care needs for youth living in rural areas. Unfortunately, the authors note that most of the recommendations issued in these reports have not been addressed.

Goodkind and colleagues (2010) conclude their review by assembling seven explanations they have identified as areas of behavioral health disparities for minority youth: (1) high levels of violence and trauma exposure and traumatic loss; (2) past and current oppression, racism, and discrimination; (3) underfunded systems of care; (4) disregard for effective indigenous practices in service provision, policy, and funding; (5) overreliance on evidence-based practices; (6) lack of cultural competence among systems of care providers; and (7) barriers to care. In one form or another, these seven explanations identified by Goodkind and her team of researchers (2010) are also found in the everyday lives of the three Native sisters.

To further examine the impact of the seven explanations on AIAN youth in need of mental health services, Goodkind and colleagues (2010) conducted a study with a sample of 71 American Indian youth, parents, and elders; 25 service providers; and four traditional healers or practitioners. In this study, the team was especially interested in exploring mental treatment models for youth that were said to be based on "indigenous healing practices and perspectives."

Following the review of the selected intervention models and the results of their study, Goodkind and her colleagues (2010) offered the following seven recommendations to help develop more comprehensive, culturally appropriate interventions in addressing mental health needs of AI youth in rural communities: (1) expand mechanisms for reimbursing for services provided by traditional healers; (2) fund infrastructures that link behavioral health and primary care health services for young clients; (3) shift emphasis from evidence-based practices to practice-based evidence; (4) require behavioral health systems to take into account the current realities of Native youth; (5) provide funding for innovative programs that connect prevention and treatment; (6) create alternative licensing and credentialing for culturally appropriate services provided by Native service providers; and (7) encourage an apology from the U.S. government for destroying the culture and strengths of American Indians.

These seven recommendations voice the importance of a movement from evidence-based to best practice approaches, interventions to help integrate a more holistic approach to addressing current mental health problems faced by Native youth as well as to advocate for developing certification processes for Native healers because "western behavioral health systems must find ways to support Native healing practices" (p. 391).

In another study, Mmari, Blum, and Teufel-Shone (2010) examined delinquent behaviors of American Indian youth and protective factors in a study conducted with three different tribal communities (urban Southwest, Midwest, and rural Southwest). The study design used by Mmari and colleagues was a social-ecological model that incorporated four levels of inquiry: the community, the school, the family, and the individual. The researchers categorized their findings to each of these four levels.

At the community level, they identified risk factors that included racism, ready access to cash or per capita payment received by youth from tribal gaming enterprises, loss of language and culture, and gangs and weapons. Mmari and colleagues (2010) observed that primary prevention and key protective factors at the community level need to give youth cultural strengths that include providing them with knowledge of their tribal language and getting them involved in traditional ceremonies or other cultural activities so that these cultural groundings can give them a stronger personal identity and a sense of belonging.

The stories of the three Native sisters highlight their disconnect with their respective Native heritage and their low levels of involvement in tribal cultural activities. Rosaline, having spent the first 10 years of her life in Mexico, faced language and cultural barriers when she started school in Arizona. Laura's education among non-Native classmates separated her somewhat from the cultural activities of her mother's tribe, and Carla's adoption placed her in a home where religious beliefs and practices of her adopted parents discouraged her from learning or being exposed to her tribal cultural activities. Active connection to tribal cultural activities such as ceremonies and language classes might have provided a more supportive environment that could have aided these girls in avoiding some of the unhealthy choices made.

At the school level, the authors identified the risk factors that could have been minimized if protective factors were available through teacher support or an environment where the youth had contact with mentors and positive role models (Mmari et al. 2010). Indeed, the three Native sisters each experienced peer pressure that was difficult to resist. Peer pressure led Laura to start cigarette smoking to lose weight and as a way to fit in. Being a pregnant teen showed Rosaline that she was popular with the boys, and it gave her a particular status in her peer group, some of whom were also pregnant. Carla's self-medication led to her submersion in a teen culture where drinking and abusing drugs was an easy way to avoid the sadness of her life. How might the lives of these three Native sisters have been different? What can make a difference in the lives of teen American Indian girls to provide them with more hopeful futures? It would seem that the recommendations offered by Mmari and (2010) are appropriate in more than one area.

Mmari and colleagues (2010), for example, also identified risk factors at the family level, a critical protective resource that was either weak or missing in the lives of the three Native sisters. For the three sisters, family support was lacking in many instances due to family disintegration, availability of drugs and alcohol, and lack of parental disciple.

The participants involved in the Mmari study were not questioned about individual-level risk behaviors and protective factors but instead were questioned about the difficulties and hardships individuals had to overcome. Overwhelmingly, the responses to these questions emphasized the importance of religion, spirituality, and teaching the young responsibility and self-motivation (Mmari et al. 2010). The findings from this study have important implications in the future design of interventions utilizing their social-ecological framework as well as stressing the importance of addressing both risk and protective factors.

From these and other studies, the researchers recommend that AIAN youth programs include the involvement of parents, a recommendation that is supported by the literature for youth of other races and ethnicities (DiClemente et al. 2001; Farrington and Hawkins 1991; Resnick, Ireland, and Borowsky 2004; Steinberg, Elmen, Mounts 1989). The distinct lack of parental involvement in the lives of the three Native sisters resulted not only in a lack of parental role models but also in a lack of firm guidance and definition of boundaries for behavior for Carla, Laura, and Rosaline. The combination of a lack of parental involvement, peer pressure, and a lack of positive role models led each of our three Native sisters into behaviors that were not healthy for them.

STRENGTHS OF NATIVE ADOLESCENTS

One example in the literature on the strengths of Native youth is found in a smoking cessation study by Horn and colleagues (2009), *Who Wants to Quit? Characteristics of American Indian Youth Who Seek Smoking Cessation Intervention*. This study was a part of the American Lung Association's Not on Tobacco (NOT) program, where the investigators compared the 2001 to 2004 profiles of Native youth with non-Native youth in the Northeastern United States. NOT was a national intervention program that was conducted in 49 states and reached over 150,000 teens between 2000 and 2005. This was an evidence-based intervention program that targeted high school students who wanted to quit smoking by taking lessons in life management skills. In this national sample, there were 91 Native youth who participated, and the sample was composed of females (50.5%) and males (49.5%), with most of the youth over age 16 (70.3%) and in the 10th grade or higher (72.5%).

A major finding from NOT was that the Native youth who had enrolled in the program were smoking with less intensity and frequency and were more ready to quit smoking than the non-Native youth participants. In addition, approximately 61 percent of the Native youth reported that they started smoking cigarettes between the ages of 10 and 14 years. The NOT findings hold important implications for future research in improving recruitment strategies in order to improve participation by Native teens in smoking intervention programs. The study uncovered previously little-known behavioral and environmental factors that influence a youth's readiness to quit smoking. The researchers found in their study that "being male, being low nicotine dependent, having previously tried to quit, and having fewer friends who smoke were strong predictors" for being a good candidate to a smoking intervention program (Horn et al. 2009:161). There is still much to learn, but this study provides insight into possible intervention design and recommendations to further investigation with a population that is currently understudied.

SUCCESSFUL INTERVENTIONS

Are there interventions out there that work to aid AIAN teens in developing healthier behaviors? The patterns followed by Carla, Rosaline, and Laura are all too familiar, but are there strategies that can help these Native sisters change? According to a recent study by Rushing and Stephens (2011), *Use of Media Technologies by Native American Teens and Young Adults in the Pacific Northwest: Exploring Their Utility for Designing Culturally Appropriate Technology-Based Health Interventions*, offers some helpful insight as to how to reach youth. Rushing and Stephens compared the use of media technology by 405 Native youth to a national sample of teens reported in a 2008 U.S. sample. The examination of the data found that the Native youth reported using computers, cell phones, and iPods or MP3 players at a greater proportion.

The study also found that interventions that were web-based and delivered through social network sites or through text messages were more appropriate for females than males, whereas intervention messages delivered through video games or online videos were more appropriate for males than females in the study. In addition, the Native youth in the study voiced an interest in seeing health messages that were culturally appropriate and that contained images similar to themselves. The findings from this study have potential implications on the future design of health promotion, prevention, or intervention for Native female youth in the Pacific Northwest—interventions that work through many different modes of delivery to help tackle the problems facing today's Native youth.

An example of community-based interventions by Kegler, Malcoe, and Fedirko (2010) was a study conducted with American Indians in Oklahoma. The intervention study included nine American Indian nations whose tribal lands were left with millions of tons of mine tailings and were subsequently designated as part of the Superfund sites in 1984. Kegler and colleagues developed a community-based intervention aimed at changing behaviors to lessen lead poisoning. The intervention involved lay health advisors and youth from the communities. The first phase of the intervention (1998–2000) involved the recruitment of 40 natural helpers who were trained on lead poisoning prevention strategies and who initiated community awareness activities that resulted in nearly 27,000 contacts and 5,000 hours of community education.

In the second phase of the study (2001–2004), 24 Native lay health advisors were trained in lead poisoning prevention and accomplished over 12,500 contacts and 3,500 hours of work. The lay health advisors also produced and administered a tribal day-care lead poisoning prevention curriculum. In addition, 120 youth were recruited from schools surrounding the Tar Creek Superfund site who worked with a high school art teacher and a junior high English teacher to conduct youth-led projects (Kegler et al. 2010). One intervention focused on emphasizing hand washing before meals and snacks for Native children. This intervention showed improvement in annual blood levels for lead while there was no improvement in the sample of white children. The researchers attributed the difference to the method of dissemination of prevention information through important systems of social networks in the Native communities.

Another example of a different community-based intervention program was conducted with a Southwestern tribal community. The study design utilized a collaborative family-based intervention involving the development of a culturally adapted curriculum designed to address a major health concern in the community—youth substance use initiation. The theoretical foundation of the curriculum included family resiliency building, cultural embeddedness, and strategies to enhance community empowerment using the public health prevention framework (Belone et al. 2011). The intervention utilized a participatory approach, first establishing a local advisory council that was very active in the research process, where it assisted with (1) the development of a culturally focused curriculum, (2) the development of process and outcome measurements, and (3) the facilitation of the intervention utilizing the culturally adapted curriculum.

It should be noted that although there are many approaches to addressing substance use initiation by youth, most of these mainstream interventions are planned and implemented with little or no attention to making the intervention culturally specific. For that reason, Belone and colleagues (2011) initiated in their public health prevention framework a culturally adapted, family-based intervention that utilized tools from another successful model used with an American Indian community (Whitbeck 2011). The aim of the Southwestern tribal intervention model was to teach youth about substance abuse and its consequences. The initial results from the pilot study intervention indicate positive improvements in cultural identity and substance use intention by American Indian youth, particularly among those who had not yet started to drink alcohol or use drugs. Again, the combination of a culturally responsive intervention and parental involvement at an early age is essential to ensure success, and if available, this type of program could have been of potential benefit to adolescent teen girls such as Carla, Rosaline, and Laura.

APPROACHES TO INTERVENTIONS

Empirically supported interventions (ESIs) have become critical to establish internal validity and effectiveness. The concern remains of how to translate findings from highly controlled efficacy trials (often in a single population) and replicate these in real-world community interventions (Solomon, Card, and Malow 2006) with diverse populations and cultures (Miller and Shinn 2005) in settings that are often resource poor with fewer staff and training opportunities

(Solomon et al. 2006). The challenge also remains to retain fidelity to the effective components of an intervention while contextualizing and adapting to the new culture and setting for enhancing external validity and program acceptance (Fixsen et al. 2005; Glasgow et al. 2006; Green and Glasgow 2006).

Because interventions tested on dominant-culture communities have been historically less effective in minority communities (Dutta 2007), excellent research has begun to be conducted in dissemination and implementation processes for ESIs. Literature suggests that programs with adaptations can enhance client participation, community support, and program outcomes (Solomon et al. 2006; Kelly, Sogolow, and Neumann 2000). The second research direction that can offer a greater possibility for a community-driven approach is that which goes beyond "tailoring" but, instead, works to create mutual learning, where the intervention can bridge or integrate community and culturally supported beliefs and practices (Solomon et al. 2006).

Among tribal populations, such culturally supported interventions often center on spiritual practices that are deeply embedded in the culture (Miller, Meyers, and Hiller-Sturmhofel 1999). One frequent explanation regarding high rates of alcohol abuse is that alcoholism was unknown prior to European contact, and therefore there was no need to develop indigenous treatments for addiction. Because alcohol and other substance abuses were not common, sanctions against the use of addictive substances were also not necessary. With no history of alcoholism and other substance abuse, the pressure of colonization did not leave much time for most tribes to set in place sanctions against alcohol or other substance abuse.

Moreover, sanctions against associated deviant behavior were further weakened by disruption of cross-generational teachings that reinforced cultural rules on expectant behaviors (Duran et al. 1998; Duncan et al. 1995). In addition, mainstream alcohol or drug prevention approaches or those initiated based on refusal skills found in ESI approaches often conflict with tribal values of fitting into one's peer group. For example, mainstream prevention programs are designed with an individualistic worldview whereas Native youth may be raised with a collectivistic worldview, placing the importance of the group before the importance of the individual. Due to the sparse and short-term funding available for AIAN youth behavioral intervention, the three Native sisters identified here did not have an opportunity to benefit from such interventions. In the best of all worlds, today's educators and health providers could learn more from studies that share information on successful interventions, interventions that can guide Native youth on a path to wellness.

INNOVATIVE INTERVENTION APPROACHES

Even though Carla's, Rosaline's, and Laura's health and future were negatively impacted by their risky behaviors, there is still hope for the future for other adolescent Native girls. Educators, health providers, and the teens themselves can benefit from findings of successful interventions. For example, the University of New Mexico's Center for Participatory Research has developed an innovative research approached called RezRIDERS (Tafoya 2010), a Native cultural adaptation and youth community involvement program to reduce alcohol and substance abuse in high-risk Native youth. Specifically, this project builds and expands upon a culturally connected American Indian facilitator and mentor network that has established an action sports program, a form of diversion intervention. The program is grounded in experiential and outdoor adventure education with an aim to build and foster leadership development instead of engaging in the use of alcohol or other unhealthy substances.

Through a sequential order of repeated exposures to activities such as snowboarding, white-water rafting, and ropes courses that are paired with lessons on traditional core values, optimism and hope for the future, self-determination, and team building, Native youth are given a chance for mutual learning with Native adult mentors. Adapting action sports through culturally connected mentorship with an emphasis on indigenous values helps revive these activities to the historical and traditional ways that AI youth used to challenge themselves in the environment coupled with lessons gained through storytelling and examples provided by elders and adult mentors. This intervention provides a controlled setting that integrates risk-prevention strategies through sports with mentorship under the guidance of skilled instructors. The program is especially aimed at high-risk youth who are unlikely to participate in team sports or after-school activities (Brave Heart et al. in press; Tafoya 2010). The success of this model holds much promise for other youth who need adult guidance and resources on how to develop sport and leadership skills as well as strategies that can help them and their friends avoid temptations associated with alcohol and other substances.

CONCLUSION

The stories shared about the three sisters, Rosaline, Carla, and Laura, reflect everyday challenges faced by some young Native women, and their stories also highlight the need for culturally relevant interventions that can help others like them overcome or avoid the negative health consequences that threaten AIAN youth and future generations. The problems of AIAN youth are well documented, but useful interventions that have been evaluated or documented with appropriate research designs are rare or lacking. It is therefore important to highlight culturally appropriate behavioral intervention studies that are promising and ensure the research results are shared with tribal communities and behavioral health service agencies and providers.

REFERENCES

Belone, L., J. Oetzel, N. Wallerstein, G. Tafoya, R. Rae, A. Rafelito, L. Kelhoyouma, I. Burbank, C. Finster, J. Henio-Charley, P. G. Maria, Y.-M. Lee, A. Thomas. 2011. "Using Participatory Research to Address Substance Use in an American Indian Community." Pp. 403–34 in *Communication Activism* (6th ed.). L. R. Frey and K. M. Carragee (Eds.). Cresskill, NJ: Hampton Press.

Brave Heart, M. and G. Tafoya. In press. "Wicasa Was'aka: Restoring the Traditional Strength of American Indian Males." *American Journal of Public Health*.

Centers for Disease Control (CDC). 2010. "Teen Birth Rates Declined Again in 2009." National Center for Chronic Disease Prevention and Health Promotion, Division of Reproductive Health. Accessed October 15, 2012. http://www.cdc.gov/Features/dsTeenPregnancy/.

DiClemente, R., G. Wingood, R. Crosby, C. Sionean, B. Cobb, K. Harrington, S. Davies, E. W. Hook, M. K. Oh. 2001. "Parental Monitoring: Association with Adolescents' Risk Behaviors. *Pediatrics* 107(6):1363–68.

Duncan, T. E., E. Tildsley, S. C Duncan, H. Hops. 1995. "The Consistency of Family and Peer Influences on the Development of Substance Use and Adolescence." *Addiction* 90(12):1647–60.

Duran, B., E. Duran, M. B. H. Yellow Horse. 1998. "Native Americans and the Trauma of History." In *Studying Native America: Problems and Prospects in Native American Studies*. R. Thornton (Ed). Madison: University of Wisconsin Press.

Dutta, A. 2007. *Development-induced Displacement and Human Rights*. New Delhi: Deep & Deep Publications.

Farrington, D. P. and J. D. Hawkins. 1991. "Predicting Participation, Early On-set and Later Persistence in Officially Recorded Offending." *Criminal Behavior and Mental Health* 1, 1–33.

Fixsen, D. L., S. F. Naoom, K. A. Blasé, R. M. Friedman, F. Wallace. 2005. "Implementation Research: A Synthesis of the Literature." National Implementation

Research Network. Accessed September 6, 2011. http://www.fpg.unc.edu/~nirn/resources/publications/Monograph/pdf/Monograph_full.pdf.

Glasgow, R. E., L. W. Green, L. M. Klesges, D. B. Abrams, E. B. Fisher, M. G. Goldstein, L. L. Hayman, J. K. Ockene, C. T. Orleans. 2006. "External Validity: We Need to Do More." *Annals of Behavioral Medicine* 31(2):105–8.

Goodkind, J. R., K. Ross-Toledo, S. John, J. L. Hall, L. Ross, L. Freeland, E. Coletta, T. Becenti-Fundark, C. Poola, R. Begay-Roanhorse, and C. Lee. 2010. "Promoting Healing and Restoring Trust: Policy Recommendations for Improving Behavioral Health Care for American Indian/Alaska Native Adolescents." *American Journal of Community Psychology* 46, 386–94. doi:10.1007/s10464-010-9347-4.

Green, L. W. and R. E. Glasgow. 2006. "Evaluating the Relevance, Generalization, and Applicability of Research: Issues in External Validation and Translation Methodology." *Evaluation and the Health Professions* 29(1):126–53.

Horn, K., N. Noerachmanto, G. Dino, K. Manzo, and M. Brayboy. 2009. "Who Wants to Quit? Characteristics of American Indian Youth Who Seek Smoking Cessation Intervention." *Journal of Community Health* 34, 153–63. doi:10.1007/s10900-008-9131-7.

Jones, S. E., K. Anderson, R. Lowry, and H. Conner. 2011. "Risks to Health among Indian/Alaska Native High School Students in the United States." *Preventing Chronic Disease* 8(4):A76. http://www.cdc.gov/pcd/issues/2011/jul/10_0193.htm.

Kegler, M. C., L. H. Malcoe, V. Fedirko. 2010. "Primary Prevention of Lead poisoning in Rural Native American Children: Behavioral Outcomes from a Community-based Intervention in a Former Mining Region." *Family and Community Health* 33(1):32–43.

Kelly, J. A., E. D. Sogolow, and M. S. Neumann. 2000. "Future Directions and Emerging Issues in Technology Transfer between HIV Prevention Researchers and Community-based Service Providers." *AIDS Education and Prevention* 12(Suppl. A):126–41.

Miller, W. R., R. J. Meyers, and S. Hiller-Sturmhofel. 1999. "The Community Reinforcement Approach." *Alcohol Research and Health: The Journal of the National Institute on Alcohol Abuse and Alcoholism* 23(2):116–21.

Miller, R. and M. Shinn. 2005. "Learnings from Communities: Overcoming Difficulties in Dissemination of Prevention and Promotion Efforts. *American Journal of Community Psychology* 34(3–4):169–83.

Mmari, K. N., R. W. Blum, and N. Teufel-Shone. 2010. "What Increases Risk and Protection for Delinquent Behaviors among American Indian Youth?: Findings from Three Tribal Communities. *Youth and Society* 41(3):382–413. doi:10.1177/0044118X09333645.

National Institutes of Health (NIH). 1998. "Drug Use among Racial/Ethnic Minorities." National Institute on Drug Abuse. NIH Publication No. 98-3888, printed 1995, revised September 1998. Accessed October 15, 2011. http://archives.drugabuse.gov/pubs/minorities/.

Resnick, M. D., M. Ireland, and I. Borowsky. 2004. "Youth Violence Perpetration: What Protects? What Predicts? Findings from the National Longitudinal Study of Adolescent Health." *Journal of Adolescent Health* 35(5):424.e1–10.

Rushing, S. C. and D. Stephens. 2011. "Use of Media Technologies by Native American Teens and Young Adults in the Pacific Northwest: Exploring Their Utility for Designing Culturally Appropriate Technology-based Health Interventions. *Journal of Primary Prevention* 32:135–45.

Solomon, J., J. J. Card, and R. M. Malow. 2006. "Adapting Efficacious Interventions: Advancing Translational Research in HIV prevention." *Evaluation and the Health Professions* 29(2):162–94.

Steinberg, L., J. D. Elmen, and N. S. Mounts. 1989. "Authoritative Parenting, Psychosocial Maturity, and Academic Success among Adolescents." *Child Development* 60(6):1424–36.

Tafoya, G. 2010. "Reducing Risk through Interpersonal Development, Education, Reflection and Sport: The RezRIDERS Curriculum." Unpublished master's thesis, University of New Mexico.

U.S. Census Bureau. 2011. "American Factfinder2 Website with Detailed Tables by Race." Accessed October 20, 2011.http://factfinder2.census.gov/faces/nav/jsf/pages/index.xhtml#none.

Whitbeck, L. B. (2001). "*Bii-zin-da-de-da:* The Listening to One Another Prevention Program." Paper presented at the Second National Conference on Drug Abuse Prevention Research: A Progress Update, Washington, DC.

CHAPTER 13

Protections to Consider When Engaging American Indians/Alaska Natives in Human Subject Research

Francine C. Gachupin

INTRODUCTION

American Indian and Alaska Native (AIAN) ancestors have been researchers and inventors for thousands of years, posing questions and utilizing answers to better understand health and well-being, disease and illness, and the interconnectedness of people and the environment. This knowledge base and accumulation of skills were passed from generation to generation and formed the basis of survival, subsistence, and adaptation to change. The changes experienced by AIANs, as a collective, over the last few hundred years have been substantive, and the long-term effects of these experiences remain unfolding and, in many instances, unknown, therefore, retaining the value of research.

The value and respect paid to beneficial innovation and discovery, however, became threatened and resisted when AIANs found themselves subjects of curiosity, observed and described without their knowledge or consent. Unfortunately, outcomes from some of these descriptions have created misinformation and misinterpretation that have added to lingering negative stereotypes and social harm.

The benefits gained from such observations went to the investigators, many of whom gained national or international recognition for their studies and publications. Early investigators included explorers, adventurers, and self-taught ethnographers. Social scientists like anthropologists followed with a more scientific agenda, although some were motivated to record customs and traditions of AIANs before they all vanished.

The emphasis in some of these early descriptions of tribal life tended to highlight what investigators saw esoteric, especially ceremonies conducted as a part of healing the ill. Some of these ceremonial aspects were described as "heathen" practices, creating a new target for missionaries and others to outlaw some of these ceremonies. By association, tribal healers also became targets of the prohibition. These attacks on medicine people and ways of healing that were a central part of tribal life helped fueled the antiresearch attitude. Research abuse, however, continued, some of it as part of medical care—for example, forced sterilization (Jarrell 1992; Milligan 1993; Online Encyclopedia 2012).

Today, the enforcement of national policies to protect study participants is slowly changing some of the Native peoples' negative perception of research. Some of this change is also due to greater role tribes are assuming in defining, permitting, and collaborating in or conducting their own research.

This chapter focuses on the current state of human subject protection policies and the applicable definition of research as a systematic investigation designed to develop or contribute to generalizable knowledge and the policy impacts on AIANs (45 CFR 46[102]). The discussion begins with the three basic ethical principles that serve as the reference for current research involving human subjects: (1) respect for persons, (2) beneficence, and (3) justice (U.S. DHHS 2012d; National Commission 1978). These three principles are meant to protect individuals from the burden of research while balancing the burden with the ability to access promising research (Summers 2011). When an investigator is proposing a research project, these three principles must be taken into account and serve as integral facets of the research.

The protection of human subjects in research is a requirement, and most of the authors contributing research studies in this book had to go through the process of obtaining approval to conduct their studies. The protection requirements are based on case instances (Beecher 1966) where individuals were subjected to brutal crimes under the guise of medical research (Berger 1990), where individuals were subjected to unethical research (Brandt 1978; Krugman 1986), or where subjects were chosen because they were in a compromised or powerless position (for example, prisoners, poor, children, elderly, or people of color)

(Makhijani and Kennedy 1994; Elliot and Abadie 2008). In order to ensure better protection of subjects participating in research, these ethical principles were established so individuals were informed of the different aspects of a particular study and were voluntarily participating once given the opportunity to assess the requirements of their participation. These principles endorse measures to protect information and minimize harms while benefits are maximized (U.S. DHHS 2012d).

NATIVE PEOPLES AND RESEARCH ABUSE

Indian country—a term that is used to refer to the collective of tribal nations across the United States—has experience with research studies gone awry where harm has been done to individuals as well as to tribes, although few have been documented in written form. The most recent case of research abuse involved the Havasupai Tribe of Arizona, a tribe that was forced to take legal action against a researcher and the researcher's academic institution for publishing data that took liberty with biological samples (without consent or tribal approval) obtained in an earlier study and for failing to follow protocol in getting informed consent for conducting unrelated health record research ("The Havasupai Case" 2007; Harmon 2010a; Harmon 2010b; Vorhaus 2010).

Indigenous communities in Canada have not been immune to research abuse either. In 2000, the Nuu-Chah-Nulth on Vancouver Island in British Columbia also made public their appeal to have specimens returned after learning samples collected for an arthritis study were being used by students and collaborators for tracing origins of the tribal members and were involved in data sharing that was unknown to the tribe (Wiwchar n.d.; Wiwchar 2004). The experiences of these tribes, only a couple among many, are important as these examples underscore the importance of ethics and the need to understand the rights and responsibilities in protecting participants in research.

POLICIES ON PROTECTION OF RESEARCH PARTICIPANTS

The protection of human subjects regulations are intended to provide reference and guidance to researchers and scientists and have both international ("Declaration of Geneva" n.d.; Declaration of Helsinki n.d.; Nuremberg Code n.d.) and national roots (45 CFR 46;

21 CFR; "Good Clinical Practice" n.d.; "Hippocratic Oath" n.d.). These policies underscore the paramount importance of the rights and welfare of individuals, even above and beyond the importance of science and society (Summers 2011).

The current oversight responsibility of human subject research begins at the federal level. The Common Rule (U.S. DHHS 2012a) refers to the shared responsibility of all federal departments and agencies that are signatories to the federal policy for the protection of human subjects and their having adopted oversight by institutional review boards (IRBs) that require informed consent requirements as written in Title 45 of the Code of Federal Regulations (CFR), part 46, Subpart A (U.S. DHHS 2012c; "Institutional Review Board" n.d.). These federal departments and agencies include the Departments of Agriculture, Energy, Commerce, Housing and Urban Development, Justice, Defense, Education, Veterans Affairs, Transportation, Health and Human Services, and Homeland Security; the National Science Foundation; the Environmental Protection Agency; the National Aeronautics and Space Administration; the Agency for International Development; the Central Intelligence Agency; and the Consumer Product Safety Commission (US DHHS 2012a).

Research funded by the DHHS, for example that of the National Institutes of Health (NIH), the Centers for Disease Control and Prevention (CDC), the Indian Health Service (IHS), are subject to 45 CFR 46. The Food and Drug Administration (FDA) also has regulations 21 CFR 56 for basic requirements for IRBs and 21 CFR 50 for informed consent, which pertain to FDA-regulated products such as drugs, devices, or biologics (21 CFR). Depending on the scope of a given project, a researcher may need approval with respect to both sets of codes.

The current version of 45 CFR 46 includes five subparts. Subpart A is the basic set of protections for all human subjects of research conducted or supported by DHHS and was revised in 1981 and 1991, with technical amendments made in 2005. Three of the other subparts provide added protections for specific vulnerable groups of subjects. Subpart B, issued in 1975 and most recently revised in 2001, provides additional protections for pregnant women, human fetuses, and neonates involved in research. Subpart C, issued in 1978, provides additional protections pertaining to biomedical and behavioral research involving prisoners as subjects. Subpart D, issued in 1983, provides additional protections for children involved as subjects in research. Subpart E, issued in 2009, requires registration of IRBs that conduct reviews of human research studies conducted or supported by

DHHS (45 CFR 46). A research project including any of these vulnerable groups of subjects must complete additional documentation on processes to ensure protection.

Academic institutions and tribes or tribal consortia receiving federal funding for research are also required to have a federal-wide assurance (FWA) (U.S. DHHS 2012b) and individual research projects reviewed by an IRB. FWA requirement state that

> All of the Institution's human subjects research activities, regardless of whether the research is subject to the U.S. Federal Policy for the Protection of Human Subjects (also known as the Common Rule), will be guided by a statement of principles governing the institution in the discharge of its responsibilities for protecting the rights and welfare of human subjects of research conducted at or sponsored by the institution (U.S. DHHS 2012b: 45 CFR 46).

TRIBAL ROLES IN HEALTH RESEARCH

In 1998, the first four tribally based epidemiology centers were funded by the federal IHS and were established at Anchorage, Alaska; Portland, Oregon; Phoenix, Arizona; and Lac du Flambeau, Wisconsin (IHS 2012c). Tribal support for these epidemiology centers continued to grow, and by 2006, 11 tribally based epidemiology centers existed across the country, including Seattle, Washington; Window Rock, Arizona; Albuquerque, New Mexico; Oklahoma City, Oklahoma; Billings, Montana; Rapid City, South Dakota; and Nashville, Tennessee (IHS 2012c). These centers were funded to manage public health information systems, to investigate diseases of concern to area tribes, to manage disease prevention and control programs, and to respond to public health emergencies. Several of these centers began research projects and became active participants in establishing FWAs or serving on IRBs (Northwest Portland Area Indian Health Board 2012; RMTEC 2012; Northern Plains Tribal Epidemiology Center 2009).

To promote more health-related research activities in Indian country, in 2000 the IHS and the National Institute of General Medical Sciences (NIGMS) of the NIH formed a joint partnership supporting the Native American Research Centers for Health (NARCH) (IHS 2012b). The goal of this initiative was stated as the following:

> The NARCH initiative supports partnerships between American Indian/Alaska Native (AI/AN) Tribes or Tribally-based

organizations and institutions that conduct intensive academic-level biomedical, behavioral and health services research. This funding mechanism develops opportunities for conducting research, research training and faculty development to meet the needs of American Indian/Alaska Native (AI/AN) communities. As a developmental process, Tribes and Tribal Organizations are able to build a research infrastructure, including a core component for capacity building and the possibility of reducing the many health disparities so prevalent in AI/AN communities. (IHS 2012b)

The NARCH initiative not only established infrastructure within tribes and tribal consortia for human subject protection but provided resources for studies that were of value to the tribal communities. Table 13.1 provides some of these NARCH research projects.

Table 13.1
NARCH Research Projects in Indian Country by Funding Sources

Alaska Native Tribal Health Consortium (ANTHC)	
Autoimmune Liver Disease in Alaska Natives	NIAID
Nicotine Exposure and Metabolism in Alaska Natives	NIDA
Tobacco-Free Alaska Native Families	NIGMS
Bronchiectasis Observational Study in Alaska Native Children	NHLBI
Prenatal Alcohol Exposure among AI/AN Infants	NIAAA
Aberdeen Area Tribal Chairmen's Health Board (AATCHB)	
Predicting Insulin Resistance in American Indian Youth (Diabetes and prediabetes in Northern Plains tribal youth)	NIDDK
Screening for Asthma among Children in Northern Plains Tribal Communities	NHLBI
Validation Study of Depression and Anxiety Measures with Northern Plains Indians	NIDA
California Rural Indian Health Board (CRIHB)	
Variation in Preventable Hospitalization Outcomes in Tribal Health Programs	AHRQ
Northwest Portland Area Indian Health Board (NPAIHB)	
Internet-Assisted Diabetes Care in Rural AI/AN (Study of self-management of Type 2 Diabetes)	NIGMS
Child Safety Seat Project	NIGMS
Community Intervention to Reduce Childhood Obesity and Caries	NIDCR

Table 13.1 (Continued)

Evidence Based Medicine to Improve Health Care	NIGMS
Black Hills Center For American Indian Health (BLCAIH)	
Contextual Issues in Traditional Lakota Healing	NCCAM
Theory-Based Colorectal Cancer Screening Intervention	NCI
Navajo Nation/Dine' College	
Navajo Ethno-Medical Encyclopedia Research Project	NCCAM
Indian Health Council, Inc. (Southern California)	
Burden and resilience among caregivers of frail elders	ORWH
Oklahoma NARCH (ONARCH): Cherokee/Chickasaw	
Clinical Trial to Improve Outcomes in Fetal Alcohol Syndrome	NIAAA
Understanding Rheumatic Disease in Oklahoma Tribal Members	NIAMS
Southcentral Foundation (Alaska)	
Ethical and Cultural Implications of Specimen Banking among Alaska Native People	NHGRI
Great Lakes Inter-Tribal Council (GLITC)	
Breast Cancer Risk and Screening Patterns in Bemidji Area American Indian Women	NIGMS
Albuquerque Area Indian Health Board (AAIHB)	
Listening to Each Other—Substance Abuse Intervention	NIDA
Tribal Cancer Control Project	NCI
Juvenile Justice Program: Incarcerated Youth at Risk	NIGMS
White Mountain Apache Tribe	
Youth suicide prevention using community-based, participatory research	ORWH
Prevention of pneumococcal spread within Apache families	NIAID

Source: IHS (2012b).

RESEARCH PROTOCOL IN INDIAN COUNTRY

When a research project is being undertaken, whether in Indian country or elsewhere, the researcher must receive approval to conduct the study through an IRB. An IRB is a committee, also known as independent ethics committee (IEC) or ethical review board (ERB), governed by 45 CFR 46, that has formal designation to review, approve, and monitor behavioral and biomedical research involving human subjects. IRBs are regulated by the OHRP within DHHS:

The Office for Human Research Protections (OHRP) provides leadership in the protection of the rights, welfare, and wellbeing of subjects involved in research conducted or supported by the U.S. Department of Health and Human Services (HHS). OHRP helps ensure this by providing clarification and guidance, developing educational programs and materials, maintaining regulatory oversight, and providing advice on ethical and regulatory issues in biomedical and social-behavioral research. (45 CFR 46.102)

IRBs are empowered to approve research plans, require modifications of research plans prior to approval, or disapprove research. The specific role and responsibility of an IRB is summarized as follows:

IRBs are most commonly used for studies in the fields of health and the social sciences, including anthropology, sociology, and psychology. Such studies may be clinical trials of new drugs or devices, they may be studies of personal or social behavior, opinions or attitudes, or they may be studies of how health care is delivered and might be improved.

The purpose of an IRB review is to assure, both in advance and by periodic review, that appropriate steps are taken to protect the rights and welfare of humans participating as subjects in a research study. To accomplish this purpose, IRBs review research protocols and related materials (e.g., informed consent documents and investigator brochures) to ensure protection of the rights and welfare of human subjects of research. The chief objectives of every IRB protocol review are to assess the ethics of the research and its methods, to promote fully informed and voluntary participation by prospective subjects who are themselves capable of making such choices (or, if that is not possible, informed permission given by a suitable proxy) and to maximize the safety of subjects once they are enrolled in the project. (U.S. DHHS 2012c)

There are three types of applications that are available to the researcher, and the investigator has to determine which application to submit to the IRB. The selection depends on two things: (1) the risk level of the study and (2) the type of research being undertaken. Depending on the proposed study, an IRB can decide if the application meets the requirement for an exemption from a full IRB review, merits an expedited review, or would require a full IRB review. The first two (exempt and expedited) are reviewed by one or two members of the IRB, most typically a chairperson or his or her designee, and are reviewed outside of a formally convened IRB committee meeting.

These studies are typically considered to be at or less than minimal risk. The regulatory definition of minimal risk is that the probability and magnitude of harm or discomfort anticipated in the research are not greater in and of themselves than those ordinarily encountered in daily life or during the performance of routine physical or psychological examinations or tests (45 CFR 46.102[h][i]).

The latter, full-review studies, are reviewed by two primary reviewers and are discussed and voted on by a fully convened IRB. Full-study applications or proposals are typically greater than minimal-risk studies.

In Indian country, many tribal or IHS IRBs review, as a committee, *all* proposed research projects irrespective of risk level or type of research being undertaken; for example, the Navajo Nation Health Research Review Board and the Alaska Area IHS IRB take this approach (IHS 2012a). Table 13.2 lists IRBs that are under the jurisdiction of the IHS.

Table 13.2
IHS IRBs

National IRB (NIRB) at IHS Headquarters—Rockville, Maryland		
Phillip Smith, MD, MPH Chair, IHS National IRB (NIRB)	IHS NIRB c/o Ms. Juanita Neconie	301-443-4700 (voice) 301-443-0114 (fax) phillip.smith@ihs.gov
Alan Trachtenberg, MD, MPH IHS Human Research Protection Administrator IRB00000646	801 Thompson Ave. TMP, Suite 450 Rockville, MD 20852	Submit projects electronically to irb@ ihs.gov
Aberdeen Area		
Elaine Miller, M. D. Chair, Aberdeen Area IHS IRB IRB00000635	115 4th Avenue, SE Aberdeen, SD 57401	605-226-7341 (voice) 605-226-7543 (fax) Elaine.miller@ ihsabr.ihs.gov
Alaska Area		
David Barrett, MD Chair, Alaska Area IHS IRB	4315 Diplomacy Drive—RMCC	907-729-3924 (voice) 907-729-2082 (fax) tjpowell@anmc.org

(continued)

Table 13.2 (Continued)

Terry Powell Administrator, Alaska Area IHS IRB IRB00000636	Anchorage, AK 99508	

Bemidji Area

Dawn Wyllie, MD, **MPH** Chair, Bemidji Area Publication Review	522 Minnesota Avenue, NW Bemidji, MN 56601	218-444-0491 (voice) 218-444-0498 (fax) dawn.wyllie@ihs.gov

Billings Area

Diane Jeanotte Chair, Billings Area IHS IRB IRB00000638	P.O. Box 36600 2900 4th Avenue North Billings, MT 59107	406-247-7125 (voice) 406-247-7231 (fax) Diane.jeanotte@ mail.ihs.gov

Nashville Area

Palmeda Taylor, PhD Cochair, Nashville Area IHS IRB **Roy S. Kennon, MD** Cochair, Nashville Area IHS IRB IRB00000640	711 Stewarts Ferry Pike Nashville, TN 37214	615-467-1534 (voice) 615-467-1585 (fax) palmeda.taylor@ihs.gov 615-467-1531 (voice) 615-467-1580 (fax) roy.kennon@ihs.gov

Navajo Nation

Beverly Becenti- **Pigman** Chair, Navajo Nation Health Research Review Board (and Navajo Area IHS IRB) IRB00000641	Drawer Box 1390 Administration Building 2 Window Rock, AZ 86515	928-697-2525 (voice) 928-871-6263 (fax) bbp_pqh@yahoo.com

Oklahoma Area

Travis Watts, Pharm. D., BCPS, CDE, Chair, Oklahoma Area IHS IRB IRB00000642	Five Corporation Plaza 3625 NW 56th Street Oklahoma City, OK 73112	405-951-3829 (voice) 405-951-3916 (fax) travis.watts@ihs.gov

Phoenix Area

Augusta Hays, MD Chair, Phoenix Area IHS IRB IRB00000643	Two Renaissance Square 40 North Central Avenue, Suite 600 Phoenix, AZ 85004	602-364-5047 or 602-364-5039 Augusta.Hays@ihs.gov

Table 13.2 (Continued)

	Portland Area	
Rena Gill,	NW Portland Area	503-326-2014 (voice)
Chair, Portland Area	Health Board	503-326-7280 (fax)
IHS IRB	2121 SW Broadway,	Rena.gill@ihs.gov
IRB00000645	Suite 300,	
	Portland, OR 97201	
	Tucson Area	
Karen Higgins,PhD	7900 South J. Stock	520-295-2532 (voice)
Chair, Tucson Area	Road	520-295-2569 (fax)
Publication Review	Tucson, AZ 85746	Karen.Higgins@ihs.gov
Committee		

Source: IHS (2012b).

TRIBAL IRBS

With considerable encouragement from within and without, an increasing number of tribal organizations and tribal communities are developing their own IRBs under 45 CFR 46. Currently, research projects conducted at IHS direct care facilities serving a tribal nation that has its own IRB must have the approval of *both* the tribal IRB *and* the IHS IRB. Projects at facilities managed by tribal nations with their own IRB and FWA require approval of only the tribal IRB. Where a tribe does have its own IRB, the following procedure is followed:

Protocols approved by Tribal Research Review Committees that do not meet the formal requirements of 45 CFR 46 for an IRB should also be forwarded to the IHS IRB for approval. A formal letter of approval from the Tribal Research Committee or IRB is required for consideration by an IHS IRB. This generally takes the place of the Council Resolution or approval letter from an authorized Tribal Health Official that would ordinarily be required. Tribal IRBs that serve a dual role as both a Tribal IRB *and* an IHS Area Office IRB (Such as the Navajo Nation's IRB) are listed under IHS IRBs (IHS 2012a).

Table 13.3 provides a listing of IRBs that are under the jurisdiction of a specific tribe or tribal consortium.

Table 13.3
Tribal IRBs

California Rural Indian Health Board (CRIHB)

Susan Dahl, MHA, RHIA, CHC, CHP Chair, CRIHB IRB	4400 Auburn Blvd., 2nd floor Sacramento, CA 95841	916-929-9761 Ext 1010 916-929-7246 (fax) susan.dahl@crihb.net
Carol Korenbrot, PhD Cochair, CRIHB IRB		919-929-9761, Ext. 1040 916-929-7246 (fax) carol.korenbrot@ crihb.net

Cherokee Nation

Sohail Kahn, MBBS, MPH Cochair, Cherokee Nation IRB **Gloria Grim, MD** Cochair, Cherokee Nation IRB	P.O. Box 948 Highway 62, 4 miles South of city Tahlequah, Oklahoma 74465	918-456-0671 X2557 (voice) 918-458-5539 (fax) Sohail-Khan@ cherokee.org

Chickasaw Nation

Sheryl Goodson, Chair Chickasaw Nation Research Review Committee (RRC) **Bobby Saunkeah, RRC Secretary**	Carl Albert Indian Health Facility 1001 N. Country Club Road Ada, OK 74820	580-421-4548 (voice) 580-421-6208 (fax) Sheryl.Goodson@ chickasaw.net 580-421-4532 bobby.saunkeah@ chickasaw.net

Choctaw Nation

David F. Wharton, MPH, RN Facilitator, Choctaw Nation IRB	Choctaw Nation Health Services Choctaw Nation Health Clinic— Idabel 902 E Lincoln Road Idabel, OK 74745	580-286-2600 Ext. 1076 580-286-1189 (fax) dfwharton@cnhsa.com

Rocky Mountain Tribal IRB

Cheryl Belcourt RMT-IRB Coordinator	175 North, 27th Suite 1003 Billings, MT 59101	406-252-2550 406-254-6355 (fax) cheryl@mtwytlc.com

Source: IHS (2012c).

This number will undoubtedly continue to increase as more tribal communities invest their resources in health-related research, especially those communities that are now or will be managing their own health programs.

TYPES OF IRB REVIEWS

All IRBs observe certain criteria for evaluating research proposals submitted to them for their review. The review outcomes include exempt applications, expedited applications, and those applications that require full review.

EXEMPT FROM REVIEW

To submit an exempt study application, the proposed research should be encapsulated within one or more of the following categories (U.S. DHHS 2012d):

1. Research conducted in established or commonly accepted educational settings, involving normal educational practices, such as:

    1-a) research on regular and special education instructional strategies, or

    1-b) research on the effectiveness of or the comparison among instructional techniques, curricula, or classroom management methods.

2. Research involving the use of educational tests (cognitive, diagnostic, aptitude, achievement), survey procedures, interview procedures or observation of public behavior, unless:

    2-a) information obtained is recorded in such a manner that human subjects can be identified, directly or through identifiers linked to the subjects; and

    2-b) any disclosure of the human subjects' responses outside the research could reasonably place the subjects at risk of criminal or civil liability or be damaging to the subjects' financial standing, employability, or reputation.

3. Research involving the use of educational tests (cognitive, diagnostic, aptitude, achievement), survey procedures, interview

procedures, or observation of public behavior that is not exempt under paragraph (b)(2) of this section, if:

   3-a) the human subjects are elected or appointed public officials or candidates for public office;

   3-b) federal statute(s) require(s) without exception that the confidentiality of the personally identifiable information will be maintained throughout the research and thereafter.

4. Research involving the collection or study of existing data, documents, records, pathological specimens, or diagnostic specimens, if these sources are publicly available or if the information is recorded by the investigator in such a manner that subjects cannot be identified, directly or through identifiers linked to the subjects.

5. Research and demonstration projects which are conducted by or subject to the approval of department or agency heads, and which are designed to study, evaluate, or otherwise examine:

   5-a) public benefit or service programs;

   5-b) procedures for obtaining benefits or services under those programs;

   5-c) possible changes in or alternatives to those programs or procedures; or

   5-d) possible changes in methods or levels of payment for benefits or services under those programs.

6. Taste and food quality evaluation and consumer acceptance studies, (i) if wholesome foods without additives are consumed or (ii) if a food is consumed that contains a food ingredient at or below the level and for a use found to be safe, or agricultural chemical or environmental contaminant at or below the level found to be safe, by the Food and Drug Administration or approved by the Environmental Protection Agency or the Food Safety and Inspection Service of the U.S. Department of Agriculture.

EXPEDITED REVIEW

To submit an expedited study application, the proposed research should be encapsulated within one or more of the following categories (U.S. DHHS 2012d):

1. Clinical studies of drugs and medical devices only when one of the following conditions is met.

1-a) Research on drugs for which an investigational new drug application (21 CFR Part 312) is not required.

1-b) Research on medical devices for which one of the following is true:

1-c) An investigational device exemption application (21 CFR Part 812) is not required

1-d) The medical device is cleared/approved for marketing and the medical device is being used in accordance with its cleared/approved labeling.

2. Collection of blood samples by finger stick, heel stick, ear stick, or venipuncture as follows:

  2-a). From healthy, non-pregnant adults where all of the following are true

  i) The participants weigh at least 110 pounds

  ii) The amounts drawn will not exceed 550 ml in an 8-week period

  iii) Collection does not occur more frequently than 2 times per week

  2-b). From other adults and children considering the age, weight, and health of the participants, the collection procedure, the amount of blood to be collected, and the frequency with which it will be collected where all of the following are true:

  i) The amount drawn will not exceed the lesser of 50 ml or 3 ml per kg in an 8 week period

  ii) Collection may not occur more frequently than 2 times per week

3. Prospective collection of biological specimens for research purposes by noninvasive means.

4. Collection of data through noninvasive procedures (not involving general anesthesia or sedation) routinely employed in clinical practice, excluding procedures involving x-rays or microwaves. Where medical devices are employed, they must be cleared/approved for marketing.

5. Research involving materials (data, documents, records, or specimens) that have been collected, or will be collected solely for non-research purposes (such as medical treatment or diagnosis).

6. Collection of data from voice, video, digital, or image recordings made for research purposes.

7. Research on individual or group characteristics or behavior (including, but not limited to, research on perception, cognition, motivation, identity, language, communication, cultural beliefs or practices, and social behavior) or research employing survey, interview, oral history, focus group, program evaluation, human factors evaluation, or quality assurance methodologies.

FULL REVIEW

If studies do not meet any of these aforementioned categories, a full study application is required (U.S. DHHS 2012d).

In the review of all proposed research, the IRB members review the application to determine if regulatory requirements are met. Table 13.4 outlines typical IRB protocol review standards; these examples are taken from the NIH (NIH 2012).

Table 13.4
NIH IRB Protocol Review Standards

Regulatory Review Requirement	Suggested Questions for IRB Discussion
1. The proposed research design is scientifically sound and will not unnecessarily expose subjects to risk.	(a) Is the hypothesis clear? Is it clearly stated? (b) Is the study design appropriate to prove the hypothesis? (c) Will the research contribute to generalizable knowledge, and is it worth exposing subjects to risk?
2. Risks to subjects are *reasonable* in relation to anticipated benefits, if any, to subjects, *and* the importance of knowledge that may reasonably be expected to result.	(a) What does the IRB consider the level of risk to be? (b) What does the PI consider the level of risk/discomfort/inconvenience to be? (c) Is there prospect of direct benefit to subjects?
3. Subject selection is equitable.	(a) Who is to be enrolled? Men? Women? Ethnic minorities?

Table 13.4 (Continued)

Regulatory Review Requirement	Suggested Questions for IRB Discussion
	Children (rationale for inclusion/exclusion addressed)? Seriously ill persons? Healthy volunteers? (b) Are these subjects appropriate for the protocol?
4. Additional safeguards required for subjects likely to be vulnerable to coercion or undue influence.	(a) Are appropriate protections in place for vulnerable subjects, e.g., pregnant women, fetuses, socially or economically disadvantaged, decisionally impaired?
5. Informed consent is obtained from research subjects or their legally authorized representative(s).	(a) Does the informed consent document include the eight required elements? (b) Is the consent document understandable to subjects? (c) Who will obtain informed consent (PI, nurse, other?) and in what setting? (d) If appropriate, is there a children's assent? (e) Is the IRB requested to waive or alter any informed consent requirement?
6. Risks to subjects are minimized.	(a) Does the research design minimize risks to subjects? (b) Would use of a data and safety monitoring board or other research oversight process enhance subject safety?
7. Subject privacy and confidentiality are maximized.	(a) Will personally identifiable research data be protected to the extent possible from access or use? (b) Are any special privacy and confidentiality issues properly addressed, e.g., use of genetic information?

(continued)

Table 13.4   (Continued)

Regulatory Review Requirement	Suggested Questions for IRB Discussion
Additional Considerations	
1. Ionizing radiation	If ionizing radiation is used in this protocol, is it medically indicated or for research use only?
2. Collaborative research	Is this domestic/international collaborative research? If so, are FWAs or other assurances required for the sites involved? Is there a Centre for Rural Education and Development (CRADA)?
3. FDA-regulated research	Is an Investigational New Drug (IND) or Investigational Device Exemption Investigational Device Exemption (IDE) involved in this protocol?

Source: NIH (2012).

When a study has been reviewed by the IRB, there are four decisions that can be made: a study can be (1) approved as is; (2) approved with contingencies (and the conditions have to be addressed before actual approval is granted); (3) deferred or tabled (usually pending additional information about the study); or (4) disapproved (U.S. DHHS 2012d; Amdur and Bankert 2002). The timeliness with which a project is reviewed is largely dependent on the investigator and the completeness of the submitted application. If required elements of the application are missing or incomplete, the IRB cannot make a determination until these omissions or clarifications are addressed.

Tribal and IHS IRBs often use the federal regulations as the floor to human subject protection and not the ceiling. Federal regulations pertain specifically to the individual, *but because tribes are collective entities with unique status, namely tribal sovereignty, tribal and IHS IRBs assess harms and benefits to extend beyond the individual to include assessment of family and community harms and benefits in review of research study protocols* (Freeman and Romero 2002).

When working with any population, researchers must be sensitive to the local culture, traditions, research priorities, and worldview of those being studied. In working with AIAN communities, researchers must receive the approval of the appropriate respective tribal government(s) or tribal organization(s) prior to implementing any study. If more than one tribe or tribal organization is involved, the researcher must obtain approval from each tribe individually. If the research involves the IHS, the researcher will need to obtain approval for the project from the local IHS service unit (IHS 2012a).

To obtain prior approval, the researcher should involve all concerned groups as early as possible in the study planning process. Once a project is approved, regular communications including updates and meetings with health directors, health boards, tribal leadership, tribal councils, and IHS should occur annually at minimum. The ongoing communication is important and, should change in tribal leadership occur, an update session should be scheduled as soon as possible to ensure the new leadership is aware and in support of ongoing activities.

A RESPONSIBLE INVESTIGATOR

There are basic elements of respect that should be adhered to when working with AIANs, including respecting tribal culture and traditions; respecting tribal sovereignty and self-determination; respecting concerns and opinions of the community; respecting local research priorities and needs; respecting individuals, families, and communities; respecting human participants' rights and dignity; respecting a tribe's right to decline participation; respecting the autonomy and decisions of the tribe; demystifying research; being accessible; and providing feedback and findings in a timely manner (Romero and Kanade 2000).

Similarly, there are basic elements of responsibility that should be adhered to when working with AIANs, including ensuring understanding and good communication regarding all aspects of the proposed research; communicating and coordinating with tribal leaders; maximizing benefits and minimizing risks; protecting human participants and sensitive data; complying with informed consent process; obtaining service unit director, tribal, IHS research committee, and IRB approval; not beginning research until all approvals are obtained; sharing results of the research with the tribes; protecting participant and tribal identity; building capacity within the community; complying with the agreed-upon protocol specifications; and complying with tribal and IHS publication clearance (Romero and Kanade 2000).

As mentioned throughout the chapter, the elements to protect human subjects in research encompass three ethical principles: respect for persons, beneficence, and justice. In working with AIAN individuals and communities, these tenets hold.

PROPOSING A STUDY

A proposal should include the following information, as applicable: a cover letter with a list of all investigators and a contact person and telephone number; a tribal resolution or tribal letter of cooperation and approval from each participating tribe; an IHS service unit director letter of support; letters of IRB approval from collaborating institutions; a detailed protocol of the study design, sampling, analyses, timelines, evaluation, and community involvement; informed consent and assent forms; and other attachments, such as a copy of scripts or surveys that will be used, material that will be distributed, and so forth. Because the completeness of all these documents is important, items that should be included in each of them are provided (Romero and Kanade 2000).

Within the protocol's introduction and background section, the researcher should provide relevant research background and explain why this activity is necessary or important; explain why it is necessary to involve AIANs as participants in the research; explain how the burdens and benefits of the research will be equitably distributed; explain if there are other equally suitable groups who could be recruited for the study; describe the potential impact of the proposed research on AIANs; and, if a resolution or support letter from the tribe has not been obtained, describe how and when they will be obtained. The resolution should be forwarded to the IRB when it is received (Romero and Kanade 2000).

Within the protocol's study design section, the researcher should provide a complete description of the study design, sequence, and timing of all study procedures that will be performed and any information for phases within the project, for example, pilot, screening, intervention, and follow-up phases. All materials that will be used in the respective procedures should be included, such as surveys, scripts, questionnaires, and similar materials. Attach flow sheets if they will help the reader understand the procedures. Describe how study procedures differ from standard care or procedures (e.g., medical, psychological, educational, etc.). If any deception or withholding of complete information is required, explain why this is necessary and attach a debriefing statement. Describe where the study will take place; a letter of approval and cooperation from each participating site is needed. For example, if the study will be conducted in the local school system, an approval letter from the school board and superintendent are necessary. Finally, discuss and detail the specifics of data ownership and access (Romero and Kanade 2000).

Within the protocol's participants section, the researcher should explain how the nature of the research requires or justifies using the participant population; provide the approximate number and ages for the control and experimental groups; describe the gender and minority representation of the participant population; describe the criteria for selection for each participant group; describe the exclusion criteria exclusion for each participant group; describe the source for participants and attach letters of cooperation from agencies, institutions, or others involved in the recruitment; explain who will approach the participants and how the participants will be approached; explain what steps will be taken to avoid coercion and protect privacy; submit advertisements, flyers, contact letters, and phone contact protocols; explain if participants will receive payments, services without charge, or extra course credit; and explain if participants will be charged for any study procedures (Romero and Kanade 2000).

Within the protocol's risks and benefits section, the researcher should describe the nature and amount of risk of injury, stress, discomfort, invasion of privacy, and other side effects from all study procedures, drugs, and devices; describe the amount of risk the community may be subjected to; describe how due care will be used to minimize risks and maximize benefits; describe the provisions for a continuing reassessment of the balance between risks and benefits; describe the data and safety monitor or committee, if any; and describe the expected benefits for individual participants, the community, and society. In addition, the protocol should describe how adverse effects will be handled; discuss if facilities and equipment are adequate to handle possible adverse effects; and explain who will be financially responsible for treatment of physical injuries resulting from study procedures, for instance, a study sponsor, the subject, an organization compensation plan, or some other entity (Romero and Kanade 2000).

Within the protocol's confidentiality and privacy section, the researcher should explain if data will be anonymous (no possible link to identifiers); explain if identifiable data will be coded and if the key to the code will be kept separate from the data; explain if any other agency or individual will have access to identifiable data; and explain how data will be protected, for instance, by a computer with restricted access, a locked file, or some other means (Romero and Kanade 2000).

If the study includes the study of drugs, substances, and devices, a list of all noninvestigational drugs or other substances that will be used during the research should be included, with information on the name, source, dose, and method of administration. As applicable, a list of all investigational drugs (IND) or substances to be used in the study should be included along with the name, source, dosage, method of administration, IND number, and phase of testing. INDs must be registered with the appropriate institutional pharmacy. A concise summary of drug information prepared by the investigator should be included, including available toxicity data, reports of animal studies, description of studies done in humans, and drug protocol. Finally, as applicable, a list of all investigational devices to be used should be provided including name, source, description of purpose, method, and FDA IDE (Investigational Device Exemption) number; if no IDE is available, an explanation as to why the device qualifies as a nonsignificant risk. Attached to the protocol should be descriptions of studies in humans and animals and drawings or photographs of the device (Romero and Kanade 2000).

The protocol is analogous to the blueprint of a house because it describes how the project will be built from its base foundation. The more descriptive and detailed the protocol, the more clearly the IRB can see how the project is expected to unfold. An IRB cannot make assumptions about a research project and will return a submission with missing information.

Another vital document for IRB consideration is the informed consent form. The informed consent is one of the primary ethical requirements underpinning research with human participants; it reflects the basic principle of respect for people. It is too often forgotten that informed consent is an ongoing process, not a piece of paper or discrete moment of time. Informed consent ensures that prospective participants will understand the nature of the research and can knowledgably and voluntarily decide whether or not to participate. Federal regulations *require* that certain information must be provided to each participant (45 CFR 46.116):

- A statement that the study involves research, an explanation of the purposes of the research and the expected duration of participation, a description of the procedures to be followed, and identification of any procedures which are experimental.

- A description of any reasonably foreseeable risks or discomforts to the participants.
- A description of any benefits to the participant or to others, which may reasonably be expected from the research.
- A disclosure of appropriate alternative procedures or courses of treatment, if any, which might be advantageous to the participant.
- A statement describing the extent, if any, to which confidentiality of records identifying the participant will be maintained.
- For research involving more than minimal risk, an explanation as to whether any compensation and an explanation as to whether any medical treatments are available if injury occurs and, if so, what they consist of, or where further information may be obtained.
- An explanation of whom to contact for answers to pertinent questions about the research and research participants' rights, and whom to contact in the event of a research-related injury to the participant.
- A statement that participation is voluntary, refusal to participate will involve no penalty or loss of benefits to which the participant is otherwise entitled, and the participant may discontinue participation at any time without penalty or loss of benefits to which the participant is otherwise entitled.

The regulations further provide that the following additional information be provided to participants where appropriate:

- A statement that the particular treatment or procedure may involve risks to the participant (or to the embryo or fetus, if the participant is or may become pregnant) that are currently unforeseeable.
- Anticipated circumstances under which the participant's participation may be terminated by the investigator without the participant's consent.
- Any additional costs to the participant that may result from participation in the research.
- The consequences of a participant's decision to withdraw from the research and procedures for orderly termination of

participation by the participant. If your study offers compensation for participation, specify the effects of termination of participation on that compensation. (The compensation should be
prorated to reflect the duration of participation rather than an
"all or nothing" so that it appears fair and noncoercive).

- A statement that significant new findings developed during the
  course of the research that may relate to the participant's willing-
  ness to continue.
- The approximate number of participants involved in the study.

Investigators may seek consent only under circumstances that provide the prospective participant or his or her representative sufficient
opportunity to consider whether or not to participate, and that minimize the possibility of coercion or undue influence. Furthermore,
the information must be written in language that is understandable
to the participant or representative. The consent process may not
involve the use of exculpatory language through which the participant
or representative is made to waive or appear to waive any of the participant's legal rights, or release or appears to release the investigator,
sponsor, institution, or agents from liability for negligence.

In a research protocol, the investigator will need to explain the
process of administering consent. The protocol should address the
following questions: Is consent obtained in a reasonably quiet, unhur-
ried setting? Is translation or a translator needed? Is an interpreter
needed? Is there a knowledgeable person present who can answer
questions in a clear manner, using layman terms? Is a copy of the consent form provided to each participant? If children (under age 18) are
involved in the study, has a parental consent form been prepared? If
the study involves minimal risk, then consent of one parent is
adequate; if it involves more than minimal risk, then permission from
both parents must be obtained. If the children are old enough to make
at least some decisions themselves (usually at least 5 or 6 years of age,
but this is specific to their culture), has a form and process for their
assent been prepared? Who will explain the research to the potential
participants? Should someone in addition to or other than the investigator be present? Should participants be reeducated and their consent
required periodically? If a waiver of some or all of the consent requirements is requested, does the importance of the research justify such a
waiver? Is more than minimal risk involved? Can the research design
be modified to eliminate the need for deception or incomplete

disclosure? Will participants be given more information after completing their participation? Would the information to be withheld be something prospective participants might reasonably want to know in making their decision about participation? If medical, academic, or other personal records will be used, has a description of access and use been provided? If audio-visual recordings, tape recordings, or photographs will be used, has a description of access and use been provided? (Romero and Kanade 2000).

In addition to a detailed discussion of the components of the consent and assent forms and the administration process, a researcher will need to include labeled copies of each form specifying its type (e.g., parental consent, child assent, regular consent), participant (e.g., community focus group members, adult vaccine recipients), and situation where it will be used, for instance, for pretest of a screening instrument or administration of a provider questionnaire.

Researchers must report results to the tribes and a service unit involved on an ongoing basis and after the investigation has been completed and the data have been evaluated. The tribes and the service units should be the first to receive the results. The forum and the setting for the presentation can be determined by the appropriate tribal boards or councils. The results of the project must be approved by the tribes, service units, and IRBs before they are presented in public forums or published (Romero and Kanade 2000).

Although involved and complicated, the protection of human subjects is navigable. In working with AIANs, or any other identifiable population, the protection of participants cannot be underestimated.

PARTNERING AGENCIES, INSTITUTES, CENTERS, AND OFFICES

- Agency for Healthcare Research and Quality (AHRQ)
- National Cancer Institute (NCI)
- National Heart, Lung, and Blood Institute (NHLBI)
- National Human Genome Research Institute (NHGRI)
- National Institute on Alcohol Abuse and Alcoholism (NIAAA)
- National Institute of Allergy and Infectious Diseases (NIAID)
- National Institute of Arthritis and Musculoskeletal and Skin Diseases (NIAMS)

- National Institute of Dental and Craniofacial Research (NIDCR)
- National Institute of Diabetes and Digestive and Kidney Diseases (NIDDK)
- National Institute on Drug Abuse (NIDA)
- National Institute of General Medical Sciences (NIGMS)
- National Center for Complementary and Alternative Medicine (NCCAM)
- NIH Office of Research on Women's Health (ORWH)

REFERENCES

Amdur, R. and E. Bankert (Eds.). 2002. *Institutional Review Board, Management and Function*. Sudbury, MA: Jones and Bartlett.

Beecher H. 1966. "Special Article: Ethics and Clinical Research." *New England Journal of Medicine* 274(24):1354–60.

Berger, R. L. 1990. "Special Article: Nazi Science–The Dachau Hypothermia Experiments." *New England Journal of Medicine* 322(20):1435–40.

Brandt, A.M. 1978. "Racism and Research: The Case of the Tuskegee Syphilis Study." *Hastings Center Report* 8(6):21–29.

"Declaration of Geneva," World Medical Association Declaration of Geneva, Adopted by the 2nd WMA General Assembly Geneva, Switzerland, September 1948 and amended by 173rd WMA Council Session, Divonne-les-Bains, France, May 2006.

"Declaration of Helskinki," World Medical Association Declaration of Helsinki, Ethical Principles for Medical Research Involving Human Subjects, Adopted by the 18th WMA General Assembly Helsinki, Finland, June 1964 and amended by 52nd WMA General Assembly, Edinburgh, Scotland, October 2000.

Elliott, C. and R. Abadie. 2008. "Exploiting a Research Underclass in Phase I Clinical Trials." *New England Journal of Medicine* 358, 2316–17.

Freeman, W. L. and F. C. Romero. 2002. "Community Consultation to Evaluate Group Risk." In *Institutional Review Board, Management and Function*. Amdur R and Bankert E (Eds.). Sudbury, MA: Jones and Bartlett, pp. 160–64.

"Good Clinical Practice," ICH Expert Working Group, International Conference on Harmonisation of Technical Requirements for Registration of Pharmaceuticals for Human Use, ICH Harmonised Tripartite Guideline, Guideline for Good Clinical Practice E6(R1),Current Step 4 version, June 10, 1996.

Harmon, A. 2010a, April 21. "Havasupai Case Highlights Risks in DNA Research," *New York Times*. Accessed February 28, 2012. http://www.nytimes.com/2010/04/22/us/22dnaside.html.

Harmon A. 2010b, April 21. "Indian Tribe Wins Fight to Limit Research of Its DNA." *New York Times*. Accessed February 28, 2010. http://www.nytimes.com/2010/04/22/us/22dna.html.

"Hippocratic Oath," National Institutes of Health, National Library of Medicine, History of Medicine Division, Greek Medicine, The Hippocratic Oath, tranlated by Michael North, 2002. http://www.nlm.nih.gov/hmd/greek/greek_oath.html, last updated February 7, 2012, accessed July 5, 2012.

Indian Health Service (IHS). 2012a. "Human Research Participant Protection in the Indian Health Service." Accessed February 28, 2012. http://www.ihs.gov/ Research/index.cfm?module=hrpp_irb.

Indian Health Service (IHS). 2012b. "Native American Research Centers for Health (NARCH)." Accessed February 28, 2012. http://www.ihs.gov/Research/index .cfm?module=narch.

Indian Health Service (IHS). 2012c. "Tribal Epidemiology Centers." Accessed February 28, 2012. http://www.ihs.gov/Epi/index.cfm?module=epi_tec_main.

"Institutional Review Board," The Belmont Report, Office of the Secretary, Ethical Principles and Guidelines for the Protection of Human Subjects of Research, The National Commission for the Protection of Human Subjects of Biomedical and Behavioral Research, April 18, 1979.

Jarrell, R. H. 1992. "Native American Women and Forced Sterilization, 1973–1976." *Caduceus* 8(3):45–58.

Krugman, S. 1986. "The Willowbrook Hepatitis Studies Revisited: Ethical Aspects." *Reviews of Infectious Diseases* 8(1):157–62.

Makhijani, A. and E. Kennedy. 1994, Winter. "Human Radiation Experiments in the United States." *Science for Democratic Action* 3, 1–7.

Milligan, B. C. 1993. "Patient's rights and sterilizations." *IHS Primary Care Provider* 18(2):36–37.

National Commission for the Protection of Human Subjects of Biomedical and Behavioral Research. 1978. "The Belmont Report: Ethical Principles and Guidelines for the Protection of Human Subjects of Research." *Report of the National Commission for the Protection of Human Subjects of Biomedical and Behavioral Research.* Maryland: Elkridge, Belmont Conference Center.

National Institutes of Health (NIH). 2012. "Information for NIH IRB Members." Accessed February 28, 2012. http://ohsr.od.nih.gov/irb/protocol.html.

Northern Plains Tribal Epidemiology Center. 2009. "Welcome to NPTEC Website!" Accessed February 28, 2012. http://aatchb.org/nptec/.

Northwest Portland Area Indian Health Board. 2012. "About the Epicenter." Accessed February 28, 2012. http://www.npaihb.org/epicenter/about_the_epicenter/.

Nuremberg Code, Trials of War Criminals before the Nuremberg Military Tribunals under Control Council Law No. 10. Vol. 2, Nuremberg, October 1946– April 1949. Washington DC: US GPO 1949–1953, pp. 181–182.

"Nuremberg Code," n.d. Wikipedia. Accessed July 12, 2011. http://en.wikipedia.org/ wiki/Nuremberg_Code.

Online Encyclopedia. 2012. "Forced Sterilization of Native Americans." Accessed March 2, 2012. http://encyclopedia.jrank.org/articles/pages/6242/Forced -Sterilization-of-Native-Americans.html#ixzz0Zl34gPPk.

RMTEC. 2012. "Rocky Mountain Tribal Epidemiology Center." Accessed February 28, 2012/ http://www.rmtec.org/.

Romero, F. C. and S. Kanade. 2000. *Guidelines for Researchers.* Portland, OR: Northwest Portland Area Indian Health Board.

Summers, E. 2011, July 7. "Developing Your Human Research Protections Program: Regulatory Compliance and Additional Considerations." personal communication.

"The Havasupai Case: Research Without Patient Consent." 2007. WhoOwns YourBody.org. Accessed February 28, 2012. http://www.whoownsyourbody.org/havasupai.html.

U.S. Department of Health and Human Services (DHHS). 2012a. "Federal Policy for the Protection of Human Subjects ('Common Rule')." Accessed February 28, 2012. http://www.hhs.gov/ohrp/humansubjects/commonrule/index.html.

U.S. Department of Health and Human Services (DHHS). 2012b. "Federalwide Assurance (FWA) for the protection of Human Subjects." Accessed February 28, 2012. http://www.hhs.gov/ohrp/assurances/assurances/filasurt.html#sectiona.

U.S. Department of Health and Human Services (DHHS). 2012c. "Institutional Review Boards (IRBs)." Accessed February 28, 2012. http://www.hhs.gov/ohrp/assurances/irb/index.html.

U.S. Department of Health and Human Services (DHHS). 2012d. "Office for Human Research Protections (OHRP)." Accessed February 28, 2012. http://www.hhs.gov/ohrp/.

U.S. Department of Health and Human Services (DHHS). 2012e. "Regulations." Accessed July 12, 2011. http://www.hhs.gov/ohrp/humansubjects/index.html.

Vorhaus, D. 2010, April 21. "The Havasupai Indians and the Challenge of Informed Consent for Genomic Research." *Genomics Law Report*. Accessed February 28, 2012. http://www.genomicslawreport.com/index.php/2010/04/21/the-havasupai-indians-and-the-challenge-of-informed-consent-for-genomic-research/.

Wiwchar D. 2004, December 16. "Nuu-Chah-Nulth Blood Returns to West Coast." *Ha-Shilth-Sa* 31(25). Accessed February 28, 2012. http://caj.ca/wp-content/uploads/2010/mediamag/awards2005/(David%20Wiwchar,%20Sept.%2012,%202005)Blood2.pdf.

Wiwchar D. n.d. "Nuu-Chah-Nulth Blood Returns to West Coast," *Canadian Association of Journalists*. Accessed February 28, 2012. http://caj.ca/wp-content/uploads/2010/mediamag/awards2005/Pages/Community%20Newspaper.htm.

Index

About the Editors and Contributors

Lorenda Belone, PhD, MPH

Tribe: Navajo Nation

Associate Scientist II/Lecture II, University of New Mexico

Dr. Belone is a research scientist at the University of New Mexico's Center for Participatory Research and Master of Public Health Program. Dr. Belone received her doctorate in 2010 from the University of New Mexico, where she currently holds the Robert Wood Johnson Center for Health Policy Postdoctoral Fellowship.

Dr. Belone has worked on several National Institutes of Health (NIH) and Centers for Disease Control and Prevention (CDC) funded research projects with American Indian communities in the Southwest. Currently, she is the principal investigator on a project investigating an intergenerational family prevention program as well as serving as a co-investigator on a national study seeking to better understand community-based participatory research projects being conducted with American Indians/Alaska Natives and other communities confronted by problems associated with health disparities.

Valarie Blue Bird Jernigan, DrPH, MPH

Tribe: Choctaw Nation of Oklahoma

Assistant Professor, University of Oklahoma College of Public Health

Dr. Blue Bird Jernigan is an artist, an activist, and a scholar. Her research interest focuses on participatory action research with indigenous communities, studies that include attention to social justice incorporated in improving health outcomes. As an artist, she uses documentary film, photography, and social media to create innovative programs aimed at community organizing and capacity building for health promotion.

Valarie has a doctorate in public health from University of California–Berkeley and attended film school at Stanford University and the San Francisco School of Digital Filmmaking. Valarie completed a postdoctoral fellowship at Stanford School of Medicine. Her film *Forty Winters* won the California Council for the Humanities Documentary Film Award in 2010. She has produced several films available online and through the Stanford Prevention Research Center. Valarie was recently named a 2011 Indigenous Film Fellow with the Indigenous Film Circle. She currently lives in Tulsa, Oklahoma, with her husband, Choctaw filmmaker Tvli Jacob, and their daughter Cedar Nuseka.

Linda Burhansstipanov, MSPH, DrPH

Tribe: Cherokee Nation of Oklahoma

President, Native American Cancer Initiatives, Incorporated
Founder, Grants Director, Native American Cancer Research Corporation

Dr. Burhansstipanov has worked in public health since 1971, collaborating with Native American organizations on a variety of health concerns that are paramount in these communities. In addition, she also taught full time at California State University Long Beach for 18 years and part time for the University of California–Los Angeles for five years.

Since leaving California, she developed and implemented the Native American Cancer Research Program at the National Cancer Institute from 1989 to 1993. She worked with the AMC Cancer Research Center in Denver for five years before founding Native American Cancer Initiatives, Incorporated (1998), a for-profit business, and Native American Cancer Research Corporation (1999), an American Indian–operated nonprofit. She serves on multiple federal advisory boards for the NIH and CDC. She currently is the principal investigator and subcontractor on more than five NIH grants. She has over 100 peer-reviewed publications, of which most address Native American cancer, public health, and data issues.

Francine C. Gachupin, PhD, MPH, CIP

Tribe: Jemez Pueblo

Operations Manager, Human Research Protections Office, University of New Mexico

Dr. Gachupin has extensive experience working with American Indian tribal communities, focusing primarily on chronic disease surveillance, public health practice, epidemiology, and research. Dr. Gachupin obtained her doctorate from the University of New Mexico and her master of public health in epidemiology from the University of Washington in Seattle. Her work has been based primarily at tribal epidemiology centers serving the Northwest, Northern Plains, and Southwest tribes.

She has been the principal investigator on several projects focused on behavioral risk factors, cancer control, diet and nutrition, mortality, injury, and population genetics.

Dr. Gachupin has served as cochair to the National IHS IRB and chair of both the Portland Area IHS IRB and the Southwest Tribal IRB. She has served on the Secretary's Advisory Council for Human Research Protections (SACHRP), the Canadian Institutes of Health Research (CIHR) Institute for Aboriginal People's Health (IAPH) Institute Advisory Board (IAB), and on data safety monitoring boards for the Strong Heart Study (SHS) and Genetics of Coronary Artery Disease among Alaska Natives (GOCADAN) Study—both funded by the National Heart, Lung, and Blood Institute (NHLBI)—and the Adult Dental Caries (ADC) Project funded by the National Institute of Dental and Craniofacial Research (NIDCR).

Jennifer Giroux, MD, MPH

Tribe: Rosebud Sioux

Medical Epidemiologist, Indian Health Service

Dr. Giroux is a mother of three, including two *hunka* (young women), and serves as a medical epidemiologist at the Indian Health Service Division of Epidemiology and Disease Prevention. Currently she is assigned to the Aberdeen Area Indian Health Service (AA-IHS) and leads the management of outbreaks for 17 tribes living in the following four-state region: North Dakota, South Dakota, Iowa, and Nebraska.

She was instrumental in developing a public health front line in Indian country and pivotal in starting the Northern Plains Tribal Epidemiology program in Rapid City, South Dakota, and the Rocky Mountain Tribal Epidemiology Center in Billings, Montana. She continues to provide public health and epidemiology leadership and technical assistance to the Northern Plains tribes and the Great Plains Tribal Chairmen's Health Board (GPTCHB), state health departments, and other organizations, with a focus on building collaborations to meet tribal public health needs.

Dr. Giroux completed her undergraduate degree at Montana State University, Bozeman, Montana, and graduated from the Indians into Medicine Program at University of South Dakota. While finishing medical school and starting a family, she worked for the Aberdeen Area IHS Epidemiology Program on the Strong Heart Study, the Sioux Cancer Study, and the Infant Mortality Study.

She completed her medical internship with the Internal Medicine Program at Merit Care, located in Fargo, North Dakota, prior to serving as an epidemic intelligence service officer for the Centers for Disease Control and Prevention (CDC). While at CDC, she spent two years learning to manage outbreaks in Indian country. She completed her master's in public health in epidemiology at the University of Minnesota and her preventive medicine residency at the Division of Tuberculosis Elimination at CDC in Atlanta, Georgia.

R. Turner Goins, MS, PhD

Tribe: Catawba Indian

Associate Professor, Oregon State University

Dr. Goins received her master's degree and doctorate in gerontology from the University of Massachusetts–Boston. She completed a National Institute on Aging postdoctoral research fellowship at Duke University's Center for the Study of Aging and Human Development. Dr. Goins also participated in the Native Investigator Development Core training program of the Native Elder Research Center at the University of Colorado–Denver.

Dr. Goins is currently an associate professor at Oregon State University's College of Public Health and Human Sciences where she is on faculty in the Health Management and Policy program, the Human Development and Family Sciences program, and the Center for Healthy Aging Research.

She has spent over a decade conducting research to understand aging-related issues with American Indian and Alaska Native communities. Specifically, her research has focused on examining determinants of functional impairment, long-term care access, and cultural aspects of elder caregiving. Dr. Goins has over 50 peer-reviewed journal articles and book chapters on these issues.

Carol Goldtooth-Begay, MPH

Tribe: Navajo Nation

Graduate Research Assistant, Native American Research and Training Center

Carol Goldtooth-Begay was born and raised in Tuba City, Arizona. Her maternal clan is *Kinyaa'aanii* (Towering House People), paternal clan is *Biih Bitoodnii* (Deer Springs People), maternal grandfather is *Tl'izi lani* (Manygoats People), and paternal grandfather is *Tl'aashchi'i* (Red Bottom People).

She received her master's in public health in policy and management in 2006 from the University of Arizona's Mel and Enid Zuckerman College of Public Health. Her bachelor's in microbiology in 1997 was from Northern Arizona University, Flagstaff, Arizona.

Her master's internship and research study was conducted with the Navajo Division of Health, on a study that examined the tribe's Breast and Cervical Cancer Prevention Program and also participated in developing a survey instrument that helped access Navajo Nation employees' knowledge, attitudes, and behaviors about cancer.

She has held several graduate research assistant positions at the University of Arizona, including one with an innovative program undertaken by the University's Arizona Cancer Center Native American Cancer Partnership. This partnership trained Native students in conducting cancer research as well as motivating them to seek a science career. She currently works for the Native American Research and Training Center as a graduate research assistant on the Arizona National Children's Study as well as on the American Indian and Alaska Native Tool Kit, a kit to be used to disseminate information about the National Children's Study to American Indian and Alaska Native communities.

Emily A. Haozous, PhD, RN

Tribe: Chiricahua Fort Sill Apache

Assistant Professor, University of New Mexico College of Nursing

Dr. Haozous received her nursing training at Yale University School of Nursing, receiving her undergraduate degree in nursing in 2002, a master's in oncology nursing in 2003, and her PhD in 2009. The title of her dissertation was "Exploring Cancer Pain in Southwest American Indians."

Since joining the faculty at the University of New Mexico in 2009, Dr. Haozous has been involved in a number of projects examining health disparity outcomes among American Indians with cancer, including two projects that examined SEER data and survival and data quality disparities, and a project developing telemedicine and distance learning for clinicians who work with American Indians experiencing cancer pain in the Seattle region.

Presently, Dr. Haozous is a regent's lecturer at the University of New Mexico, and is a Robert Wood Johnson Foundation nurse faculty scholar. As a nurse faculty scholar, Dr. Haozous is working a project that will develop and test digital stories about cancer prevention with American Indian women.

Jennie R. Joe, PhD, MPH

Tribe: Navajo Nation

Professor Emeritus, (retired) Department of Family and Community Medicine, University of Arizona.

Dr. Joe received her graduate degrees from University of California–Berkeley (public health, anthropology, and a doctorate in medical anthropology). Her undergraduate degree was from the University of New Mexico (BSN). She served as a Kellogg fellow and was recipient of the social justice Robert F. Kennedy fellowship. As a graduate student, she taught at Dine' Community College, and following her graduation from the UC Berkeley, she joined the Department of Anthropology and American Indian Studies at UCLA. In 1986, she was invited by the University of Arizona to help launch a series of studies on disabilities and rehabilitation intervention for Native peoples with disabilities. Her tenure at the University of Arizona included joint faculty appointment in American Indian studies.

Dr. Joe has been engaged in a longitudinal study of one Navajo community impact by forced removal and relocation. Her other research activities have included Native peoples and type 2 diabetes; breast and cervical cancer screening; childhood diabetes; culturally based substance abuse treatment programs; disability and rehabilitation; and health disparity and its impact on American Indians and Alaska Natives.

Professor Joe was a founding member of the Board of Trustees for the Smithsonian's National Museum of American Indians and has continued to serve on a number of national and international organizations, including the Institute of Medicine, Safety Monitoring Board for the Strong Heart Study, and Canadian Institute on Health Research's Institute on Aboriginal People's Health. She served and continues to serve on a number of editorial boards, including UCLA's *American Indian Culture and Research Journal* and *Interreligious Insight: A Journal of Dialogue and Engagement.*

Judith Salmon Kaur, MD

Tribe: Choctaw/Cherokee

Professor of Oncology, Mayo Clinic, Rochester, Minnesota

Dr. Kaur is one of only two American Indian medical oncologists in the country. Currently she is the medical director for the Native American Programs of the Mayo Clinic Comprehensive Cancer Center. At Mayo, Dr. Kaur directs the Native C.I.R.C.L.E., a national resource center that provides and develops culturally appropriate cancer education materials for laypersons, allied health, and clinicians working in Native communities. The Spirit of Eagles is another program that is part of Dr. Kaur's program, a community networks program with outreach nationally to American Indians and Alaska Natives, the only national program working with AIAN populations.

As a professor of oncology in the Medical School at the Mayo Clinic, Dr. Kaur's research, in addition to her clinical work, includes a special interest in women's cancers, particularly breast and cervical cancer. Currently she directs the Mayo Clinic Hospice Program and Palliative Care Task Force.

In 2007, Dr. Kaur was awarded Physician of the Year by the Association of American Indian Physicians. In the following year, 2008, she was appointed to the National Cancer Advisory Board by President George W. Bush (a four-year appointment) and also became a Fellow of the American Academy of Hospice and Palliative Care. Dr. Kaur is one of the medical directors for Mayo Clinic's Hospice program and the research director for the Palliative Care Program and course director for an Intensive Case-based Training in Palliative Care program for the Indian Health Service.

Teresa D. LaFromboise, MA, PhD

Tribe: Miami

Professor, Counseling Psychology in the School of Education, Stanford University

Dr. LaFromboise is a fellow of the American Psychological Association and the Association for Psychological Science. She specializes in stress-related problems of American Indian and Alaska Native youth. Much of her current attention is focused upon cultural humility as a theoretical orientation in developing and implementing interventions in suicide prevention.

She is a recognized contributor to American Indian mental health initiatives, having published extensively in that area. She has also authored a number of prevention intervention manuals including *Circles of Women: Skills Training for American Indian Professionalization* and *American Indian Life Skills Development Curriculum (AILS)*.

Dr. LaFromboise's awards for *AILS* include recognition from the Department of Health and Human Services as a SAMHSA Program of Excellence, the Carter Center for Public Policy at Emory University, as well as recognition in *Intervention Ready for Prime Time* and by the First Nations' Behavioral Health Association as one of the Ten Best Practices. The *AILS* is also listed in SAMHSA's National Registry of Evidence-based Programs and Practices as well as in the Department of Justice's Registry of Effective Programs.

She teaches courses in cultural psychology, racial and ethnic identity development, psychology, American Indian/Alaska Native mental health, and counseling theories and interventions from a multicultural perspective. She has served as the chair of Native American Studies at Stanford University for 10 years. She most enjoys mentoring students and consulting with personnel in community and school-based programs for the empowerment of Native youth.

Terry M. Maresca, MD

Tribe: Mohawk

Medical Director, Snoqualmie Tribe, Washington

Dr. Maresca has served American Indian people as a board-certified family physician since 1987 in both reservation and urban settings. Her training and clinical practice blends both traditional indigenous plant medicine work with Western medicine approaches to health.

As the former director of the Native American Center of Excellence at the University of Washington, she continues to teach electives in Indian health issues at the medical school. She is active in cross-cultural curriculum development and holds a faculty position with the Seattle Indian Health Board's family medicine residency training program.

Dr. Maresca is a past president of the Association of American Indian Physicians and was named American Indian Physician of the Year in 1997. When not teaching or providing health care to people, she manages a tribal medicinal herb garden and strives to maintain her vital relationship to the world of healing plants and cultural teachings.

Bayley J. Marquez, BA, MA

Tribe: Chumash

Research Assistant, Stanford University

Bayley Marquez is from Santa Ynez California, graduated from Stanford in 2007, and spent the next three years teaching high school in northern New Mexico on the Navajo Nation. She returned to Stanford in 2010 to pursue a master's degree in international comparative education, writing a master's thesis on representations of American Indians/Alaska Natives in high school social studies curriculum. She has plans to pursue a PhD at Stanford, focusing on American Indian education.

Mary Rogers, MS, PhD, LAC

Senior Associate, Sundance Research Institute, Bethesda, MD, and Sundance, WY

Dr. Rogers' position with the Sundance Research Institute allows her to provide support and specialized technical assistance and services assisting communities, tribes, and other organizations to achieve their goals to improve the health and well-being of their citizens.

Her areas of expertise include curriculum design and program evaluation, substance abuse, and crisis intervention. Rogers recently served as the co-principal investigator on a two-year CDC grant to develop strategies, techniques, and curriculum for teachers, human services workers, the justice system, and mental health providers who work with youth or adult students or clients who may have fetal alcohol syndrome. In addition, Dr. Rogers recently completed serving as principle investigator for a five-year NIH grant that explored cultural resilience and adolescent risk behaviors among American Indian young men and women.

Previously, Rogers was a law enforcement officer in South Dakota, was a juvenile crisis intervention specialist with the Bismarck Police Department, North Dakota, and has served as a domestic violence advocate. Dr. Rogers also has held teaching positions in North Dakota, served as assistant professor and chair of criminal justice and alcohol and drug studies in California, and was assistant professor of human services in South Dakota. She currently holds adjunct faculty positions with the University of South Dakota and the University College at Maryland University.

Teshia G. Arambula Solomon, PhD

Tribe: Choctaw Nation of Oklahoma

Associate Professor, Department of Family and Community Medicine and Director of the Native American Research and Training Center, College of Medicine, University of Arizona

Dr. Solomon has over 20 year experiences in health-related research and training involving minority populations. She previously held positions as director of the Southern Plains Inter-Tribal Epidemiology Center at the Oklahoma City Area Inter-Tribal Health Board and as assistant professor both at the University of Texas School of Public Health and the University of Oklahoma College of Public Health.

She earned her doctorate from University of Texas–Austin in health promotion. Her research has focused on improving the health of disenfranchised populations, particularly American Indians, creating an environment where communities are empowered to advocate for the health of their people through education and training, research, and science. Her work involves research in cancer, fetal alcohol syndrome, and maternal and child health and development. She also works to train Native investigators and institutionalize indigenous methods of scientific inquiry into the mainstream research enterprise to decrease health disparities in disenfranchised populations.

Irene S. Vernon, PhD

Tribe: Mescalero-Apache/Yaqui

Professor and Chair, Ethnic Studies Department, and Assistant to the College of Liberal Arts Dean, Colorado State University.

Dr. Vernon was appointed in the 2009 as the associate provost of special projects at Colorado State University, a position that included responsibility for a number of projects including developing family-friendly resources and RAMS for Diversity activities.

Dr. Vernon is trained in Native American studies as well as in ethnic studies and has been engaged in ethnic studies program reviews and serves as a manuscript reviewer for a number of journals and presses. Dr. Vernon has membership in several professional health societies such as the National Association of Ethnic Studies, National Minority AIDS Council (NMAC), Colorado Public Health Association, Racial and Ethnic Populations Ad Hoc Committee, National Institute of Health, and Indigenous HIV/AIDS Research Training Council and was recently nominated to the Office of AIDS Research Advisory Council.

Dr. Vernon has been actively involved in the field of health for over 16 years and is the author of *Killing Us Quietly: Native Americans and HIV/AIDS* (2001) and several other journal articles. Her research interest and work is in Native American health, particularly HIV/AIDS, with other subinterests in health disparities and issues related to the Native American transgender population. As part of her scholarly work, Dr. Vernon also provides capacity-building assistance aimed at mobilizing communities around HIV/AIDS prevention in Native communities throughout the United States.

Nina S. Wampler, DSc, MPH

Tribe: Eastern Band of Cherokee

Assistant Research Scientist, Family and Community Medicine, University of Arizona

The main focus of Dr. Wampler's research career has been community-based participatory research that examined the epidemiology of chronic diseases among Native Americans, including cancer, tobacco control, and aging-related illnesses. Her research and academic training has prepared her to pursue this goal by providing a strong background in epidemiology, health policy, and quantitative analysis.

After receiving her doctorate in epidemiology from Boston University School of Public Health in 2001, Dr. Wampler was one of four Native American postdoctoral fellows at the University of Colorado in the Native Elder Research Center funded by the National Institute on Aging.

Her more current research fellowship at the University of Arizona has been on a project examining the information sharing between smoking cessation (*Quitlines*) in the United States and Canada under the study "Knowledge Integration in *Quitlines*: Networks Improving Cessation (KIQNIC)," a study housed in the Behavioral Health Division of the Arizona Cancer Center, University of Arizona, in Tucson.

Dr. Wampler is married to Dr. John Doty, and they reside in Pine, Colorado. They have two children, Emma, 26, who is a senior financial analyst in Boston, Massachusetts, and Matthew, 27, who is a doctoral student in electrical engineering at Northwestern University in Illinois.

Rosita Kaahani Worl, PhD

Tribe: Tlingit

Vice Chair, Sealaska Corporation; President, Sealaska Heritage Institute

Rosita Worl is Tlingit from the Thunderbird Clan and House Lowered from the Sun of Klukwan, Alaska. She is a child of the Sockeye Clan. She is an enrolled member of the Central Council of Tlingit and Haida Indians and is a member of the Sealaska Corporation, organizations that are federally recognized entities.

Dr. Worl holds a doctoral degree in anthropology from Harvard University and is the president of the Sealaska Heritage Institute, an institute dedicated to preserving and enhancing the culture of the Tlingit, Haida, and Tsimshian. Dr. Worl also serves on the Board of Directors of Sealaska Corporation, which was created by Congress to implement the aboriginal land claims of the Alaska Natives.

She served as a professor of anthropology at the University of Alaska and was formerly the publisher and editor of *Alaska Native News*, a publication that she founded with her family and that was published for eight years. Dr. Worl serves on the Board of Directors of the Alaska Federation of Natives, Cultural Survival, and the Indigenous Language Institute.

She was a founding board member of the Smithsonian's National Museum of American Indians and was appointed to President Clinton's Northwest Coast Sustainable Development Commission. Dr. Worl now serves on the Smithsonian's National Museum of Natural History Arctic Studies Advisory Committee.

Dr. Worl's scholarly activities have included extensive research throughout the circumpolar Arctic, and she has served on the National Science Foundation Arctic Program Committee; the National Science Committee overseeing the social scientific studies of the *Exxon Valdez* oil spill; the Scientific Committee of the Arctic Eskimo Whaling Commission; and as science advisor to the International Whaling Commission in 1979. She has written a number of landmark studies and reports published by foundations, universities, federal organizations, and Alaska Native organizations on bowhead whale and seal hunting as well as other impacts of industrial development on Native communities, repatriation, and Tlingit law.